TIGHTROPE WALKING

Books by the same author

Second to None: The Royal Scots Greys 1918–1945
El Alamein
Tobruk
The War Lords (ed.)
Harding of Petherton
The Apostles of Mobility
War Since 1945
A Policy for Peace
The Seven Ages of the British Army
Dilemmas of the Desert War
Twentieth Century Warriors
Out of Step

TIGHTROPE WALKING
British Defence Policy since 1945

MICHAEL CARVER

HUTCHINSON
London

This edition first published in 1992 by
Hutchinson

Random Century Group Ltd
20 Vauxhall Bridge Road, London SW1V 2SA

Random Century Australia Pty Ltd
20 Alfred Street, Milsons Point, Sydney, NSW 2061, Australia

Random Century New Zealand Ltd
PO Box 40–086, Glenfield, Auckland 10, New Zealand

Random Century South Africa Pty Ltd
PO Box 337, Bergvlei, 2012, South Africa

BRITISH LIBRARY CATALOGUING-IN-PUBLICATION DATA
Carver, Michael
Tightrope walking: British defence policy since
1945.
I. Title
355.00941
ISBN 0–09–174682–5

Set in 11/12.5 Plantin by Intype, London
Printed and bound in Great Britain by
Butler & Tanner Ltd, Frome and London

CONTENTS

PROLOGUE

Why tightrope walking? Because British defence policy is a perpetual balancing act: between commitments and resources; between Europe and the wider world; between Europe and the Commonwealth; between links with Western Europe and North America; between, in simplified terms, a continental and a maritime strategy – the resources to be allocated between maritime and land operations and the air support of both: within the navy, between surface, sub-surface and airborne effort: within the army, between the requirement to fight a sophisticated modern army, like that of the Soviet Union, and that of low-intensity operations, like those in Northern Ireland: within the air force, between air defence, strike, reconnaissance, transport and tankers; and within strike, between attacks on the enemy's navy, his army, his air force and non-military targets: within all three services, between nuclear and conventional; between the front-line units and all that is needed to maintain them in active operations, possibly far away from Britain; between sophistication and simplicity, which involves a choice between quality and quantity; between equipment and manpower, and, in the latter, between numbers and the demand for 'quality of life', which has many aspects, varying from housing and welfare of families to opportunities for sport and adventure; between the traditional appeal of the past and the challenge of the future; between boredom and danger or disruption of family life; between the armed forces themselves and their various sub-divisions; between the demands of peacetime and those of war; between the need to offer an attractive career and that of ensuring both that the fighting element is young enough to bear its strains and that short service provides reserves; between regular, standing forces and reserves, voluntary or other; between the national strength which comes from a flourishing economy and that derived, both in the political and the military sphere, from strong and effective armed forces; between what it all costs and other demands on the public purse, most of which have more popular appeal, especially at election time.

The object of defence policy is to provide those who direct affairs with the greatest possible freedom of action in furthering the interests of the nation. The locust years of the 1930s demonstrated that it was impossible to pursue an effective policy for that purpose when the nation was not only desperately weak in military terms itself, but unable or unwilling to commit itself firmly to an alliance which might have helped to maintain one. Our nation's greatest failing has long been a nostalgic devotion to the past. If we do not shake ourselves out of it, we shall fall off the tightrope. I hope that the chapters which follow will illustrate that.

1

POST-WAR DISILLUSION:
1945–1951

Wɪᴛʜ ᴛʜᴇ sᴜᴅᴅᴇɴ end of the Second World War, brought about by the explosion of two atomic bombs on Japan in August 1945, both the politicians of the Labour Party, by then in power, and the military chiefs who served them, indulged in day-dreams about defence which were as sharply in contrast to each other as they were unrealistic. The principal Labour politicians, Attlee, Bevin, Morrison, Cripps and Dalton, had served in Winston Churchill's wartime administration, had been privy to all the discussions which had taken place about how Europe, the Commonwealth and the world were to be organized when Germany and Japan had been defeated, and, with perhaps the exception of Cripps and Dalton, tended to take a realistic view of the prospect. They knew that, without American financial help, Britain was bankrupt; that the restoration of British authority over areas in which it had been exercised without great effort before the war was likely to be much more difficult in future, particularly in regions which had been affected, directly or indirectly, by the Japanese attempt to establish a Greater East Asia Co-Prosperity Sphere. They were as keen as Winston Churchill had been to maintain Britain's position and standing as a world power which had made a unique contribution to victory over the Fascist alliance. They were also, particularly Bevin, as concerned as Churchill had been that all the hopes that victory would usher in an era of peace were at risk from the uncompromising attitude adopted by the Soviet Union, whose immense military power sat menacingly in the heart of Europe, while the United States of America announced their intention of withdrawing within two years the only forces that could counterbalance it.

But these Labour ministers had to take account of strong feelings within their party, feelings which their success in the 1945 General Election showed were shared by the general public: that the sacrifices and privations endured during six years of war should be rewarded by an easing of all the restrictions which had made wartime life so dreary for those who had stayed at home, and that the aspirations should be met of those who sought a reformation of society in the direction of a more equal share in national resources and a more compassionate attitude to those who were less well endowed, whether or not they believed that state socialism was the best method of achieving those aims. Many of those who thought that way admired the achievements of the Soviet Union and were not inclined to regard their former ally as immediately transformed into a potential enemy. Both the leaders and the great body of their supporters pinned their hopes on new international organizations and procedures to realize the aims so hopefully set out in the joint declaration made by Roosevelt and Churchill in August 1941, known as the Atlantic Charter, which became the basis of that of the United Nations Organization.

The service chiefs took a sharply different view. They were all concerned to apply what they saw as the lessons of the war. They felt keenly the handicaps they had suffered as a result of their services' unpreparedness for war in 1939. They knew from bitter experience how long it had taken to develop and equip forces capable of tackling a major enemy, and were determined that the experiences of 1939 to 1941 should not be repeated. The lessons they drew from this differed sharply, depending on the service to which they belonged. Alanbrooke, who served on as Chief of the Imperial General Staff, head of the army as well as acting as chairman of the Chiefs of Staff, until June 1946, was influenced by two factors: the extent to which Britain had depended on the Commonwealth for the provision of troops, and the atomic bomb. He shared with Professor Sir Henry Tizard, one of the government's principal scientific advisers, a concern that Britain was so vulnerable to atomic attack that its resources, human and industrial, should be dispersed throughout the Commonwealth, principally to the 'white' dominions. He linked this to the concept that defence should be organized on a regional basis, each of the dominions taking a leading part in the defence arrangements of its region.

But the world tour which he undertook in the last months of 1945 made him realize that his concept was unrealistic. Wavell in India convinced him that it would not be possible for Britain to maintain her authority over the sub-continent by force and that it would be a major defence liability instead of the asset, with its great volunteer army, that it had been hitherto. In this, Alanbrooke's hopes received a severe setback. As he flew further east, he found to his disappoint-

2

ment that Australia, with New Zealand, showed no enthusiasm for assuming a greater responsibility for defence in that region. By the time he handed over the post that he had held for five and a half years to Montgomery in June 1946, his vision of a shared Commonwealth defence, strengthened by a dispersion of Britain's resources, had faded into oblivion.

His successor took a more robust but equally unrealistic view. On taking over as CIGS, Montgomery was appalled to discover that the Prime Minister, Attlee, thought that Britain should make no attempt to maintain her military position in the Middle East, or expect to be able to traverse the Mediterranean and the Suez Canal in the event of a clash with the Soviet Union, but should plan on using the Cape route to maintain sea communications with the Indian Ocean. Montgomery was determined that the army should not suffer from something like the permanent prolongation of the 'No war within ten years' rule that had left it disastrously ill-equipped and unprepared for war in 1939. Without bothering to discuss the strategic background with his colleagues in the Chiefs of Staff Committee, let alone with any of his or their political masters, within a month of assuming office he issued a directive, laying down that the regular army 'must within five years be adequately equipped to handle any small troubles that might arise' and that it and the Territorial Army – the two together described as 'The Balanced Whole' – must be ready 'as regards equipment, manpower, ammunition, reserves etc.' to fight a major war, and that that situation must be maintained thereafter.* Having failed to persuade his colleagues, Admiral Sir John Cunningham and Marshal of the Royal Air Force Lord Tedder (who was also chairman of the Chiefs of Staff), to join him in producing an agreed memorandum on strategy, he characteristically produced one himself within two weeks. He recommended that:

a. We should attempt to build up the strength of our potential allies in Europe to establish a Western Bloc which, by holding the land armies in the West, would keep the war away from Britain.

b. We should fight for the North Africa coastline and thus enable our communications through the Mediterranean to be kept open.

c. We should fight for the Middle East, which with the United Kingdom would form the bases for the launching of such a

*Nigel Hamilton, *Monty. The Field Marshal 1944–1976*. London, 1986, p. 652.

tremendous air offensive against Russian resources as to make it impossible for her to carry on the war.

In spite of the faith in strategic bombing which the last recommendation implied, Tedder and Cunningham refused to go along with Montgomery or to allow his paper to be forwarded to the Prime Minister. Their views about future defence needs reflected their service backgrounds. Cunningham, a conventional sailor, thought that the war had proved that Britain's traditional maritime strategy – what Liddell Hart had described as 'The British Way in Warfare' – was the one to follow and that a commitment before a war had started to deploy and maintain an army on the continent of Europe was a fatal error. In 1914 it had led to a limitless drain on our resources, which had restricted those available to the navy, when the ultimate threat to our existence was a maritime one: the interruption of our ability to bring to our ports and pass through them the supplies needed to keep our overpopulated island alive. We should pay heed to the advice of Francis Bacon, that: 'He that commands the sea is at great liberty and may take as much or as little of the war as he will, whereas those that be strongest on land are many times nevertheless in great straits.'* There is no denying the navalist contention that, once Britain had provided a contingent to fight alongside an ally on the continent, the commitment was liable to escalate beyond the control of the British government, with the result that it would reduce the effort available for maritime operations; but it disregarded the danger that a power which dominated the land of the continent of Europe could build a powerful navy and deploy it, with overwhelming air support, in the seas all round Britain and across our trade routes. Britain's strategic problem had always been to strike the right balance between a continental commitment and the exercise of sea power.

The airmen, led by Lord Tedder, had little sympathy for either the army's or the navy's view. Although there might be argument about how much the strategic bombing of Germany had contributed to victory, there could be no doubt about the effect of the two atomic bombs dropped on Japan. Strategic bombing with nuclear weapons would certainly be decisive, and would make it impossible to conduct long-drawn-out campaigns either on land or at sea. The Chiefs of Staff had looked forward to cooperation with the United States in the development and production of atomic bombs, to deliver which

*Essays. 29. Of The True Greatness of Kingdoms.

4

the air staff were producing specifications for new bomber aircraft;* but the passage of the McMahon Act through the US Congress in August 1946 put paid to that. The influences which persuaded Attlee, and the few colleagues whom he made privy to the matter, to proceed with plans to develop British nuclear weapons on our own were not solely military.

They were strongly moved by the fear that the USA might have a monopoly of nuclear power as a source of energy, on which high hopes were then placed. Nevertheless it had been assumed by all those in the know that Britain, after the war, would produce her own atomic bombs. The agreement between Churchill, Roosevelt and the Canadian Premier, Mackenzie King, at Quebec in 1943 had led them to expect that the US government would share the secrets of the technique of manufacture, but it became clear to Attlee, when he visited President Truman in Washington in November 1945, that he was going to have difficulty in obtaining an assurance to that effect. Truman was under pressure from Congress, which had reacted sharply against the suggestion by Colonel Stimson, the War Secretary, that basic scientific data about the bomb should be shared with Russia. Congress was determined that responsibility for the nuclear programme should be transferred from military to civilian control. Their suspicion that Attlee's socialist government was too friendly to communism added to these pressures. In the months that followed, as the McMahon Bill made its way through Congress, Attlee received either negative answers to his representations to Truman, or none at all.

The McMahon Act came as a second blow to Anglo-American relations: the sudden end of Lend-Lease without any forewarning or discussion, only seven days after Japan's surrender, had been the first. Little wonder therefore that both the politicians and the military felt they could not rely on American help in the future, and that having one's own atomic bombs and the means to deliver them was the only viable deterrent against Soviet aggression. In reporting to the Prime Minister on 1 January 1946, the Chiefs of Staff re-emphasized their advice that the ability to retaliate in kind was the best defence against atomic attack. 'We must be prepared,' they wrote, 'for aggressors who have widely dispersed industries and populations. This means that in order to be effective as a deterrent we must have a considerable number of bombs at our disposal. It is not possible now to assess the precise number which we might

*To be eventually produced as the V-bombers, Valiant, Victor and Vulcan.

require but we are convinced we should aim to have as soon as possible a stock in the order of hundreds rather than scores.'* A firm decision was not taken until a year later, when it was provoked by a paper from Marshal of the Royal Air Force Lord Portal, who had been appointed Controller of Production, Atomic Energy, in the Ministry of Supply. He needed a firm decision before a number of important technical decisions could be made. The only Ministers present at the meeting at which the decision was made were Attlee (Prime Minister), Bevin (Foreign Secretary), Morrison (Lord President of the Council), A. V. Alexander (Defence), Addison (Dominions) and Wilmot (Supply). The Cabinet was not informed.

But it would be five years at least before Britain could hope to produce a bomb and nearly ten before any significant number, and the aircraft to deliver them, would be available. Meanwhile the varied and conflicting hopes of the political and military chiefs had to be subordinated to the needs of the moment. The 1946 Defence White Paper (Cmd 6743), having stated that 'The great strides . . . in Science and Technology, including the atomic bomb, cannot fail to affect the make up of our forces', had to admit that 'for 1946 the question of fundamental reorganization does not arise'. In the same paper the government congratulated itself on having, by demobilization, reduced the forces from a strength of 5.1 million, when they took over, to 2.2 million by 30 June 1946, setting as a target by the end of the year half that figure, with a further 100,000 under training.

The commitments which had to be met, most of them by the army, were, however, not being reduced at the same rate. The paper listed them as:

a. our share of forces to ensure the execution by Germany and Japan of the terms of surrender;
b. our share of the forces of occupation of Austria;
c. provision of forces to assist the Greek nation in its recovery;
d. provision of forces to carry out our responsibilities in Palestine;
e. liquidation of Japanese occupation in Allied territories in South East Asia;
f. maintenance of internal security and settled conditions throughout the Empire;
g. safeguarding of our communications and the upkeep of our bases.

*Margaret Gowing, *Independence and Deterrence. Britain and Atomic Energy 1945–52*. London, 1974, Vol. I, *Policy Making*, p. 169.

Hopes that voluntary recruitment would make it possible to meet these commitments without prolonging wartime conscription were doomed to disappointment. By September, on his return from a visit to the USA which itself angered both his fellow Chiefs of Staff and his political bosses, Montgomery decided that it was essential that conscription should continue at a length of 18 months' service. Failing to enlist the support of Tedder and Cunningham for the preparation of a paper setting out the manpower problem, he tackled Attlee directly, and was told to prepare a paper for the Defence Committee himself. The upshot was Cabinet approval, announced in the King's Speech at the State Opening of Parliament on 6 November 1946, that a bill would be introduced as Montgomery had recommended. There was strong opposition to it in both the Labour and the Liberal Parties, and it was only through the support of the Conservatives that Attlee succeeded in getting the bill through the Commons on 1 April 1947. As a sop to the considerable section of government supporters who were opposed to it, the period was reduced from 18 to 12 months two days later.

Before Montgomery's entry like a bull in a china shop into what was called 'The Central War Machinery', the new administration had considered what changes were needed to replace the idiosyncratic arrangements which Winston Churchill had introduced when he became Prime Minister in 1940 and combined the post with that of Minister of Defence. A further White Paper (Cmd 6923) stated that the Prime Minister would retain supreme responsibility for defence and that a Defence Committee, chaired by him, would take over the functions of the pre-war Committee of Imperial Defence. The Minister of Defence would be deputy chairman of the Defence Committee and would preside over meetings with the Chiefs of Staff 'whenever he or they may so desire'. He would be responsible to Parliament for:

(i)   the apportionment in broad outline of available resources between the three services in accordance with strategic policy laid down by the Defence Committee, including general policy for research and development and correlation of production programmes;

(ii) the settlement of questions of a general order in which a common policy for the three services is desirable;

(iii) the administration of inter-service organizations such as Combined Operations Headquarters and the Joint Intelligence Board.

7

The single-service Secretaries of State and their Chiefs of Staff therefore remained firmly entrenched in the Admiralty, the War Office and the Air Ministry.

The commitment described as 'maintenance of internal security and settled conditions throughout the Empire' included not only the restoration of British authority in those areas which had been over-run by the Japanese, notably in South East Asia, but also the thorny question of the future of India. Attlee's Labour administration was dedicated to granting independence and sought some federal sol-ution which could be established peacefully. But the mission sent to India in March 1946 was no more successful than had been previous attempts since the Cripps Mission of 1942 in finding a solution which would reconcile the conflicting demands of Congress, led by Nehru, and Jinnah's Muslim League. As the deadlock continued, Wavell, the Viceroy, suggested that, from March 1947, power should be handed over to Congress in those provinces in which they had a majority, while he continued to exercise authority in those with a Muslim majority, as well as in the two important ones with a Hindu majority in the north-west, bordering on what would become Paki-stan. A year later Britain would withdraw altogether. He told the Cabinet that the only alternative to this so-called Breakdown Plan was to reinforce the Indian Army with four or five British divisions and try and hang on to power for another 15 years. Neither choice was acceptable to Attlee who turned to Mountbatten to replace him, in the hope that he could find a way out of the impasse. He had been impressed by Mountbatten's judgement in the handling of events in Burma after the war in contrast to that of the Governor, Sir Reginald Dorman-Smith, who had shown himself inflexible and unimagin-ative in dealing with the Burmese nationalists. Whatever happened, the army in 1946 could not count on an early release from its commitment in the sub-continent.

As long as that commitment lasted, the Middle East fell into the category of 'safeguarding our communications and the upkeep of our bases' in addition to its own intrinsic strategic importance as a source of oil supply. In 1946 we still had troops in Iran, holding them there until Soviet forces were withdrawn from the north of the country. Potential troubles simmered also in Iraq, Palestine, Egypt and the Sudan. The base from which all these could be dealt with, the huge installation established in the Suez Canal Zone of Egypt during the war, was itself under threat. Egypt was demanding renegotiation of the 1936 Anglo-Egyptian Treaty, which covered Britain's right to station military forces in Egypt, including the

Suez Canal Zone, and her position in the Sudan. There had been nationalist riots in Cairo and Alexandria in November 1945, leading to the resignation of the Egyptian government in February 1946. Attlee had initially been sceptical about the need for Britain to retain a major military presence in the area. In response to a proposal by the Foreign Secretary and the Chiefs of Staff in August 1945 that Britain should be granted UN trusteeship in order to retain a military presence in the former Italian colonies of Cyrenaica and Somaliland, Attlee composed a memorandum in which he wrote:

1. At the back of all the argument is the idea of the defence of the British Empire leading to conclusions as to the importance of our retaining control of strategic areas in the Middle East.
2. Quite apart from the advent of the atomic bomb which could affect all considerations of strategic area, the British Commonwealth and Empire is not a unit that can be defended by itself. It was the creation of sea power. With the advent of air warfare the conditions which made it possible to defend a string of possessions scattered over five continents by means of a fleet based on island fortresses have gone. In the nineteenth century the passage of the Mediterranean could be secured by sea power with Gibraltar, Malta and Egypt as its bases. In the air age the neutrality, if not the support, of all countries contiguous to the route are needed. This is only one example.
3. The British Empire can only be defended by its membership of the United Nations organization. If we do not accept this, we had better say so. If we do accept this we should seek to make it effective and not at the same time act on outworn conceptions. If the new organization is a reality, it does not matter who holds Cyrenaica or Somalia or controls the Suez Canal. If it is not a reality we had better be thinking of the defence of England, for unless we can protect the home country no strategic positions elsewhere will avail.*

Attlee's views were to be considerably modified in the course of the following years of his administration, as the threat to British interests in the Middle East, principally oil, developed, potentially from the Soviet Union and actually from nationalist movements and American pressure; but in January 1947 he was still inclined to consider

*PRO CAB/129/Vol I/C.P.(45)144 dated 1 September 1945, quoted in Kenneth Harris, *Attlee*, London, 1982, Appendix IV.

withdrawal from the Middle East, provoking a threat from the Chiefs of Staff to resign if the government decided on that course.*

By then the major commitment in the area was in Palestine. The Labour Party had traditionally supported the Zionist cause and tended to sympathize with the demand to open the door of immigration to Palestine to the many thousands of Jews who had survived the holocaust in Europe, a demand strongly supported personally by President Truman, who pressed Britain to admit 100,000. But Bevin in the Foreign Office, backed by the Chiefs of Staff, resisted this, keenly sensitive to Arab feeling. August 1945 saw the formation of an alliance between the different Jewish armed resistance movements, which proceeded to increase their activity. By January 1946 this led to the deployment of 80,000 troops, rising to 100,000 by February 1947, when Bevin announced that the government was not prepared to sacrifice more British lives in trying to sustain an impossible burden, and that Britain would hand over the problem to the United Nations and leave when the Mandate expired on 15 May 1948. On 18 February, three days after that announcement, the British Ambassador in Washington presented a note to General Marshall, the US Secretary of State, informing him that Britain had decided to withdraw her troops from and terminate her economic aid to Greece and Turkey.

But as these burdens were being shed in Burma, India and the Middle East, new ones were being shouldered in Europe. The Marshall Plan for economic aid to Europe, arising in part from the British decision about Greece and Turkey, and the decision of the British and American governments to merge their occupation zones in Germany, carrying out financial and economic reforms there, brought to a head the conflicting and apparently irreconcilable views of the Western powers on the one hand and the Soviet Union on the other about the future of Germany. Talks between the Foreign Ministers finally broke down on 23 December 1947 and Bevin feared that the Russians might try and impose their solution by force. At that time the only plan on the files to deal with that eventuality was to withdraw the allied occupation forces from Germany. Bevin acted quickly to change matters and to try and ensure that the Americans, and if possible the 'white' dominions of the Commonwealth, were involved. He asked Montgomery to initiate military staff talks between the British, US and French Commanders-in-Chief in Germany 'with a view to ensuring concerted action in the event of any

*Viscount Montgomery, *Memoirs*. London, 1958, p. 436.

attempt by the Russians to move into Western Europe', and himself to go and talk with his French opposite number, General Revers, about it. While Bevin acted quickly on the diplomatic front with the support of his French colleague, Georges Bidault, and the Canadian Prime Minister, Lester Pearson, the Chiefs of Staff instructed their joint planners to review the strategy they should recommend. They came up with a paper which stated that 'The supreme object of our defence policy is the defence of the United Kingdom and the development of an offensive capability,' and their conclusion was:

> From the point of view of the countries of Western Europe, there is no doubt that they would be encouraged and fortified if we adopted a continental strategy, but this, in our view, is quite impracticable, at least until 1957. The retention of a foothold in Europe might be a practicable strategy, but requires much more detailed examination and discussion with the Americans. At present our view is that the disadvantages outweigh the advantages. We therefore conclude that, from our point of view, the best strategy appears to be the air strategy, since that gives us the best chance of preventing war and achieving ultimate victory and provides for at least some support to the countries of Western Europe. In any case we recommend that, in the forthcoming talks (in Washington) we should enter into no commitment to send land and air forces to the continent.*

This was not to the liking of Montgomery, who, contrary to the hallowed ritual of the procedure of the Chiefs of Staffs Committee, submitted a rival, and remarkably prescient, paper of his own. Its salient points were the need to develop the three western zones of occupation into one West German State, which could be accepted into Western Union (the organization based on the Brussels Treaty, then in process of negotiation) and contribute to its military strength. In order to persuade the French to accept the resurrection of their former enemy, Britain must commit herself to fighting alongside France on land on the line of the Rhine. The aim should be to build up a Western Union strong enough to hold a Soviet attack until American help could be deployed.†

When the two papers were considered by the Chiefs of Staff, Tedder and Cunningham supported the view of the joint planners.

*PRO DEFE4.10. JP(48)16(Final) of 27 January 1948.
†Hamilton, *Monty*, Vol. III, p. 702.

The issue was then referred to what was called a Staff Conference, a meeting of the Chiefs of Staff with Attlee, Bevin and Alexander. The minutes record that Tedder and Cunningham 'considered that it would prove financially and economically impossible to place an army on the Continent on the outbreak of war, especially as in any future war we should have to be prepared for full-scale operations from the beginning . . . it was open to doubt whether it was militarily sound to attempt to hold an enemy, with such predominant superiority in manpower, on the Continent.' They suggested that our support for Western Union should be limited to air and naval support. Tedder said that 'he could not believe that Western Union would collapse if we withheld a specific promise to fight on land on the Continent.' Cunningham agreed, and said:

> Our traditional policy was to encourage and assist our Continental allies to provide land forces but to refrain from engaging in any land operations ourselves at the outset, in order to leave ourselves free to wield our maritime power. Nowadays, of course, we could use air power as well, and he feared that any commitment to engage in land operations was bound to detract from our air and sea power. The only times we had broken away from our traditional policy had led to the tragedies of Mons and Dunkirk.

Even Montgomery seemed to have been affected by the concept of limited liability, although he stuck to his plea that we must line up with the French from the start. He said that Western Union would need 23 divisions by D + 14 and 48 by D + 30, and optimistically declared that France could produce 30, while we need only provide two. Attlee sided with Tedder and Cunningham and suggested that we should plan an offensive from the Middle East, while Bevin failed to give full support to Montgomery, saying that 'he would like the Chiefs of Staff to consider how the forces of the United Kingdom, France, the Benelux Countries and possibly Italy should be organized and rationalized so as to form an effective whole', and registered his dislike of Montgomery's idea of the resurrection of Germany.*

They were of course influenced by knowledge of the decision, taken a year previously, that we should develop our own atomic bomb. Reliance on an 'air strategy' must be seen in that light; but it would be at least nine years before we would be in a position to deliver any number – the joint planners' date of 1957 was linked to

*PRO DEFE4.10. COS(48) 18th Meeting.

that – and our Western European allies, and indeed the British public, did not even know that the decision had been made. One wonders how Cunningham thought that we were going to 'encourage and assist our Continental allies to provide land forces' if we did not, and how he would have proposed to 'wield our maritime power' against the Soviet Union advancing to the Rhine. Attlee's suggestion of an offensive against the Soviet Union launched from the Middle East seems equally unrealistic, unless he envisaged solely an aerial one, once atomic bombs were available.

As a first step, primarily to convince the Americans that the nations of Western Europe were prepared to make an effort to cooperate in their own defence, the Brussels Treaty was signed in March 1948 by Britain, France, Belgium, the Netherlands and Luxemburg, forming a Western European Union, for which a military command structure was created, headed by a Commanders-in-Chief Committee, established at Fontainebleau in France. With sighs of relief on all sides, Montgomery left Whitehall to assume the post of Chairman of the Committee, in which he clashed with the French Commander-in-Chief of the Land Forces, Marshal de Lattre de Tassigny, as sharply as he had with his colleagues in London.

A series of events persuaded the Americans to agree not only to a binding North Atlantic Alliance, but also to the establishment of an integrated military command organization, the principal command posts of which were to be held by them, Eisenhower returning from retirement to become the first Supreme Allied Commander Europe with his headquarters near Paris. The Western Union command organization was absorbed as a subordinate headquarters covering what was known as the Central Front, that is from the Alps to the Kiel Canal, Montgomery leaving it to join Eisenhower as his deputy. Although the North Atlantic Treaty, setting up the Alliance, was signed in April 1949, Eisenhower's headquarters* was not established until June 1950, after the Korean War had started.

When discussions about the North Atlantic Alliance had started, neither the Americans nor the British imagined that they were committing themselves to the permanent presence of their armies on the continent. Both hoped that they could limit their contribution to naval and air support once the armies of the continental European members of the Alliance had been built up by US military aid, while their economies were supported by the Marshall Plan. The events that prompted the Americans to commit themselves to a greater

*Supreme Headquarters Allied Powers Europe – SHAPE.

degree were the communist coup in Czechoslovakia in February 1948; the crisis over Berlin, culminating in the Soviet blockade in July, which, relieved by the airlift, lasted until May 1949; the crude pressure which the Soviet Union applied to Norway to try and prevent her joining any Western European grouping; the explosion of the first Soviet nuclear device on 23 September 1949, and, coinciding with it, Mao Tse-tung's final victory over Chiang Kai-shek and the latter's departure to Taiwan. By this time France had become thoroughly bogged down in Indo-China, and hopes that she would provide the bulk of the armies needed to face the Russians in Europe had faded. Far from being able to reduce the British forces, the equivalent of two divisions stationed in Germany as occupation forces, Attlee's government, in dire financial straits, was faced with the need to strengthen them and convert them into operational formations with effective logistic support. Hitherto they had been supplied with their purely occupational needs through the port of Hamburg. This clearly made no sense if they had to be prepared to fight invading Soviet armies. Nevertheless it was some years before a viable line of communications was established, based on Antwerp.

During this period yet another commitment arose, which was to last a long time and absorb a great many soldiers. On 16 June 1948 an emergency was declared in Malaya to counter the activities of the so-called Malayan Races Liberation Army, a communist rebellion led by Chin Peng, who had been decorated for his wartime resistance to the Japanese. It was almost entirely confined to the Chinese inhabitants of the country. While all this was in train, the government was struggling to reduce defence expenditure and the size of the forces. At the end of 1946 the strength of the services had been 1,427,000 and the target set for 31 March 1948 was just over one million. The estimated cost for the year 1947/48 was £899m. The Defence White Paper of February 1948 (Cmd 7327) proposed a further reduction from 940,000 at the beginning of the financial year 1948/49 to 716,000 by the end, the navy staying at 146,000, the RAF reducing from 261,000 to 226,000 and the army taking a major cut from 534,000 to 345,000. The estimates for this amounted to £692m, but later in the year the Minister for Defence, A.V. Alexander, tried to reduce it to £600m. This, combined with his refusal to do anything to encourage regular recruiting, led to two major rows with the Chiefs of Staff, Montgomery, before he went off to his Western Union post, demanding that National Service be extended to 18 months, although he made it clear that he thought that two years was needed.

These representations were effective. On 23 September 1948 Emmanuel Shinwell, Secretary of State for War, announced that more resources would be devoted to defence. Release from the forces would be deferred for three months and National Service, when the act came into force on 1 January 1949, would after all be for 18 months. Manpower overall would be reduced, but by less than had been planned; army strength would come down from 416,000 at the start of the 1949/50 financial year to 391,000, its call-up of national servicemen during the year being set at 120,000. With £200m devoted to new equipment, the defence budget for the year was estimated at £760m, representing 7 per cent of national income. None of this was popular with the government's supporters, but Attlee and Bevin were anxious that, while the North Atlantic Treaty was being negotiated, Britain should be seen to be setting a good example within the Western European Union. It was not easy for them to hold their position through the financial crisis which they faced in August 1949, which led to the devaluation of sterling. Cuts in government expenditure were fiercely resisted by departmental ministers. Alexander threatened to resign if there were cuts in defence, and Aneurin Bevan if they fell on the social services. In the end all suffered some reductions, but, after the Labour government was returned in the General Election of February 1950,* the defence budget was increased, in response to the need to strengthen, both in quality and quantity, the forces to be assigned to the new NATO command structure. Although manpower was to fall again by April 1951 to 682,100, of which 356,600 would be in the army, expenditure would rise to £780m, of which £193m would be for the navy, £304m for the army and £223m for the air force.† The March 1950 Defence White Paper (Cmd 7985) stated that 'a thorough review has been undertaken from an inter-service point of view of our present forces and the money allocated to their upkeep and development. The conclusion reached is that the existing balance between the forces is about right.'

But the government was not able to rest there. On 25 June 1950 North Korea invaded the South and within a month had driven the American and South Korean soldiers to the south-east corner, penning them into an area only 80 miles by 50. The British government's reaction was to send part of the Far East Fleet and an infantry

---

*The result was Labour 315, Conservative 298, others 12.
†It was hoped that some of the dollar cost of this would be met by US military aid.

brigade from the Far East, to be joined later by one from the United Kingdom. Together with a Canadian brigade and units from Australia and New Zealand, they were later to form the Commonwealth Division. The first reaction of the Chiefs of Staff was to think that it might be a Soviet-inspired diversion to draw in US and Allied defence effort, thus weakening NATO in Europe, where they might be planning their main offensive. They were therefore initially reluctant to send land or air forces, but were overruled. It was clear to Attlee that we could not expect the Americans to support our position in the Far East, including in Hong Kong, about which they had always, as anti-colonialists, been lukewarm, nor could we hope to influence their action, unless we made an acceptable contribution to what was technically a United Nations Force, quite apart from the Labour Party's devotion to attempts to strengthen that organization. The Chiefs of Staff were no keener on the use of nuclear weapons. At their meeting on 28 June they concluded that:

It might be suggested by the Americans that in the event of their participation being insufficient to restore the situation in Korea, an atom bomb should be dropped in North Korea. If the proposal should be made, ministers would wish to know the views of the Chiefs of Staff. There was general agreement from the military point of view that the dropping of an atomic bomb in North Korea would be unsound. The effects of such action would be worldwide, and might well be very damaging. Moreover it would probably provoke a global war.*

In this atmosphere, soon after the whole of China had come under communist rule and when there were real fears that the Soviet Union, allied to her, might be planning a worldwide offensive, Attlee and Bevin decided that Britain must sacrifice her desire for better social conditions and brace herself for a programme of rearmament. There must be no repetition of the 1930s. Vegetius's maxim – 'If you want peace, prepare for war' – must be the order of the day. An immediate increase in the defence budget of £100m was announced and, before the House of Commons rose for the summer recess in August, Shinwell, who, after the election, had succeeded Alexander as Minister for Defence, announced a three-year programme to strengthen the forces, costing £3,400m, which was increased to £3,600m when Parliament was recalled on 12 September, the period

*Quoted in Max Hastings, *The Korean War*. London, 1987, p. 73.

of National Service being extended at the same time to two years. Five days later General MacArthur dispelled the atmosphere of gloom which had pervaded the Korean scene by his successful amphibious operation at Inchon, followed by the recapture of Seoul. As he drove the North Korean army back to the Manchurian frontier on the River Yalu, those in the Labour Party who had supported the rearmament programme began to doubt if it was necessary, the divisions within the Party being accentuated by the resignation on health grounds of Stafford Cripps as Chancellor of the Exchequer. Attlee's choice of Arthur Gaitskell as his successor angered Aneurin Bevan and the left of the party, sowing the seeds of the trouble which was to erupt a year later.

The feeling of relief about Korea was rudely shattered towards the end of November when Chinese communist forces launched a counter-offensive across the Yalu, driving MacArthur's army right back behind the 38th parallel, which divided North from South Korea. MacArthur demanded the right to bomb targets in China in retaliation, and President Truman made some remarks which were interpreted as meaning that he contemplated using nuclear weapons. Attlee was greatly concerned on two grounds: both that a general war against China should be avoided and that nuclear weapons should not be used. He sought assurance that the 1943 Quebec agreement that neither country should use the weapon without the agreement of the other would be adhered to. Ernest Bevin not being fit to travel, Attlee went himself to Washington to see Truman, taking the line that all nations which had contributed to the UN Force in Korea should be consulted and that there should be unanimity among them before a decision was taken to use an atomic bomb. So concerned was he that he went so far as to suggest to Truman that a ceasefire should be negotiated and that UN forces should be withdrawn from Korea. He failed in that plea, but Truman assured him that he had no intention of giving in to MacArthur and becoming involved in a general war with China, nor was he contemplating the use of nuclear weapons. In a private conversation, he assured Attlee that he would be consulted before nuclear weapons were used, but his Secretary of State, Dean Acheson, reminded him of his constitutional position: that he could not commit himself to consult others before authorizing the use of nuclear weapons in defence of the United States or its forces or interests. However, on his return to London, Attlee reported to the Cabinet that the President 'had entirely satisfied him about the use of the bomb. He had assured the Prime Minister that he regarded the atomic bomb as in

17

a sense a joint possession of the US, the UK and Canada, and that he would not authorize its use without prior consultation with the other two governments save in an extreme emergency – such as an atomic attack on the US which called for immediate retaliation.'* Unfortunately there was no agreed record of this, the US authorities refusing to accept the British record of what had transpired, or to commit themselves beyond the wording of the communiqué issued, which had simply said that it was the President's hope that world conditions would never call for the use of the atomic bomb, but that he had told the Prime Minister that it was also his desire to keep him at all times informed of developments which might bring about a change in the situation. They maintained that this superseded the undertaking to consult which the President had given the Prime Minister before Acheson had reminded him of his constitutional position, as well as the Quebec agreement, of which there was no official agreed record.

Attlee's report to Cabinet did not satisfy the Chiefs of Staff, especially the Chief of the Air Staff, Sir John Slessor, who was very concerned that the US might launch atomic bomb attacks by aircraft based in the UK, as they had been since the Berlin crisis, without the air staff having any idea of their plans. He called for an immediate joint study of the strategic use of the atomic bomb, including disclosure of American plans to the British air staff. It could not be left to last minute *ad hoc* discussion, as had been the case over Korea. The Chiefs of Staff and the Foreign Office were also concerned about the apparent American view that use of the bomb would solve all problems. Britain's vulnerability alone compelled them to regard its use as a 'last resort', only to be turned to if all else failed and the alternative would be worse than war, such as capitulation to Soviet communism. The issue was not resolved until October 1951, when both the US and British governments accepted the formula that the use by the Americans of air bases and facilities in the United Kingdom in an emergency 'naturally remains a matter for joint decision in the light of the circumstances of the time'.†

In return for what Attlee thought that he had obtained from Truman, he had to make a contribution himself. It was to agree to an announcement that 'the military capabilities of the US and the UK should be increased as rapidly as possible.' The American interpretation of this was that Britain should expand her three-year

*Harris, *Attlee*, pp. 465–6.
†Gowing, *Independence and Deterrence*, pp. 314–19.

£3,600m programme to one of £6,000m. Attlee faced considerable opposition within his Cabinet to any further increases, and Bevin's illness meant that he had to bear the burden of arguing against Bevan almost alone. In the end the programme was increased to £4,700m, doubling the pre-Korean-war rate of expenditure and bringing it to 14 per cent of national income. When the programme was debated in the House of Commons on 14 February 1951, Aneurin Bevan, to everyone's surprise, defended it with fervour. This was less than a month before Attlee persuaded a reluctant Ernest Bevin to leave the Foreign Office, five weeks before his death, to be succeeded by Herbert Morrison.

The latter was soon faced by a new crisis in the Middle East, stemming from the advent to power as Prime Minister of Iran in May 1951 of the nationalist Dr Mossadeq, intent on nationalizing the oil industry, wholly owned by the Anglo-Iranian Oil Company. When the US government urged that force should not be used for fear of provoking Soviet intervention, Morrison, smarting from the recent defections of Burgess and Maclean, suspected that American oil interests were trying to oust Britain's. He took a jingoist line, sending a parachute brigade and additional naval forces to the eastern Mediterranean. Taking advantage of Morrison's absence in July, Attlee took direct control of the affair himself and sent an emissary, Richard Stokes, to talk to Mossadeq. By the time that he had advised that negotiations should be opened with Iran, the refinery at Abadan had been shut down. Morrison still favoured military action, but the Cabinet supported Attlee in rejecting it, except for the purpose of saving lives, and in deciding to refer the matter to the United Nations, while the expatriate employees of the Anglo-Iranian Oil Company abandoned Abadan.

By this time the government's narrow majority in the House of Commons and its internal divisions combined to raise demands for a general election. Attlee had already announced, on 5 September, that Parliament would be dissolved a month later. The result of the election which followed was Conservative 321, Labour 295, Liberals 6, Irish Nationalists 2, Irish Labour 1, giving Winston Churchill, who returned to power one month before his 77th birthday, an overall majority of only 17.

2

IMPERIAL ECHOES: 1951–1955

W HEN THE OLD warhorse returned to power, he decided to revert to his wartime method of dealing with defence matters by assuming also the portfolio of Minister of Defence. After a few months, however, he realized that he could not carry the double burden and appointed the soldier whom he had for long admired most, Field Marshal Alexander, who, since the end of the war, had been Governor-General of Canada. It did not prove to be a happy appointment. Alexander's experience of Whitehall was limited to one year in a minor staff appointment in the War Office 20 years before, and he carried no political weight. As the constitutional powers of the Minister at that time were limited to the timid formula which Attlee had devised, his actual power depended on that. Even if Alexander had been inclined to take a strong independent line, which he was not, his lack of political weight would have made it difficult.

It was ironic that one of the first acts of Churchill's Conservatives, who had criticized their Labour predecessors for hesitation in rearmament, but without whose support Attlee would never have pushed his programme through Parliament, was to decide that the country could not afford it, and that it must be reduced. It had certainly been ambitious. The navy was planning to build six new fleet aircraft-carriers, but the bulk of its programme was devoted to modernization of ships of all kinds constructed during the war. The cost of both new construction and modernization had escalated alarmingly, the new county class cruisers involving eight times as much effort as their predecessors and the cost of radar and radio equipment for one aircraft-carrier 15 times as much. The latter had to be converted to steam catapults and angled decks for launching the aircraft, the first jets, Sea Venoms, taking off in 1952.

The rearmament programme had come at a difficult time as far as aircraft for both the navy and the RAF were concerned. In general it had been decided that, with the exception of the Venom fighter and the Canberra bomber, the introduction of new types should be delayed until major technical advances could be included. The pressures on research and development resources exerted by the nuclear programme had meant that insufficient effort was devoted to research in the aircraft field. The rearmament programme, however, was based on a front-line strength for the RAF of between 3,000 and 4,000 aircraft, including a commitment to provide one-third of the 4,000 planned by NATO for the air defence of Western Europe. The result was a proliferation of production and development contracts among the 16 British aircraft firms, with their seven subsidiaries, all of whom ran into difficulties over the supply of skilled labour, of machine-tools and of materials. The appearance in Korean skies in November 1950 of the Russian Mig–15 fighter, significantly superior to any British fighter at the time, had come as a severe shock, and it was not until the USA and Canada agreed in 1952 to supply Britain with 400 F86 Sabre jets that the RAF was able to fill the gap until its own Hunter belatedly entered service in 1956, the Swift having fallen by the wayside.

The army's target had also been ambitious. It was planning to form ten active divisions, four of which – three armoured – would be stationed in Germany. The Territorial Army was to form 12, including one armoured and one airborne, as well as manning the anti-aircraft and coastal defences of the United Kingdom. This involved a major re-equipment programme, a significant item in which was the excellent Centurion tank, with its powerful new 105-mm gun. Although the actual results of this ambitious programme, in terms of new equipment available to combat units, were not yet great, the strain it was placing on the economy caused considerable concern in Whitehall. The rearmament programme was absorbing too great a proportion of industrial effort in every field and, in the view of the Treasury, leading the nation into bankruptcy with a balance of payments deficit approaching £600m towards the end of the year. Rab Butler, Chancellor of the Exchequer, demanded austerity measures and a sharp reduction in defence expenditure. Some immediate economies were made, the defence share of industrial production being cut from 20 to 15 per cent. Nevertheless the targets, in terms of size, for all three services were maintained in the February Defence White Paper (Cmd 8475), their strength expected to increase to 900,000 from the 809,000 it had been at the beginning of the financial year. This would be achieved, it was hoped, by an increase in regular strength of some 100,000, the National Service figure staying at 319,000. This was estimated to cost £1,377.2m of which £332.3m was for the navy, £491.5m for the army, £437.6m for the RAF, £98.5m for the Ministry of Supply (most of it for the benefit of the RAF) and £17.3m for the diminutive Ministry of Defence.

The stalemate that had been reached in Korea, combined with the establishment of NATO's military organization, served to dispel the more pessimistic fears of an imminent worldwide Soviet offensive, so that the urgency of the rearmament programme seemed less acute. Churchill, however, was alarmed to discover how much of the army's strength was dispersed overseas and how little was available for home defence. Egged on by Liddell Hart, he conjured up the threat of a sudden Soviet paratroop descent on the south-east of England, a danger which nobody else took seriously. Nevertheless it resulted in a resurrection of the Home Guard and attempts to organize fighting units from administrative installations in that area. Public response was lukewarm, only 25,000 volunteering out of the target figure of five times that number. Although the direct threat of a Soviet invasion seemed less imminent, the indirect one of communist subversion of countries on Soviet and Chinese borders, which might either come under communist influence or open their doors to Soviet or Chinese forces, was a permanent source of anxiety during the 1950s, notably in the Far East, but also in the Middle East.

The principal themes which dominated British defence policy while Churchill was Prime Minister from 1951 until he handed over, reluctantly, to Anthony Eden in April 1955, were, first, the problems arising from the attempt to rearm Germany and bring her somehow into NATO; second, the Middle East; third, the outbreaks of subversion in the colonies – Malaya, Kenya and Cyprus; and, finally, the part to be played by nuclear weapons, in particular British ones.

From the earliest days of the North Atlantic Alliance, the Americans had insisted, with good reason, that Western Europe could not be defended without a contribution from West Germany, and had made it clear that they would not commit their army to NATO plans unless that were achieved. This pressure provoked the proposal by the French Prime Minister, René Pleven, in October 1950 for a European Defence Community which would raise and control a European Army, in which there would be no national units larger than battalions, although this was later modified in the course of negotiations to brigade-sized ones. Churchill himself might have been thought of as the father of the concept. In a speech to the Assembly of the Council of Europe in Strasbourg on 11 August 1950, he had said:

We should now send a message of confidence and courage from the House of Europe to the whole world. Not only should we reaffirm, as we have been asked to do, our allegiance to the United Nations, but we should make a gesture of practical and constructive guidance by declaring ourselves in favour of the immediate creation of a European army under a unified command, and in which we should bear a worthy and honourable part.*

He made it clear at the time to Duncan Sandys, his son-in-law, that he had in mind national contributions of division strength. 'It would seem that about sixty divisions should be formed at once and stationed in Europe with another forty ear-marked as reinforcements for the ninetieth day after general mobilization,' he wrote.† But once in office he poured scorn on the Pleven Plan, describing the European Army as 'a sludgy amalgam' and unfairly stating on a number of occasions that it would entail mixing up 'companies or even platoons'. He and Eden were entirely in agreement that Britain could no more join the European Defence Community and Army than it could the European Coal and Steel Community, forerunner of the EEC, although we would have 'the closest association with it' under NATO. Eden made this clear in a speech at Columbia University on 11 January 1952, while he and Churchill were visiting Washington to discuss matters with President Truman and his Secretary of State, Dean Acheson.

The American and British peoples [he said] should each understand the strong points in the other's national character. If you drive a nation to adopt procedures which run counter to its instincts, you weaken and may destroy the motive force of its action . . . You will realize that I am speaking of the frequent suggestion that the United Kingdom should join a federation on the continent of Europe. This is something we cannot do. We know that, if we were to attempt it, we should relax the springs of our action in the Western democratic cause and in the Atlantic association which is the expression of that cause. For Britain's story and her interests lie far beyond the continent of Europe. Our thoughts move across the seas to the many communities in which our people play their part, in every corner of the world.

*Anthony Eden, *Full Circle: Memoirs*. London, 1966, p. 30.
†Martin Gilbert, *Never Despair: Winston S. Churchill 1945–1965*. London, 1988, p. 544.

These are our family ties. That is our life: without it we should be no more than some millions of people living on an island off the coast of Europe, in which nobody wants to take any particular interest.*

However, Eden came under great pressure from his French colleague, Robert Schuman, for some closer relationship between Britain and the EDC. This was applied at the NATO conference at Lisbon in February 1952, which accepted the ambitious goal proposed by Eisenhower of over 90 divisions, and at which Churchill's trusted colleague Lord Ismay was appointed the first Secretary-General. Schuman pressed for at least a treaty relationship between both Britain and the USA and the EDC, which would apply the same automatic commitment to its defence as that contained in the Brussels Treaty; but neither Eden nor Acheson would concede this, arguing that it went beyond that of the North Atlantic Treaty, which was in any case limited to 20 years. In spite of the low opinion of the European Army as a military organization shared by Churchill, Eden, his Permanent Under-Secretary Sir Ivone Fitzpatrick, the British Chiefs of Staff and Field Marshal Montgomery (until he changed his mind to the intense annoyance of Churchill in 1953), the British government continued to press its fellow members of the Western European Union and the Germans to join the 'sludgy amalgam', while refusing to do so itself. While Eisenhower was SACEUR (Supreme Allied Commander, Europe), according to Eden he approved Britain's stance.† As French hesitations continued, Eden and Acheson concocted a formula which made it possible for France to sign the EDC Treaty on 27 May 1952, the day after the signature of 'contractual agreements' between the Federal Republic of Germany and the three occupying powers, Britain, the USA and France. The Anglo-American statement, published the same day, stated: 'If any action from whatever quarter threatens the integrity or unity of the Community, the two governments will regard this as a threat to their own security. They will act in accordance with Article 4 of the North Atlantic Treaty.'‡

But that was not the end of the matter. The EDC Treaty still had to be ratified, and opposition to it in France was widespread. Much

*Eden, *Full Circle*, p. 36.
†Eden, *Full Circle*, p. 32.
‡Article 4 states: 'The Parties will consult together whenever, in the opinion of any of them, the territorial integrity, political independence or security of any of the Parties is threatened.'

of it came from fear of a renascent military Germany, while the establishment of the EDC might encourage the Americans and British to take their armies away; some from the hope that, with the death of Stalin in March 1953, the attitude of the Soviet Union would change; and some, particularly among the military, that it would restrict France's freedom of action in dealing with problems in overseas territories, the situation in Indo-China at that time being critical. The Americans became increasingly impatient as the prospect of German rearmament receded. Eisenhower had left SHAPE in June 1952 to run successfully as the Republican candidate for the Presidency, and his Secretary of State, John Foster Dulles, applied increasing pressure on the French to ratify and on Britain to become more involved in order to bring this about. The fact that Eden, as a result of the botched operation on his gallstones, was out of action from mid-April until the end of September 1953, and that, unknown to the public, Churchill, as a result of a stroke, was virtually in the same state from 23 June until the same time, meant that Britain made no positive moves during the period. The issue was tackled again at the conference in Bermuda in December 1953 attended by Eisenhower, Dulles, Churchill, Eden and the French Prime Minister, Joseph Laniel, and Foreign Minister, Georges Bidault. Dulles spoke of 'an agonizing reappraisal' of American commitment to NATO if the treaty were not ratified. Churchill, in an emotional appeal, confused matters by reverting to his plan for an organization based on divisions, at the same time suggesting that, unless the EDC came into being immediately, 'We ought to establish an arrangement under NATO that would give us at once twelve German divisions.'* On the sidelines Dulles put pressure on Eden for a greater commitment by Britain.

The Soviet Union tried to put a spanner in the works by proposing a four-power conference on the future of Germany, which the USA and Britain resisted, finally giving way to French insistence that only proof of Soviet intransigence would enable them to achieve ratification. Fortunately Molotov, in the conference of Foreign Ministers held in Berlin from 25 January to 19 February 1954, proved true to form. By this time Eden saw that the long period of uncertainty was weakening the position of the German Chancellor, Konrad Adenauer, and that it was urgent that the Federal Republic should be established as a fully independent sovereign state with the least possible delay, and an end be put to 'contractual agreements'.

*Gilbert, *Never Despair*, pp. 926–7.

The Foreign Office therefore began to put pressure on the Chiefs of Staff to agree to some form of direct permanent participation by British armed forces. At their meeting on 3 March 1954 the Chiefs concluded that they were 'extremely reluctant to go beyond the formula for association of United Kingdom land formations with those of the EDC at a previous meeting (COS(54)7th); but if considered vital politically, it could be accepted. A division would be a suitable formation.'* At a meeting a few weeks later (COS(54)33rd) they approved a statement that: 'In order to promote the integration of the armed forces placed under the command of SACEUR, the United Kingdom agrees to the inclusion, if SACEUR so requests, of British formations and air force units in European formations, and vice-versa, where military considerations make this desirable and logistic considerations make it practicable.' At that meeting they pressed for a ban on the German possession of a submarine or strategic bomber force and of any fissile material. The Foreign Office opposed that as discrimination.

This coincided with the row in France when Marshal Juin, her senior soldier and Commander-in-Chief of NATO's Central Front, came out publicly in opposition to the European Army, although not to the concept of a European Defence Community, and was deprived of his French posts as a result.† The fall of Dien Bien Phu on 7 May, followed by the Geneva conference on Indo-China, preoccupied both the French Prime Minister, Pierre Mendès-France, and Eden, who chaired it, until 21 July. In the hope of getting the National Assembly to ratify, the former pressed for amendments to make the Treaty more anti-German, but Churchill and Eden persuaded him to present it unamended. When he did so at the end of August, the Assembly rejected it by 319 votes to 264, with 43 abstentions.

The crisis this provoked persuaded Eden to drop his objection to admitting Germany and Italy into the Western Union, and he saw this as the solution to the acceptance of the Federal Republic into the North Atlantic Alliance on the same basis as other members. Mendès-France tried to insist that this could only be agreed if safeguards against a German threat were incorporated into the Brussels Treaty, but Adenauer insisted that there must be no discrimination, although he was prepared voluntarily to accept limits

---

*PRO DEFE4.69.COS(54) 22nd meeting. Confidential annex.
†He offered to resign his NATO post, but General Gruenther, SACEUR, refused. He was reinstated in his national posts in July.

on German forces. Eden therefore refused the French demands, but sought some way of countering their fears, while under pressure from Dulles not to abandon the EDC, objecting to the Brussels Treaty solution as not being supranational. He said that: 'Congress had been sold an idea that the EDC could be built up so as to be able to stand alone, and US forces could be withdrawn,' a concept as objectionable to the British as it was to the French. Eden now concluded that the key lay in a firm British undertaking,

first, to maintain on the Continent the effective strength of the British forces then assigned to the Supreme Allied Commander Europe: that is four divisions and a tactical air force or whatever SACEUR regarded as equivalent fighting capacity; and, secondly, not to withdraw those forces against the wish of the majority of the Brussels Treaty powers, who should take their decisions in the knowledge of SACEUR's views.

This revolutionary British commitment to the continent satisfied all concerned, including Dulles, who was persuaded to accord the Brussels Treaty the pledge of support which, with Britain, the USA had promised to the EDC. Eden did not at first intend to get Cabinet approval for what must be regarded as one of the most important decisions of defence policy in Britain's history before he revealed it to his Western Union colleagues and the USA, but Churchill persuaded him to do so, having some reservations about it himself. The Cabinet gave its approval on 28 September and, after some hiccups, the French National Assembly voted in favour on 29 December 1954. The way was at last open for a German contribution to NATO. Eden had come a long way since his speech at Columbia University in January 1952.

In contrast to the meeting of minds between Churchill and Eden over policy towards the EDC and the ECSC, they were almost continuously at loggerheads over Middle Eastern policy, and particularly about negotiations with Egypt over revision of the Anglo-Egyptian Treaty. Ghosts from the past haunted Churchill. He had never become reconciled to what he regarded as a pusillanimous 'scuttle' from India and opposed anything that looked like the same from Egypt; or from the Sudan, still officially an Anglo-Egyptian condominium, to the establishment of which he had contributed in a minor way by his participation, as a young cavalry officer, in the Battle of Omdurman in 1897. He had always supported the Zionist cause and instinctively sided with Israel against Arab lobbies. He

27

wished to buttress our position in the Middle East, and especially on the Suez Canal itself, of so much strategic interest to Britain, by involving the Americans in some form of Middle East Defence organization on the lines of NATO, associating them with our Canal base.* Eden not only realized that direct American involvement was a forlorn hope, but actively disliked it. He suspected American interest in the Middle East to be driven by the desire of US oil firms to undermine our own oil interests. This was already evident in Iran, where they supported Mossadeq on the grounds that, if they did not do so, he would fall under Soviet influence. Although Eden was as keen as Churchill to maintain Britain's standing as a world power and her influence in the Middle East, and as anxious as the Americans to exclude communist influence from the area, he believed that the best way to achieve both aims was to keep on good terms with Arab rulers and to come to a peaceful agreement with Egypt. From the beginning of Churchill's administration, there were riots and attacks on British installations in the Canal Zone, culminating in serious assaults on foreign property in Cairo on 24 January 1952. The British garrison on the Canal was increased to a total of 80,000 and a plan was prepared by the Chiefs of Staff to despatch troops, if necessary, to protect British lives in Cairo and Alexandria. Tension eased when a coup by Egyptian army officers in July 1952 deposed King Farouk and took over the government, headed by the seemingly moderate Major-General Neguib. However he proved no more willing than his predecessors to consider joining some military alliance with Britain, which would preserve the base, but he was prepared to drop Egypt's claim to any form of sovereignty over the Sudan, once it was granted independence. This removed one of the obstacles to agreement over the Canal base, but negotiations were difficult and protracted. Churchill, supported by the right-wing faction of the Conservative Party known as the Suez Group, constantly objected to any further concessions and called for threats of military action. It had become clear that there was no prospect of direct American involvement, and the Chiefs of Staff came round to the view of the Foreign Office that, without willing Egyptian cooperation, the base was more of a liability than an asset, as well as being vulnerable to nuclear attack. With increasing demands on military manpower elsewhere and with Rab Butler, the Chancellor of the Exchequer,

*At one time the USA, France, Turkey, Australia and New Zealand were prepared to discuss such a concept, linked to the need to ensure the security of and free passage through the Suez Canal; but Egypt's refusal to participate put an end to the idea.

repeating his warnings about Britain's financial straits and the need to reduce defence expenditure, the Chiefs of Staff themselves were keen to run down the base, the first step being to transfer the military headquarters and certain key installations to Cyprus. In November 1953 the reasonable Neguib, who had nevertheless lent his support to anti-British propaganda, was replaced by the hardline Colonel Nasser, whom the Americans at first attempted to woo with offers of military supplies, until Eden's violent protests induced them to stop.

By this time it had become clear that there was no hope of persuading Egypt to join any military alliance, and Britain's demands were reduced to the stationing of 7,000 uniformed soldiers in peacetime to maintain and secure the base installations. Even this was eventually abandoned and heads of agreement were signed in Cairo on 27 July 1954, the treaty itself three months later. It was to last for seven years and provided for the withdrawal of British forces within 20 months, to be replaced by British and Egyptian civilian technicians. Egypt agreed that Britain could reactivate the base and put it on a war footing in the event of an armed attack on Egypt or any other member of the Arab League, or Turkey. The parties would consult in such an event. At the same time Egypt undertook to respect the 1888 Constantinople Convention on freedom of navigation through the Canal. Up to the last minute Churchill tried in vain to associate the US government with this agreement, making an impassioned plea to Eisenhower when he and Eden visited Washington in June 1954, while in private he described it as 'Anthony's policy of scuttle'. Relations between the two at the time were strained as a result of Churchill's constant postponement of his declared intention to hand over the reins of government to Eden. The most that he had been able to achieve in Washington was an assurance that, as Eden reported to the Cabinet on their return on 7 July, 'US aid to Egypt would be conditional on Egyptian fulfilment of any agreement relating to the Canal Zone base and that the US would support publicly the principle of free transit through the Suez Canal'. Churchill assured the Cabinet that he was now satisfied that the withdrawal of British troops from Egypt could be fully justified on military grounds.

> Our requirements in the Canal Zone [he explained] had been radically altered by the admission of Turkey to the North Atlantic Treaty* and the extension of a defensive Middle Eastern front as

*In October 1951.

29

far east as Pakistan. Furthermore the advent of thermonuclear weapons had greatly increased the vulnerability of a concentrated base area and it might not be right to continue to retain in Egypt 80,000 troops who would be better placed elsewhere. It was also relevant that the conditions in the Canal Zone were damaging both to the morale of the Forces and to recruitment.*

No hint of scuttle.

The mention of 'a defensive Middle East front as far east as Pakistan' was something of an exaggeration. Dulles had toured the area in May 1953 and had concluded that the Arab states, members of the Arab League, could not form a sound basis for an organization to contain the spread of Soviet influence in the Middle East. Turkey held a key strategic position. The only other candidate – at the far end of the area – was Pakistan. Prompted by promises of US aid, Pakistan began discussions with Turkey on a mutual security pact in February 1954, which was concluded in May. In a brief, approved by the Chiefs of Staff for a meeting with the head of the Australian navy in April, the following comments were made:

> *The Turko-Pakistan Pact* . . . has no military value at present . . . it might eventually lead to the formation of some effective organization for the defence of the area . . . [there have been] . . . recent signs of interest in the pact on the part of Iraq whose attitude may also have the desirable effect of reducing Egypt's influence in the Arab League. Whatever befalls, we could not accept the exclusion of the United Kingdom from any planning that may take place because we provide the one directive and cohesive force in the area for which there is no substitute.
> *Persia*: The Persians are so lacking in fighting qualities that it would be dangerous to plan on their being able to offer any effective resistance whatever. Her Majesty's Government has recently advised the Persians not to contemplate joining the Turko-Pakistan pact until they are considerably stronger.†

The attitude of 'Persia' had been changed by the coup, engineered by the British and American secret services, in August 1953 which enabled the Shah to get rid of Mossadeq and take power into his own hands. Nuri es Said, the pro-Western Prime Minister of Iraq,

---

*Gilbert, *Never Despair*, p. 1018.
†PRO.DEFE4.69.COS(54) 42nd meeting.

first tried to persuade Nasser to transform the Arab League into an alliance with Britain and the USA, but received a sharp rebuff. Having failed also to persuade Syria and the Lebanon to cooperate with Iraq in joining the Turko-Pakistan Pact, he went it alone and signed up on 24 February 1955, the agreement becoming known as the Baghdad Pact. This was welcome to Britain as holding out hope of preserving the right to maintain the RAF stations at Habbaniya and Shaiba in Iraq when the 1930 Anglo-Iraqi Treaty expired in 1957. Britain therefore adhered to the Pact, but nobody else did so, the French fearing that it would adversely affect their relations with Syria and the Lebanon, while the USA also refrained for fear of unfavourable reactions from other Arab states, although they associated themselves with it two years later. When, after the revolution in Iraq in 1958, leading to its departure from the Pact, it was converted into the Central Treaty Organization (CENTO) and Iran also joined, the Americans participated more fully. The formation of the Baghdad Pact coincided with a severe defeat which Israel inflicted on Egypt in the Gaza strip, after which Nasser turned more definitely away from any pro-Western association towards the Soviet Union, from whom, through Czechoslovakia, he obtained arms.

By this time Eden had replaced Churchill as Prime Minister and, at the General Election in May 1955, increased the Conservative majority in the House of Commons to 59. Macmillan had replaced Alexander as Defence Secretary in October 1954, but now became Foreign Secretary, his place being taken by Selwyn Lloyd. Macmillan had hoped that, as a vote-catcher for the election, he would have been able to announce a reduction in the two-year length of National Service, but while the reduction of strength in the Canal Zone had been delayed, new commitments were being added. Although the situation in Malaya had been transformed by General Templer, who had been High Commissioner and Commander-in-Chief since the ambush of Sir Henry Gurney in 1951, there were still the equivalent of 23 battalions (the majority Gurkha) deployed there in 1954. In 1952 the Kikuyu rebellion, known as Mau Mau, erupted in Kenya and by 1955 10,000 soldiers, half British and half African, were in action there. In April 1955 a further commitment was added when the EOKA* revolt broke out in Cyprus.

In October, when the retiring Chief of the Imperial General Staff, Field Marshal Harding, was appointed on the Templer model as Governor, the army's strength in Cyprus was raised to 12,000, to be

*Ethniki Organosis Kuprion Agoniston – National Organization of Cypriot Fighters.

increased a few months later to 17,000. In addition to these national commitments, a further international one had been accepted in the Far East in the form of membership of the South East Asia Treaty Organization (SEATO). This had arisen out of the 1954 Geneva conference and the consequent division of Vietnam. It was designed by Dulles to form a segment of a worldwide ring of containment of the communist powers, and, although Britain did not assign any specific forces to its plans other than some of those already stationed in the Far East, the commitment to reinforce them, if the plans had to be implemented, justified the service departments in their arguments to preserve forces capable of being deployed overseas and for the maintenance of the bases to support them. The War Office's interpretation of this commitment was the need to be able to deploy up to two divisions in either the Middle or the Far East and to maintain them there in action for six months.

But all these commitments ran counter to the government's wish, strongly urged by Butler at the Treasury, to reduce defence expenditure and, if possible, for electoral reasons, if for no other, reduce the period of National Service and eventually bring it to an end altogether and rely on voluntarily recruited forces. The Chiefs of Staff were forced by the determined and intelligent Chief of the Air Staff, Sir John Slessor, to face up to this dilemma in July 1952. His own solution to the problem was clear – greater reliance on nuclear weapons, used both strategically and tactically. He maintained that long campaigns on land or at sea were not possible in the nuclear age; and that we could not in any case afford to maintain the apparatus to conduct both nuclear and conventional war. We should get rid of commitments that involved us in the latter in the Middle and Far East, enabling us to create a strategic reserve based in the United Kingdom and restoring strategic freedom of action to deploy land and air forces to meet Cold War threats wherever they might arise. Reserve forces, only capable of being employed some time after mobilization, were no longer appropriate. Our contribution to NATO's land forces should be restricted to the three armoured divisions already stationed in Germany. When the Germans raised their 12 divisions, they should also be armoured and should be backed, not by traditional reserve infantry divisions, but by a highly trained Home Guard armed principally with anti-tank guns and with light automatics as their personal weapons. The war-winning weapon was the strategic bomber, delivering nuclear weapons. The purpose of the land and air forces was to contain the enemy's forces while the bomber force wreaked destruction on the enemy's homeland. Its ability to do so, and the threat that it would, was the only sure deterrent to war.

His colleagues, Admiral Sir Rhoderick McGrigor and Field Marshal Slim, were not prepared to accept this concept without qualification, particularly as Slessor saw the navy's aircraft-carrier force, with all the other ships needed to escort it, as the principal target for economies. They insisted that, after the initial exchange of nuclear weapons, there might be a period of 'broken-backed' war, when the two sides would continue the struggle, on land and especially at sea, among the ruins left by the nuclear exchange. They also emphasized that there were many situations short of full-scale war which called for the deployment of forces from all three services in which the use of strategic bombing, nuclear or conventional, was not appropriate. Nevertheless they accepted the general emphasis on nuclear weapons as the only valid deterrent to war and counter to the Soviet and Chinese superiority in numbers, if the deterrent failed to prevent it. Agreement between the three of them was reached on a definition of Britain's defence needs as to have sufficient conventional and nuclear forces 'to exercise influence on Cold War policy, to meet NATO obligations, to prepare for war in case the deterrent failed, and to play a part, albeit a small one, in the main deterrent, the air offensive'.*

At this stage none of them, and nobody within the government, appeared to challenge the need for Britain to manufacture her own nuclear weapons and the means to deliver them. This was partly on military grounds: that the Americans might not aim at targets which we considered of high priority to our defence, and that, unless we had our own nuclear delivery force, we would be unable to influence their use of them; also that there could be situations outside the NATO area, in the Middle East in particular, where the Americans might not be directly involved. But there was also strong political support on the grounds both of making it possible to influence the Americans and of not being dependent on them. Above all it was founded on the concept, shared by both Conservative and Labour, and passionately held by Churchill and Eden, of Britain's standing as a world power. The two parties saw it in different lights, but both attached great importance to the Commonwealth and the responsibilities that went with Britain's position in it. The Conservatives saw it as an area in which we wielded influence and as reinforcing Britain's status and influence in the world, Labour as a responsibility

*Gowing, *Independence and Deterrence*, pp. 440–43.

for less fortunate people, who should be guided and led towards running their own affairs, while being helped economically and in every other way to reach that status. Churchill expressed his view clearly in addressing the boys of his old school, Harrow, on 7 November 1952, a month after the successful test of Britain's first 'nuclear device' on Monte Bello island off the west coast of Australia. 'We in this small Island,' he said, 'have to make a supreme effort to keep our place and status, the place and status to which our undying genius entitles us.'

Churchill had hoped that, when he came to power, he would be able to persuade the Americans to be more cooperative in nuclear matters than they had been with Attlee's administration. He was disappointed. All that he had been able to obtain was the agreed formula about consultation over the use of American bombers based in Britain which stemmed from the informal understanding between Truman and Attlee.* His hopes were raised again when Eisenhower won the Presidential election in November 1952.

On 2 November there had been a large explosion on Eniwetok Atoll in the Pacific, which, two weeks later, the US authorities announced had been a 'thermo-nuclear weapon', but Churchill was given no more information than that bald public statement. It was not until he met Eisenhower in Bermuda in December 1953 that a serious discussion between them took place on nuclear matters, Churchill pressing for a resumption of wartime cooperation. Although the details of what was agreed, if anything, have not been released, it appears that Eisenhower expressed himself 'sympathetic' to exchange of intelligence about Soviet nuclear developments and agreed that the aim of the meeting had been 'to facilitate a climate for closer working relationships on matters of atomic weapons'. At that meeting Eisenhower said to Churchill that 'atomic weapons were now going to be regarded as a proper part of conventional armament and that he thought this a sound concept'. Churchill agreed. Eisenhower went on to say: 'If there were a deliberate breach of the (Korean) armistice by the Communists', the United States 'would expect to strike back with atomic weapons at military targets.' Churchill raised no objection and said that it 'put him in a position to say to Parliament that he had been consulted in advance and had agreed'. When Eisenhower repeated this next day, Eden was greatly concerned and persuaded Churchill to reverse his position. It was at this meeting also that the Americans were told that the first

*See p. 18.

British atomic weapon had been delivered to the RAF and that we 'did not intend to do any work on hydrogen bombs', as it was thought possible to obtain sufficient destructive power of one or possibly two megatons yield from 'boosted fission weapons' and that in Britain's view 'few targets needed a larger yield'.*

It was not until February 1954 that a statement by the Chairman of the Joint Congressional Committee on Atomic Energy, Sterling Cole, revealed that the explosion 15 months before had in fact been a successful test of a hydrogen bomb and described some of the effects. Two weeks later a second test took place on Bikini Atoll, and the fact was immediately publicly announced. Churchill was taken aback by Cole's statement. When he spoke about it in the House of Commons five months later, he said:

> Considering what immense differences the facts he disclosed made to our whole outlook for defence, and notably civil defence, depth of shelters, dispersion of population, anti-aircraft artillery, and so forth – on which considerable expenditure was being incurred – I was deeply concerned at the lack of information we possessed, and in view of all the past history of this subject, into which I do not propose to go today, I thought I ought to have a personal meeting with President Eisenhower at the first opportunity.†

He did write a long letter of protest to Eisenhower in the second week of March.

The American revelation, followed by news that the Soviet Union had exploded a similar bomb on 12 August 1953, sparked off a public debate about the morality of this terrible weapon and calls for the government to try and persuade both superpowers to abandon it. The Labour Party took this line in the House of Commons on 5 April 1954, Churchill strongly defending the American right to possess H-bombs. Having revealed, with Eisenhower's permission, the 1944 Quebec Agreement between himself and Roosevelt that Britain and the US 'will never use this agency against each other' nor 'against third parties without each other's consent', he infuriated the opposition, and upset some of his own supporters, by saying that the opposition's attitude came ill 'considering that the abandonment of our claim to be consulted and informed as an equal was the act of the Socialist administration'. That was certainly an unfair

---

*Gilbert, *Never Despair*, pp. 918, 924, 929.
†House of Commons *Hansard*, 12 July 1954.

accusation considering the attempts Attlee had made to persuade the Americans to abide by the agreement. Churchill argued that objection to American reliance on the H-bomb would lead to their abandonment of support for Western European defence. 'The United States would withdraw from Europe altogether, and, with her three-quarters of hydrogen bases already spread around the globe, would face Russia alone.'* Three weeks later, when the French forces in Indo-China faced a crisis at Dien Bien Phu, the US government proposed Anglo-American intervention. Eden was adamantly opposed and was supported by Churchill and other Ministers. Informing the US Admiral Radford, who had flown to Paris and London to ask for this, of the decision, Churchill said: 'The British people would not be easily influenced by what happened in the distant jungles of South East Asia; but they did know that there was a powerful American base in East Anglia and that war with China, who would invoke the Sino-Russian Pact, might mean an assault by hydrogen bombs on these islands.' To his doctor, Lord Moran, he gave different reasons: 'It is no good putting in troops to control the situation in the jungle. Besides, I don't see why one should fight for France in Indo-China when we have given away India.'†

On 16 June, eight days before his departure to see Eisenhower in Washington, Churchill presided over a meeting of the Defence Policy Committee of the Cabinet which decided to initiate the production of British H-bombs. The Cabinet was not informed, although Eisenhower personally was told on the first day of the Washington visit. As Churchill had hoped, it led to a promise of greater cooperation on nuclear matters. The secret was revealed to the Cabinet on his return on 6 July. Churchill's justification for the decision was:

We could not expect to maintain our influence as a world Power unless we possessed the most up-to-date nuclear weapons. The primary aim of our policy was to prevent major war; and the possession of these weapons was now the main deterrent to a potential aggressor. He had no doubt that the best hope of preserving world peace was to make it clear to potential aggressors that they had no hope of shielding themselves from a crushing retaliatory use of atomic power. For this purpose the Western Powers

*House of Commons *Hansard*, 5 April 1954.
†Gilbert, *Never Despair*, pp. 973–4.

must provide themselves, not only with a sufficient supply of up-
to-date nuclear weapons, but also with a multiplicity of bases from
which a retaliatory attack could be launched. They must put
themselves in a position to ensure that no surprise attack, however
large, could wholly destroy their power of effective retaliation.*

The Cabinet's response was by no means unanimously enthusiastic, objections being raised on grounds of expense, of the danger
of encouraging other nations, perhaps Germany, to follow our example, and of morality. All were dismissed on the argument that they
would not be greatly more expensive than the fission weapons they
would replace; and that the other objections applied equally to those
weapons, which we had already begun to produce. The Cabinet
deferred final approval until a further meeting at the end of the
month, when it was given.

The public first knew of the decision from the Defence White
Paper published in February 1955 (Cmd 9391), introduced by Churchill in a speech in the House of Commons on 1 March which was
intended as his swan-song. Speaking approvingly of Attlee's decision
to make the atomic bomb, 'owing to the breakdown in the exchange
of information with the United States in 1946', he said that he had
tried to live up to his standard. There was 'no absolute defence
against the hydrogen bomb' nor was there any method in sight 'by
which any nation, or any country, can be completely guaranteed
against the devastating injury which even a score of them might
inflict on wide regions'. 'Which way shall we turn,' he asked, 'to
save our lives and the future of the world? It does not matter so
much to old people; they are going soon anyway; but I find it
poignant to look at youth in all its activity and ardour and, most of
all, to watch little children playing their merry games, and wonder
what would lie before them if God wearied of mankind.' The great
powers, he suggested, should seek 'a balanced and phased system of
disarmament', but meanwhile we must depend on American nuclear
superiority to prevent the Iron Curtain being extended to the Atlantic and the Channel. He went on to say:

Unless a trustworthy and universal agreement upon disarmament,
conventional and nuclear alike, can be reached and an effective
system of inspection is established and is actually working, there
is only one sane policy for the free world in the next few years.

*Gilbert, *Never Despair*, p. 1019.

That is what we call defence through deterrents. This we have already adopted and proclaimed. These deterrents may at any time become the parents of disarmament, provided that they deter. To make our contribution to the deterrent we must ourselves possess the most up-to-date nuclear weapons, and the means of delivering them.

It may well be [he said towards the end of his speech] that we shall, by a process of sublime irony, have reached a stage where safety will be the sturdy shield of terror, and survival the twin brother of annihilation . . . The day may dawn when fair play, love for one's fellow men, respect for justice and freedom, will enable tormented generations to march forth serene and triumphant from the hideous epoch in which we have to dwell. Meanwhile, never flinch, never weary, never despair.*

The White Paper put it in more prosaic terms.

Overshadowing all else in the year 1954 has been the emergence of the thermo-nuclear bomb . . . New and revolutionary problems are posed requiring courage and imagination for their solution. Nevertheless our problem is still fundamentally a dual one. We have to prepare against the risk of a world war and so prevent it: it is on the nature of these preparations that the existence of thermo-nuclear weapons has its main effect. At the same time we must continue to play our part in the defence of the interests of the free world as a whole, and particularly of the Commonwealth and Empire, in the 'cold war', and we must meet the many other peacetime commitments overseas arising from our position as a great Power with world-wide responsibilities.

After reporting the decision to proceed with the development and production of thermo-nuclear weapons, the paper said that their existence 'greatly increases the difficulty of defence'. If used in war, they would cause 'destruction on an unprecedented scale' and their effects would mean that war 'would be a struggle for survival of the grimmest kind'.

In these circumstances [it said] our immediate duty and our policy are clear. To build up our forces, in conjunction with those of our allies, into the most powerful deterrent we can achieve. By this

*House of Commons *Hansard*, 1 March 1955.

means to work for peace through strength. Thus we shall hope to obtain real disarmament and relaxation of tension. But we must also equip and train our forces and so organise the country as to enable us to survive and to defeat the enemy if all our efforts for peace should fail. Nevertheless our long-term policy remains unchanged.

That policy had been set out in the February 1954 Defence White Paper (Cmd 9075). It had opened with a forecast that, provided the defence effort of Britain, her Commonwealth partners and allies was built up and maintained, a prolonged period of cold war was more likely than a major fighting war; but the maintenance of a defence effort 'at the maximum which our economic capabilities permit' imposed a heavy economic burden. The armed forces could not 'be provided with all those things which ideally they should have'. If a global war were forced upon us, 'it must be assumed that atomic weapons would be employed by both sides'. There would be an intense period of nuclear exchange, followed by one of 'broken-backed warfare'. 'Our forces must be able to withstand the first shock. Our reserve forces must be capable of rapid mobilization behind the shield which our active forces provide and be ready to perform their combat tasks at the earliest possible moment.' Referring to atomic weapons, the paper said that 'it will be some years yet before we have enough of these new weapons to bring about any radical modification in the pattern of the United Kingdom defence effort.' We would still need troops on the ground and air forces. 'Within a total budget, we may not be able to afford both new weapons and conventional forces of their present size.' A gradual change should be brought about with greater emphasis on the RAF, 'because of the need to build up the strategic bomber force and because of the importance of guided missiles in air defence'. Expenditure on the army would tend to decline, although that would depend on commitments which the army 'as an instrument of Government policy' had to meet.

The navy would continue to concentrate on building up and modernizing its anti-submarine and anti-mine forces and on the completion of the aircraft-carriers under construction, which would be fitted with the new angled deck. All this was estimated to cost £1,554m and absorb manpower which, by 1 April 1955, would have fallen to 844,300 of whom 283,500 would be National Servicemen, and 24,000 women. But in spite of the statement in the 1955 White Paper that 'our long-term policy remains unchanged', there *had* been a significant change. At their meeting on 7 April 1954 the Chiefs of Staff agreed that 'the current concept of a future war, which grew from the previous review,* that there would first be an intense phase and then a "broken-backed" one, was unrealistic. Once war had started it would be waged with all resources available until some conclusion was reached.'† Churchill's finale as Prime Minister ended on a sombre note.

*The Global Strategy Paper. COS(52)361.
†PRO DEFE4.69. COS(54) 35th meeting. Confidential annex.

3

SUEZ AND SANDYS: 1955–1961

MACMILLAN HAD ONLY been Minister of Defence for six months when, on Eden's appointment as Prime Minister, he was transferred to the Foreign Office, but the impressions he had gained in his short tenure were to have significant results when he succeeded Eden as Prime Minister in January 1957. He was intensely frustrated by the Minister's lack of power over the service departments, exacerbated by the fact that Churchill not only interfered in the detail of defence matters but, presiding over the Defence Committee, dealt directly with the service Secretaries of State and their Chiefs of Staff. This prevented Macmillan from attempting to initiate the radical changes which he realized were necessary if defence expenditure was to be kept under control and which he was persuaded were made possible by the advent of the H-bomb. One of the obstacles to this was the commitment that, on Eden's initiative, had just been undertaken to maintain the strength of the army and air force stationed in Germany *ad infinitum*. Not only did that impose a high degree of inflexibility on the defence programme, but, since the 1952 'contractual agreements' with the Federal Republic, the additional expense of stationing these forces in Germany could no longer be charged to occupation costs and had to be paid in Deutschmarks. Argument about a German contribution to this was to continue for many years, resisted by the Federal Republic, especially when it was raising its own forces. One nuclear matter was dealt with in his time. In March 1955 Eisenhower and Dulles had publicly tried to draw a clear distinction between strategic, thermo-nuclear weapons and smaller tactical fission ones, suggesting that the latter should be regarded as 'conventional' when used against military targets. Eden, Macmillan and the Chiefs of Staff were united in opposing this, pointing out that:

> it would be fatal to give the impression that so long as no hydrogen bomb was dropped on Allied territory, none would be used against

41

Russia, or that the only likely victims of nuclear weapons in a new global war would be the armed forces and not the civilian populations and centres of government and industry . . . The Russians must be left in no doubt that the use against the West of any of their nuclear weapons would immediately bring upon them retaliation from the whole Allied armoury.*

Macmillan's views impressed Eden, who, on becoming Prime Minister, addressed himself to these matters. The 1955 Defence White Paper had estimated expenditure for the coming financial year at £1,554m and Selwyn Lloyd told him that, on current plans, it was expected to rise by 1959 to £1,929m. Eden's immediate reaction was to look for economies in conventional preparations for global war and specifically in the commitment to NATO which he had been instrumental in affirming. Some immediate economies were initiated. In the navy these were centred on reserves of various kinds, including scrapping battleships, which Churchill had resisted; in the army largely by reducing the manpower of units and cutting logistic support; in the air force by reductions in the medium bomber force and in Fighter and Coastal Commands. The Swift fighter had already been cancelled and some guided missile projects went the same way.

These cuts were expected to reduce planned expenditure in the financial year 1956/57 to £1,535m, manpower falling from the 823,630 it had been on 1 April 1955 to 700,000 by the end of 1957. The February 1956 Defence White Paper (Cmd 9691) reflected the change in the Chiefs of Staff's view about 'broken-backed' war, emphasizing the importance of immediate readiness for war and stating: 'We can no longer rely on meeting our needs for men or munitions by mobilizing reserves of untrained manpower or of industrial capacity.' The tasks of the forces were: 'First to make a contribution to the Allied deterrent commensurate with our standing as a world Power'; second, to play their part in the cold war; third, 'They must be capable of dealing with outbreaks of limited war should they occur'; and, finally, 'They must also be capable of playing their part effectively in global war should it break out. This will have to include support to the civil authorities.' One of the ways of doing this was the Mobile Defence Corps, which had been established in the previous year, intended to be 'specially trained in, and equipped for, fire-fighting and rescue and ambulance duties'.

*Harold Macmillan, *Tides of Fortune*. London, 1969, pp. 571–2.

The plan was to reach a strength within four years of 48 reserve battalions, each of 600 men, drawn from National Servicemen who had served in the army or air force and still had a reserve liability. They would receive one month's full-time training and 15 days' reserve training a year thereafter. The 1956 paper announced that the target had been reduced to 36 battalions and fire-fighting training dropped. The Corps was disbanded in 1959 when the end of National Service was in sight.

The 1956 paper explained that reduction in the size of the forces was necessary if defence expenditure was not to rise and undermine the economy. The forces would become 'smaller but harder-hitting'. The navy 'plan to make immediately available in any part of the world a force of aircraft-carriers equipped with modern aircraft and supplemented by cruisers and escorts', but the emphasis would be on anti-submarine warfare and fitting guided missiles to ships of various kinds. The army would bear the brunt of manpower reductions, one method of achieving them being the slimming down of divisions, particularly armoured ones, and the distribution of tanks and artillery to infantry brigades. In the air force an increasing role would be allotted to surface-to-air missiles in air defence: 'Close defence of vulnerable areas is an outdated concept. Our aim is a guided weapon system which can break up enemy attacks before they penetrate over the coastline and which can be integrated with our fighter defence.' By this means defence expenditure could be held at just under £1,500m after allowing for £50m from US military aid. It was hoped to extract a similar sum from the Germans as a contribution to 'support costs' of the forces in Germany. Manpower was expected to fall to 772,000 by 1 April 1956 and 735,000 by 1957, the National Service element falling from 285,000 to 253,000.

Eden told Selwyn Lloyd to initiate a major review of longer-term defence needs, which was considered by the Defence Policy Committee early in July. The conclusion was to place even greater reliance than hitherto on nuclear weapons, certainly for the defence of Europe. The role of the conventional forces of NATO was partly political – to maintain the solidarity of the alliance – and partly as a shield. Eden even went so far as to pose the question about the shield in a letter to Eisenhower on 1 July:

Need it be capable of fighting a major land battle? Its primary military function seems now to be to deal with any infiltration, to prevent external intimidation and to enable aggression to be identified as such. It may be that it should also be capable of imposing some delay on the progress of a Soviet land invasion until the full impact is felt of the thermo-nuclear retaliation which would be launched against the Soviet Union.*

Eden's eyes were focused on the eventual abolition of National Service. To this end changes were made in the pay codes of all three services, designed to reward a commitment to longer periods in the hope of improving both recruitment of regulars and their retention with the colours. The army had carried out its own review of how many soldiers would be needed in an all-regular army, making certain assumptions about reduction in commitments, and had concluded that 220,000 were needed. Lloyd tried to force it down to 185,000 and a compromise was reached between the two figures. It was hoped that the reduction might be achieved by the abolition or reduction of some fixed bases overseas, in addition to that in the Canal Zone; by the transfer of responsibility for their security to colonies moving towards independence, using locally recruited forces, and by the use of air transport both for routine troop movements and for emergency deployment. As a move towards the latter, Comet and Britannia aircraft were ordered for the RAF's Transport Command. These measures had the full support of Macmillan, who, much to his regret, had been transferred to the Treasury in the ministerial reshuffle of December 1955 to replace Butler, his place at the Foreign Office being taken by Selwyn Lloyd, who was succeeded as Minister of Defence by Walter Monckton. The latter was now given greater responsibility for concerning himself with the contents of the separate service programmes as well as their cost, and, to help him, an independent chairman of the Chiefs of Staff Committee was appointed, the Chief of the Air Staff, Marshal of the Royal Air Force Sir William Dickson, becoming the first occupant of the post.

Eight days after Eden had written to Eisenhower, Nasser announced that he was taking possession of the Suez Canal in order to use its revenues to finance the construction of the Aswan Dam, the USA and Britain having withdrawn their offers to contribute when Egypt quibbled at the terms on which the World Bank offered a loan. Eden felt outraged after all the effort he had put into his Middle Eastern policy based on peaceful agreement with Egypt. Sensitive to the criticism that he had followed a course of appeasement and determined to be seen, particularly by his own party, as a

*Eden, *Full Circle*, p. 373.

worthy successor to Churchill, he took a firm line. In a letter to Eisenhower immediately after a Cabinet meeting on 27 July, he wrote: 'My colleagues and I are convinced that we must be ready, in the last resort, to use force to bring Nasser to his senses. For our part we are prepared to do so. I have this morning instructed our Chiefs of Staff to prepare a military plan accordingly.'[*] At a hastily summoned meeting the evening before, attended by the Chiefs of Staff, Mountbatten, who was acting as chairman in the absence through sickness of Dickson, later claimed that he had recommended the immediate despatch of 1,200 marines from Malta to 'seize Port Said and the first 25 miles of the Causeway along the Canal',[†] but he was certainly not supported by his colleagues, General Sir Gerald Templer and Air Chief Marshal Sir Dermot Boyle, nor by the Ministers present, Eden wishing to make sure that the whole Canal should be secured. Formal planning was initiated on 27 July, the French being brought into it in great secrecy.

One of the principal difficulties they faced was that any seaborne expedition had to start from Malta, six days' sailing for slow landing-craft to Alexandria or Port Said, as Cyprus had no port capable of acting as a mounting base. A second was the very limited unloading facilities at Port Said. Both British and French planners would have liked to deploy a major airborne operation, but Britain had neither sufficient trained airborne troops nor the aircraft to carry them, and the French could not provide more than a limited number, withdrawn from Algeria. The combination of these factors produced a ponderous plan to land three divisions, one airborne and two seaborne, at Alexandria, to be joined there by the British 10th Armoured Division, still stationed in Libya and moving from there by land. The whole force would total 80,000 men, of whom 34,000 would be French. They would then advance along the desert road to Cairo, cross the Nile, topple Nasser and move on to the Canal. It involved the call-up of 20,000 reservists and the 'take-up' of merchant shipping. The earliest date for a landing would be 17 September, provided that preparations were put in hand immediately and a firm decision to despatch the expedition made by 2 September. The force could be ready to advance from Alexandria towards Cairo a week after landing, and it was expected that victory would be achieved within eight days thereafter, a remarkably optimistic estimate.

[*]*Full Circle*, p. 428.
[†]Philip Ziegler, *Mountbatten*. London, 1985, p. 537.

45

The preparations were put in hand, but the political and diplomatic background, which would either make them unnecessary or provide an acceptable justification for their implementation, became confused, as support for either firm political action to internationalize the operation of the Canal or military action to 'force Nasser to disgorge' became weaker internationally, including within the Commonwealth, and most significantly from the US government. Instead of trying to find a diplomatic way out of the impasse, a task at which he was so experienced and skilled, Eden was tempted by the French to seek a solution in collusion with Israel, which, although using military means, could be represented as the action of a peacekeeping force. That was one of the reasons why the plan was changed to a combined airborne and amphibious landing at Port Said, followed by a rapid advance along the canal to Suez. Sayed Idris, the aged King of Libya, had in any case objected to the use of 10th Armoured Division. Dickson, when he returned to chair the Chiefs of Staff, suggested that this force would be virtually unopposed, air action in the preceding days having brought Nasser to give way or be replaced. Eden hoped, and expected, that, although it was clear that the USA, with a Presidential election imminent, would not give their direct support to Anglo-French military action, they would not openly oppose it.

As discussion continued throughout September, the Chiefs of Staff were told to prepare a 'Winter Plan'. It involved releasing merchant shipping and transferring stores to naval vessels. This was to take place off the coast of Scotland and some ships were already on their way there, when a combination of frustrating discussions at the United Nations and pressure from France and Israel caused Eden to agree to execute the Anglo-French plan in combination with an Israeli attack at the end of October. The latter was launched on the 29th, RAF bombers starting their attacks on the Egyptian Air Force two days later. On 5 November British and French paratroops landed at Port Said, followed up next day by the amphibious landing. Resistance was negligible, and by midnight General Stockwell's leading troops were 23 miles down the west bank of the Canal, 78 from Suez, when, under pressure from the USA and the UN, a ceasefire was ordered. Under the same pressure, all British and French troops were withdrawn by Christmas, but the Canal was not opened to traffic, after all the blockships had been removed, until 25 March 1957.

By that time Macmillan had succeeded Eden as Prime Minister: indeed, on that very day, accompanied by his Foreign Secretary,

Selwyn Lloyd, he was in conference with Eisenhower and Dulles in Bermuda, doing his best to heal Anglo-American relations. He had appointed Duncan Sandys as Minister of Defence and strengthened his hand by stating that he was responsible for 'the formulation of a general application of a unified policy relating to the Armed Forces of the Crown as a whole and their requirements'. The Chairman of the Chiefs of Staff was also to act as the Minister's Chief of Staff: proposals and advice from them and from the separate service Secretaries of State were to be forwarded to the Defence Committee through the Minister. This shift of power to the centre was strongly opposed by Templer and Boyle, but not by Mountbatten, who sympathized with it and correctly assumed that he would be Dickson's successor.

Different deductions were drawn from the experience of Suez, according to the colour of uniform. The navy thought that it demonstrated the importance of being able to deliver, and give air support to, a force by sea as rapidly as possible, Mountbatten being particularly enthusiastic for one of his pet projects, landing marine commandos by helicopter from a converted carrier, which had been done for the first time and with marked success. More traditional admirals felt that this tactic made no contribution to the exercise of sea-power and feared that it would compete in demands on money and manpower with the construction and manning of new cruisers. The army thought that the affair proved the need to maintain a strategic reserve in the United Kingdom, capable of conducting limited war operations, and of providing the means to deploy it rapidly by air or sea, or both; and that more airborne troops and aircraft capable of delivering them were needed. The air force believed that their operations had been decisive in reducing opposition to token dimensions, and that the whole affair had shown that we could not rely on the Americans and must have our own nuclear delivery force. Instead of such a force being regarded primarily as a contribution to the allied deterrent, it must be truly independent. Mountbatten and Templer did not share Boyle's insistence on this point.

Macmillan and Sandys were convinced that it proved that the line taken in the July 1956 review, which was basically that put forward by Slessor in 1952, reinforced by the emergence of the H-bomb, had been proved correct, although nuclear weapons had not proved relevant. The whole apparatus, on the lines of the forces employed at the end of the Second World War, had appeared irrelevant and unsuited to the sort of politico-military operations with which we had been, and might in the future be, faced. Their reaction was too slow and cumbersome: they could not operate effectively without a string of static bases, which were both expensive and often politically embarrassing to maintain. These bases were difficult, if not impossible, to use if the local government or people did not cooperate. The key to greater value for money in defence lay in reliance on nuclear weapons to prevent, or if that failed, to win a major war against the Soviet Union and/or China; on missiles to deliver them and to provide air defence; and on air transport to move soldiers and their equipment to trouble-spots making it possible to abandon, or at least greatly reduce, bases overseas. Forces designed on these lines could be manned entirely by voluntarily recruited manpower.

Sandys wasted no time in attempting to put these concepts into practice and found himself immediately involved in a head-on clash with the Chiefs of Staff, the unfortunate Dickson finding himself caught between the Scylla of his uncompromising and determined Minister and the Charybdis of three Chiefs of Staff defending their services with equal vigour. Sandys set an overall manpower target of 375,000 to be achieved by 1962. He tried to force a limit of 165,000 on the army, which was all that he, advised by his civil servants, estimated that the army would be able to sustain by voluntary recruitment, but was forced in the end to accept 180,000, later extended to 182,000. Mountbatten had the advantage that he had recently finished a radical study of the navy's future, known as 'The Way Ahead', which laid considerable emphasis on anti-submarine warfare, on arming ships with missiles in place of guns, and on new forms of propulsion, including nuclear power for submarines. After an initial battle with Sandys, he achieved most of what he wanted for the navy, and thereafter concentrated on trying to ensure that the latter did not give way to pressure from Mountbatten's colleagues against the reductions Sandys proposed to impose on them, thus reducing the share of the cake available for the navy. Templer and Boyle complained that Sandys took no notice of their advice and imposed solutions on them which would have disastrous effects on their services and on their ability to meet their commitments, which were not being reduced at the same time. Relations between them and Sandys were unrelievedly bad throughout his time as Minister.

The 1957 Defence White Paper (Cmd 124) did not appear until April, following the Bermuda Conference and discussions within NATO and the Western European Union which had preceded it. It started with a reference to scientific advances which 'must fundamentally alter the whole basis of military planning', and went on to describe how large a share of the national effort defence and its industrial support had absorbed in recent years – 10 per cent of GNP, 7 per cent of the working population, 12.5 per cent of the output of the metal-working industries, 'an undue proportion of qualified scientists and engineers' – and the burden that maintaining forces overseas placed on the balance of payments. Turning to nuclear weapons, it stated:

It must be frankly recognised that there is at present no means of providing adequate protection for the people of this country against the consequences of an attack with nuclear weapons. Though, in the event of war, the fighter aircraft of the Royal Air Force would unquestionably be able to take a heavy toll of enemy bombers, a proportion would inevitably get through. Even if it were a dozen, they could with megaton bombs inflict widespread devastation.

It went on to say that, although the free world depended on the nuclear capacity of the United States for protection, 'There is a wide measure of agreement that [Britain] must possess an appreciable element of nuclear deterrent power of her own', announcing that our own megaton weapon was about to be tested and that it was intended that 'ballistic rockets' would supplement the V-bombers in delivering it. It was revealed that American medium-range missiles (Thor) were to be stationed in the United Kingdom, manned by RAF crews, until we had produced our own. This had been proposed by the US authorities in January and the 'dual-key' terms agreed in Bermuda in March.

But 'nuclear air power is not by itself a complete deterrent.' Frontiers had to be firmly defended on the ground. Britain must provide her fair share, but 'cannot any longer continue to make a disproportionately large contribution.' After consultation with our allies in NATO and WEU, it had been decided that the army in Germany would be reduced from 77,000 to 64,000 within the next 12 months and, subject to further consultations with allies, 'further reductions will be made thereafter.' In fact Macmillan had proposed a reduction to 50,000, but had met with strong objections from both the French and the Germans, as well as from the NATO command, and had extracted a *quid pro quo* from Adenauer of £50m towards support costs in return for halving the proposed reduction. It was supposed to be compensated for by an 'increase [in] the proportion of fighting units' – by reorganizing divisions into brigade groups and

49

cutting logistic support – and by the addition of 'atomic rocket artillery' in the form of the American Corporal missile. The air force in Germany and light bomber squadrons based in England and assigned to NATO would be halved by the end of the financial year, again to be compensated for by furnishing some of the remaining squadrons with atomic bombs. Much was made of the contribution to NATO and 'the defence of the free world' from Britain's military presence elsewhere. 'Apart from its own importance, the Middle East guards the right flank of NATO and is the gateway to the African continent' (whatever that might mean). 'In the event of emergency, British forces in the Middle East area would be made available to the Alliance. These would include bomber squadrons based in Cyprus capable of delivering nuclear weapons.' As a result of the termination of the treaty with Jordan, British forces were being withdrawn and those in Libya would be 'progressively reduced'. In the Far East we had commitments to the external defence of Malaya, where the emergency was to all intents and purposes over, and to SEATO and ANZAM.* To this end, 'it is proposed to maintain in this theatre a mixed British and Gurkha force and certain air force elements, together with a substantial garrison in Hong Kong and a small naval force based in Singapore.' Although it was described as small, it was stated that British naval strength east of Suez would be maintained 'at about its present level' and would normally include one carrier group in the Indian Ocean. With American agreement, the one infantry battalion still in Korea would be withdrawn.

The aim was to put the armed forces, excluding locally recruited overseas ones, onto an all-regular footing at a strength of about 375,000 by the end of 1962. There were bitter pills to swallow for all three services. The navy bridled at the phrase that 'The role of naval forces in total war is somewhat uncertain', even though it was heavily qualified on the grounds that 'the nuclear battle might not prove immediately decisive'. The army was appalled at the prospect of a reduction to well under half its current strength, less even than its current strength of regulars. The air force, although given a degree of priority, viewed with dismay the emphasis on missiles taking the place of aircraft. The Battle of Britain Boys in Blue reacted very unfavourably to paragraph 62, which stated: 'Work

*Australia, New Zealand and Malaya – a vaguely defined defence agreement between Britain and those countries to cooperate in the defence of Malaya and the surrounding area.

will proceed on the development of a ground-to-air missile defence system which will in due course replace the manned aircraft of Fighter Command . . . the RAF are unlikely to have a requirement for fighter aircraft of types more advanced than the supersonic P1 (later known as the Lightning) and work on such projects will stop.' The Bomber Boys were safe for the moment, but the possibility of the missile also supplanting them lay in the statement that 'high priority will . . . continue to be given to the development of British nuclear weapons suitable for delivery by manned bombers and ballistic rockets. Nuclear warheads are also being evolved for defensive guided missiles.' But the development of a supersonic manned bomber (Avro-730) would be abandoned, 'having regard to the high performance and potentialities of the Vulcan and Victor medium bombers and the likely progress of ballistic rockets and missile defence'. The reserve forces were equally hard hit. The Territorial Army was to be confined to Home Defence and units of the Royal Naval Volunteer Reserve and the Royal Auxiliary Air Force were to be disbanded, the former merging with the Royal Naval Reserve and being limited to the provision of individual reservists, as would the Royal Air Force Volunteer Reserve.

Apart from the blows these decisions inflicted on their services, the Chiefs of Staff deeply resented that they did not stem from their advice – far from it – but from that of the Minister's own scientific and civil service staff. This made them even more suspicious than they were already of any moves to grant greater power or authority over the separate service departments to the Ministry. Over the next few years they were to fight a running battle on this issue with the Minister, who was strongly backed by the Prime Minister and also by Mountbatten, both before and after he succeeded Dickson in April 1959 as Chief of the Defence Staff, as the post had been renamed in July 1958 in the face of strong opposition from Templer and Boyle.

The February 1958 Defence White Paper (Cmd 363), over which there had again been fierce arguments between Sandys and the Chiefs of Staff, revealed what the 1957 decisions entailed in practice. Having 'reviewed the role of the navy' within NATO, which the previous year had been described as 'uncertain', the point was made that, within the alliance, it was not necessary for Britain's contribution to be balanced within itself. In the Atlantic and the Mediterranean it would be based on two aircraft-carriers, two cruisers and 'a number of destroyers, frigates and submarines'. East of Suez it would be based on one of these groups and one 'commando carrier' as they came to be known. An important announcement was that 'a low-level tactical bomber' (later known as the Buccaneer) 'was being developed for the Royal Navy and its adoption by the RAF is being considered'. This drew the curtain slightly aside on an intense argument between Mountbatten and Boyle, the former proposing that the RAF's ambitious project, the TSR2,* should be dropped in favour of the Buccaneer. He lost the battle then, but, ironically, the TSR2 was later to be cancelled and, when eventually the navy lost its fixed-wing aircraft, the Buccaneers were transferred to the RAF and first saw action over 30 years later as laser-marking aircraft in the Gulf War. Although the navy still hotly disputed the concept that a war would be, as Thomas Hobbes described the life of man, 'nasty, brutish, and short', they came fairly well out of the struggle, their future manpower target, at 88,000, being only 10,000 below their current strength.

The army faced a major upheaval in a reduction from its current strength of 325,000 to 165,000, involving the disbandment of 51 'teeth-arm' units, 21 from the Royal Artillery, many of them anti-aircraft, 17 from the infantry, 8 from the Royal Armoured Corps and 5 from the Royal Engineers. With the reluctant agreement of fellow members of the Western European Union and of NATO, the strength of the British Army of the Rhine was to be reduced even further to 55,000. A total of 100,000 UK-recruited men were to serve elsewhere overseas in the Middle and Far East. That traditionally minded infanteer, Gerald Templer, agonized over the problems this posed, agreement finally being reached that infantry regiments would be grouped together organizationally in 'brigades', which would share a training depot for recruits and within which officers might serve in any of the regiments. A number of regiments, based on areas in which recruiting was difficult, were amalgamated into 'large regiments'. In the cavalry, six amalgamations were planned of regiments which had escaped that fate in 1922.

The proposed reduction in the RAF, partly compensated for by the planned increase in Transport Command, would bring its strength down from the 182,000, at which it then stood, to 135,600. These cuts were expected to reduce the proportion of GNP devoted to defence to 7 per cent, the estimated cost being reduced to £1,420m (after receipts of £63m from the USA and Germany, the latter providing only £12m) instead of the £1,644m which Sandys claimed it would have been if the changes had not been initiated.

*Tactical Strike and Reconnaissance.

It was not long, however, before events began to cast doubt on whether his aim could be achieved. In October 1957 the Soviet Union launched its satellite Sputnik into space, proving that it had the capability to produce ballistic missiles which could deliver megaton weapons onto targets in America. Reliance on the deterrent value of the threat of nuclear attack on the Soviet Union in the event of any form of attack by her in Europe would be much less credible if she could retaliate against targets in the USA. Within a few years this was to lead to strong pressure from the USA on European members of NATO to strengthen their conventional forces and not to regard them just as a trip-wire to set off a strategic nuclear attack on the Soviet Union and to hold the ring while that was being delivered.

The next perturbation stemmed from the repercussions of Nasser's apparent victory in the Suez affair within the Arab world. The most serious manifestation was the rebellion in Iraq in July 1958 in which the king, his uncle the former regent, and Nuri es Said were killed and power seized by a group of army officers headed by Brigadier Kassem. Lebanon and Jordan felt threatened, the Americans responding to the former's appeal for help and sending two brigades of Marines there, while Macmillan sent two parachute battalions to Amman to support King Hussein, Israel having agreed to their overflight through her airspace. Another battalion was subsequently sent by sea from Aden to Aqaba. Members of the Conservative Suez Group, including, it was believed, some Ministers, wanted to invade Iraq and reverse the coup, but the military and political realities soon put paid to that idea. The rulers of the small sheikhdoms of the Persian Gulf, almost all British protectorates at that time, became restive, as they felt threatened by the effect of the anti-British propaganda, launched from Cairo and Baghdad, on their populations, especially on the large number of Palestinian workers on whom they depended. Almost all Britain's oil supplies then came from the Gulf states, the most important of which was Kuwait, which furnished half of the total. The fields there belonged to Kuwait Oil, of which a 50 per cent share was held by British Petroleum, in which the British Government had a controlling interest. Ghosts of Suez raised their heads again, but that affair and the subsequent coup in Iraq had resulted in a barrier to military air movement, the RAF having lost its bases, landing and overflying rights in the area, except in Cyprus and Libya.

There were two rival schools of thought as to how to ensure the security of oil supplies in the Persian Gulf. One was to back the traditional rulers with guarantees of military support, stationing British forces in or near their territories, if required, while helping them to build up their own forces in cooperation with each other. The other was to disengage ourselves, so that we were no longer a target for anti-Western, and particularly anti-British, propaganda, relying on the hope that it would defuse local subversive movements and that, whether the traditional rulers remained or were replaced by some other system, democratic or not, the need to exploit oil resources would persuade whoever was in power to act in a sensible way. The first school prevailed and, to overcome the logistic and movement problems of deploying land and air forces to the area, plans were set in hand to construct in Kenya a cantonment to house a brigade and associated troops with a logistic base, from which the brigade could be deployed and supplied into South Arabia and the Persian Gulf, as well as in East Africa if necessary.

Hitherto the only armed forces in Aden and the sheikhdoms in its hinterland had been local levies, supported by the RAF, acting on the policy of 'air control' which had been introduced in Iraq in the 1920s on the advice of T. E. Lawrence when Winston Churchill had been Colonial Secretary. It had made possible a dramatic reduction in the army garrison of that 'mandated territory'. But the inability of air control to deal with a revolt against the Sultan of Muscat and Oman in 1957 led to the despatch of army and Royal Marine units to Aden, who remained there, as the neighbouring Yemen, influenced by the general Arab ferment, became a source of subversion in Aden itself. As Aden became transformed into a forward base for possible operations in the Gulf, and with the transfer of the navy's amphibious squadron (still equipped with Second World War craft) from the Mediterranean, and the abolition of the navy's East Indies Command, based in Ceylon, pressure from the other services, combined with the advent of Mountbatten to the post of Chief of the Defence Staff, led to the transformation of the RAF headquarters in Aden to that of a fully fledged joint service Commander-in-Chief. This placed it on a par with the truncated British Defence Coordinating Committee Middle East in Cyprus, which, after the withdrawal from Jordan, exercised command of little more than the garrison of Cyprus and the RAF station at El Adem in Libya. Hardly had the brigade and the new base been established in Kenya than it became apparent that Kenya was going to move towards independence much more quickly than anyone had imagined, under the influence of Macmillan's decision to bow to the wind of change in Africa. It was also becoming clear that Kenya was a long way from the Gulf and, for a quick response to a crisis, the troops and their stores should be kept nearer to where they were needed.

Step by step, therefore, troops and aircraft were stationed further forward, first from Aden to the Gulf and then from Kenya to Aden. This paid off in 1961, when Iraq threatened the newly independent Kuwait, with whose ruling sheikh the British government had just concluded a defence agreement to replace that of 1899 with the government of India. By a stroke of good fortune HMS *Bulwark*, the first of the commando carriers, with a Royal Marine commando embarked, was carrying out trials in the Indian Ocean and joined another commando and a battalion flown from Aden, followed by the brigade from Kenya. This rapid concentration deterred the Iraqi threat to absorb Kuwait into the province of Basra. The force was withdrawn and replaced by a small Arab one when Kuwait was admitted to the Arab League on 20 August. This effective action appeared to demonstrate the soundness of the policy of building up a force based partly in Aden and partly in the Gulf itself, linked to defence agreements with the rulers, those of the Trucial States in the southern Gulf being persuaded to come together ten years later in the United Arab Emirates.

Macmillan's Conservative administration increased its majority in the House of Commons from 67 to 107 at the October 1959 General Election and Duncan Sandys was transferred to the Ministry of Aviation, being replaced by Harold Watkinson. Having attempted, with little success, to sort out the aircraft industry, Sandys was moved in July 1960 to the Commonwealth Relations Office where he was to pursue with his accustomed vigour the policy of signing defence agreements with newly independent colonies which committed Britain to come to their assistance in meeting threats to their security, external or internal, and, in some cases, allowed her to maintain forces or installations or to make use of facilities in their territory. Macmillan judged that the atmosphere in which defence matters were conducted in Whitehall needed calming and that, with Mountbatten installed as Chief of the Defence Staff, Templer replaced by Festing, who had served amicably with Mountbatten in South East Asia, and Boyle by the milder-mannered Sir Thomas Pike, he could be confident that things would move in the direction he intended. Sandys's last Defence White Paper (Cmd 662, February 1959), entitled 'Progress of the Five-Year Plan', struck an upbeat note, emphasizing progress in modernizing the equipment of all three services: on new aircraft, fixed and rotary wing, and guided missiles for the Royal Navy, the first of the new *Tiger* class cruisers,

and 'preparations' for the first nuclear-powered submarine, its introduction having been made possible earlier than expected as a result
of a deal Mountbatten had made, when First Sea Lord in 1955, with
the US Admiral Rickover for the provision of an American nuclear
power plant.

The army was to receive the American Corporal missile to launch
American tactical nuclear warheads, and also the British Thunder-
bird anti-aircraft missile. While the RAF's strategic and tactical
transport fleet was being improved, largely by adapting civil transport aircraft, such as the Britannia, the Argosy and the Twin Pio-
neer, the number of Vulcan and Victor bombers was increasing, as
was the stock of megaton and kiloton nuclear weapons to be delivered
by them and by the old Canberra, which was to be replaced by the
TSR2 and another future 'General Purpose aircraft for the support
of the army and other tactical operations'. The development of
'propelled stand-off bombs' (Blue Steel) was said to be continuing
satisfactorily. So also, although the word 'satisfactorily' was not
used, was that of the ballistic missile Blue Streak, which was said to
be 'best suited to British needs'. In the air defence field, the Lightning fighter would be in service in the following year, equipped with
the Firestreak air-to-air missile, while the defence of bomber bases
would be increasingly entrusted to the Bloodhound ground-to-air
missile, and a 'more advanced weapon with higher performance'
was being developed. All this was estimated to cost, after receipt
of £12m from Germany (US military aid was no longer available)
£1,453m in 1958/59 and £1,502m in 1959/60. Although an increase
from the previous year in cash terms, it represented a slight fall both
in real terms and in the percentage of GNP, which itself was rising.

It was to be left to the unfortunate Watkinson to face disappointment with this rosy picture of technical progress taking the place of
manpower in defence. The costs of both Blue Steel and Blue Streak
kept on escalating and their likely in-service dates went back and
back, so that their technologies were likely to be out of date by the
time they came into service – Blue Streak was liquid-fuelled – and
there was no hope of foreign sales of either. When, therefore, in
March 1960 the US Government offered to supply the RAF with
the air-to-surface missile Skybolt, it appeared to be a better solution.
It would cash in on the investment in the 180 V-bombers, which
would thereby be able to deliver their weapons without having to
penetrate far into Soviet air defences, to which they looked like
being increasingly vulnerable. This would be preferable to replacing
them with expensive ballistic missiles. Blue Streak was therefore

cancelled, although Blue Steel was kept in reserve until Skybolt became available. The decision did not go uncontested. Mountbatten favoured the more radical solution, suggested to him by the US Admiral Arleigh Burke and favoured by his scientific adviser, Solly Zuckerman, which was to replace the RAF's V-bombers as deliverers of strategic nuclear weapons by the US Polaris missile fired from nuclear-powered submarines, a solution hotly contested by the air staff. Mountbatten did not have long to wait before events moved in his direction. As early as October 1960 Watkinson learned that the Skybolt programme was in trouble, and warnings to this effect increased after John Kennedy had been installed as President of the USA in January 1961 and appointed Robert McNamara as his Defence Secretary. But it was not until towards the end of 1962, some months after Peter Thorneycroft had replaced Watkinson as Minister of Defence, that McNamara made it clear that Skybolt was not likely to enter service with the US Air Force. This left the 'Independent British Deterrent' high and dry at the very time that Macmillan was involved in negotiations with de Gaulle about Britain's entry into the EEC.

It made the ringing phrases about the importance of Britain's capability, contained in the 1961 and 1962 Defence White Papers, sound hollow. The February 1961 paper (Cmnd 1288) stated:

We make our own contribution to the strategic nuclear deterrent forces of the West. Making full allowance for the growth of nuclear power in the world, our contribution still provides a valuable degree of strength and diversity to the Western forces as a whole. It involves dispersal and reduces reaction time. It provides powerful backing for our alliances. The Government believe that it is in the national interest that we should continue to share the burden and responsibility of maintaining this important element in the total power of the Western deterrent. Our contribution also substantially increases our influence in negotiations for a nuclear test agreement, disarmament, and the reorganization of NATO strategy . . .

We expect that our main contribution to the Western deterrent over the next decade will be provided by weapons carried in aircraft; and the task of replacing the present type of V-bombers with improved Mark II versions is well in hand. To counter probable improvements in fighter and missile defences these aircraft will be given an increasing 'stand-off' capability over this period. The missiles, which carry the British-made warhead from the aircraft to its target, must be of such type and characteristics as will present the greatest diversity of attack.

The 1962 paper (Cmnd 1639), entitled 'The Next Five Years', considered 'War in the Nuclear Age' at some length. Although it asserted that 'we must continue to make it clear to potential aggressors that we should strike back with all the means that we judge appropriate, conventional and nuclear', and that 'the Government do not believe that a major war could long continue without one side or the other resorting to nuclear weapons', a new note of caution was struck in that the possession by the Soviet Union of a growing and longer-range nuclear arsenal meant that an automatic resort to nuclear weapons would not necessarily be the right reaction to aggression. While continuing to discard the concept of a prolonged conventional or 'limited' war, the paper stressed the need to find the right balance between nuclear and conventional forces, with more than a hint that conventional response might be the right one in certain circumstances. Mountbatten personally believed this. He could see no sense in initiating a nuclear exchange, whether at the strategic or the tactical level, and did not therefore favour insistence that Britain's deterrent force must be independent. He could not envisage Britain employing her own nuclear weapons when the Americans were not using theirs.* The 1962 paper argued:

> Our contribution to the Western strategic deterrent remains significant. It is by itself enough to make a potential aggressor fear that our retaliation would inflict destruction beyond any level which he would be prepared to tolerate. Moreover, it adds considerably to the flexibility and dispersal of the total nuclear forces available to the West and thus to the retaliatory power. The efficacy of our deterrent will therefore be maintained throughout the 1960s by using our V-bombers and fitting them with stand-off weapons, Blue Steel in the first instance and later Skybolt.

The same paper went on to say:

> The Government do not believe that the defence of Europe could be left to long-range nuclear weapons alone, nor that its fate could be decided by long drawn out fighting limited to conventional forces. The Government wish to ensure that NATO forces are

*Ziegler, *Mountbatten*, pp. 561, 591, 595–6.

58

balanced and NATO strategy flexible. Our contribution to the shield is a heavy burden on the balance of payments . . . We hope to negotiate adequate means for relieving the strain on the balance of payments . . . During this period (the present decade) the proportion of those forces to be stationed on the mainland of Europe and in Britain respectively must depend to a large extent on the balance of payments position.

This reflected a continuing struggle for reimbursement from the Federal Republic of Germany for a contribution to support costs.

In 1958 Macmillan had threatened to reduce the strength of the army in Germany yet further to 45,000, but had retreated in the face of strong protests within NATO and especially from Adenauer, concerned at the renewed threat from the Soviet Union about access to Berlin. Macmillan agreed to maintain a nominal strength of 55,000 in return for a German contribution of £12m a year up to 1960. After a major row over this issue when Britain faced yet another financial crisis in July 1961, agreement was reached in 1962 on an increase to £50m. It was to continue to be a source of dispute as the American demand for a greater contribution by the European members of NATO to the conventional forces of the alliance was pressed. These were anxious and difficult years for the alliance, overshadowed by the Soviet attitude to Berlin and the recognition of East Germany. The failing health of Eisenhower and Dulles, the aged Adenauer's resistance to any agreement with the Soviet Union, and de Gaulle's return to power, complicated the business of maintaining a united alliance front. Macmillan was irritated by the fact that Britain faced grave economic difficulties while Germany, bearing a much lower financial burden for her defence, prospered. He accused France and Germany of constantly urging tough measures over Berlin, while making little contribution themselves. He was determined that NATO should not be pushed over the brink about Berlin by pressure from them or from the hawks in the Pentagon and the US State Department who wanted a show-down with the Soviet Union before she had deployed Intercontinental Ballistic Missiles capable of delivering megaton weapons onto American cities. Macmillan's visit to Moscow to talk with Khrushchev in February 1959 was undertaken with this in mind.

4

OVERSTRETCH: 1962–1965

IN THE NASSAU meeting in the week before Christmas 1962 Macmillan seized victory out of the jaws of apparent defeat on the nuclear issue. He owed it partly to his own skill as a diplomat and politician, but also to the favourable impression he had made on Kennedy during the tense period of the Cuban missile crisis two months before. Kennedy had found the much older man calm, reassuring, firm and resolute in his support. He therefore felt that he owed a debt of gratitude and was prepared to act on it at Nassau in the face of opposition from almost all of his advisers, especially Robert McNamara. Few American authorities were keen on other nations developing their own nuclear weapons. That nuclear guru, Henry Kissinger, had at first favoured it, but had more recently changed his position. In his book *Nuclear Weapons and Foreign Policy*,* he had written: 'The possession by our European allies of nuclear weapons . . . will improve the overall position of the free world', but, in *The Necessity for Choice*,† published three years later, he reversed his view, writing: 'Independent retaliatory forces in Europe stand in danger of producing an illusory feeling of security which in some respects magnifies the danger . . . They can deter only if the Soviet Union is convinced that conflict on a certain scale will unleash the United States' strategic forces. Far from making us dispensable, the effectiveness of separate retaliatory forces depends upon the likelihood of US intervention. Their function would not be substantially different from that of the tripwire.'

That was just what McNamara was determined to prevent. He was having enough trouble trying to curb the excessively ambitious nuclear plans of all three of the US armed forces and to restrain their bellicosity. He was insistent that the USA should not find itself involved in a nuclear version of August 1914, when the rigidity of

*New York, 1957, p. 198.
†New York, 1960, pp. 112–14.

the military plans deprived the political leaders of all freedom of action. It would be bad enough to have that freedom removed by American generals: it would be intolerable for that power to be in the hands of foreigners; and, if Britain were liable to exercise that form of blackmail, it would be far worse if de Gaulle's France, who had exploded her first device in the Sahara desert in 1960, were to do so; and worse still if, through France, as many in the United States suspected, Germany might acquire the same capability. Not only would that be disastrous in itself, but the fact that the Soviet Union might view it in the same light could provoke her to pre-empt that situation arising. That would undo the relaxation in US–Soviet relations which the peaceful solution of the Cuban crisis appeared to have brought about.

Thorneycroft suspected that McNamara's cancellation of Skybolt was deliberately designed to deprive Britain of her independent nuclear role, and his suspicions were confirmed when, a week before the Nassau meeting, McNamara held out the hope that Polaris might be made available as part of the multilateral nuclear force (MLF) which the Americans were suggesting as a means of satisfying the potential nuclear aspirations of NATO's European members. It would consist of merchant ships, manned by crews of several nations, equipped with Polaris and under NATO command, a proposal which evoked no enthusiasm anywhere. In the event Kennedy forced McNamara to agree to let Macmillan have Polaris provided that the force equipped with it would give support to SACEUR and be targeted in accordance with his plans, and would also be 'available for inclusion in a NATO multilateral nuclear force', to which Macmillan managed to add the crucial qualification 'except where Her Majesty's Government may decide that supreme national interests are at stake'. Ever thereafter the British government, whatever its political hue, was able to play either the NATO or the independent card according to the mood of the time and the audience they were addressing. The only aspects which remained truly independent were the design and production of the warhead (although there was American help in the design) and the fact that the missile could not be fired by the all-British crew without the authority of the Prime Minister.

It was not only the existence of independent nuclear forces which McNamara feared might force the hand of the United States, but also the weakness of NATO's conventional forces. It must not be assumed, he argued, that, as soon as enemy forces crossed the Iron Curtain, the Americans would employ nuclear weapons. Once that happened, there was no sure way of controlling an escalation which would lead to megaton weapons landing on American cities. That awful prospect had been faced over Cuba. NATO must therefore have strong enough forces to impose a long enough delay to make it possible for political discussion to take place, and the dire consequences of continuing to be brought home to the aggressor. This concept had already been promulgated within the NATO command system and led to prolonged discussion about strategy. It was hard to reconcile it with the conflicting desire of European members to avoid a long war, conventional, nuclear or both, and to ensure that it was made clear to the Soviet Union that any military adventure into NATO territory did carry the risk that megaton weapons would land on *her* cities. Nor did Europeans relish the prospect, which always seemed to arise when US and Soviet nuclear arsenals appeared to balance each other, that Europe could be engulfed in war while the homelands of the USA and the USSR remained inviolate. The delicate negotiations on this subject were to last for many years, resulting in a compromise called 'flexible response'. This was intended to mean that the alliance would choose its response according to the action of the enemy, meeting tit for tat, but always threatening to go one higher up the scale and demonstrably having the capability and will to do so. The possession of that capability was called 'escalation dominance' and could justify an infinity of forms of nuclear weapon and means of delivery.

For Macmillan, this pressure to increase NATO's conventional strength came at a very embarrassing time, just when he was trying to whittle down Eden's 1954 commitment and rely on the nuclear threat to take care of European defence, and before his new strategy of reduction in bases and reliance on air transport to rush troops from Britain to distant trouble-spots elsewhere in the world (helped by relying also on bowing to the wind of change to reduce the need for such action) had been realized. In fact, as we have already seen in respect of the Gulf, that strategy was not working out as had been hoped. New bases were being created and more troops stationed overseas. The 1962 Defence White Paper gave considerable prominence to East-of-Suez commitments, as Watkinson had done when introducing its predecessor. He had then said:

We do not propose to leave the Arabian Peninsula and our treaty obligations there. We do not intend to leave places like Hong Kong defenceless or to abandon those members of the Commonwealth in whose defence we have agreed to share . . . I have made it plain that the Government have no intention of backing out of our world obligations. I am not ashamed to stand at this Box and say that I am proud that the nation still has some responsibilities in the world.*

The 1962 paper reflected a major strategic review initiated by the Chiefs of Staff in the autumn of 1961, in which they had looked forward to the next decade. They estimated that the growing atomic power of the West and the differences between the Soviet Union and China made war in Europe very unlikely, and that the principal threat to our interests would be in Africa and Asia, arising from the combination of nationalism and communist exploitation of it. It was in those areas that our forces were most likely to be engaged. There were limits to the extent that we should be able to undertake such engagement. Only one major operation at a time and not more than one such a year could be supported, while a limited number of minor ones could be maintained in a given period of time. The review was both a justification of the forces which the Chiefs of Staff wished to preserve and a warning to the government to limit commitments to those which their reduced resources could adequately meet.

Their review complemented, but to a marked degree diverged from, a similar attempt to judge what the needs of the 1960s would be, which had, with great secrecy, been put in hand by Macmillan in 1958, known as the Future Policy Study. He insisted that it should be conducted by officials at a medium level, who should not be subject to overriding instructions from their superiors, official or political, although the report would be submitted to him through the former. It was to answer the questions: what will the world be like in ten years' time; what will Britain's position be; what policies should a future government try and pursue in the light of the answers to those questions? The report was completed early in 1960. It forecast a decline in Britain's power and status and stressed the need for us to defend our interests not so much by the use of our own resources as by combining with friends and allies. We should face a delicate balancing act between the USA, Europe and the Commonwealth. The Atlantic Alliance was vital, but we could not make an absolute choice between relations with North America and those with Western Europe. Our aim must be to bind them together, and for that we must not distance ourselves from our European neighbours. The Commonwealth was another matter. It was not and

*House of Commons *Hansard*, 28 February 1961, Colns 1508–9.

never would be comparable as a source of power with the USA or Western Europe. With the right policies and some luck, it could be useful to us, but sentimentality must not blind us to the facts, and that, in some respects, it could become more of a liability than an asset. Some of the report's recommendations would not have been favourably received by many Conservative politicians or by their military advisers, such as that 'we should work towards terminating our political obligations in the Persian Gulf, if this can be done without causing too much damage', although they might have agreed that 'we should try to engage the Americans further in the defence of the area'; but neither would they have liked the suggestion that 'we should give up the idea of intervening by force in order to prevent a country (e.g. Iraq) going Communist or because it had acted harmfully against British interests (e.g. the Persian Gulf).'* That is perhaps why, although circulated by the Prime Minister as a Cabinet paper (C(60)35), it appears never to have been discussed by that body.

It was not only to the Middle East and Africa that attention was being drawn. The 1962 White Paper included a long section about the Far East, much of it relating to the proposed formation of Malaysia out of Malaya, which had gained independence in 1957, the colony of Singapore, which had enjoyed 'internal self-government' since 1959, the colonies of Sarawak and North Borneo, and, it was hoped, the protectorate of Brunei, the last three forming the northern side of the large island, most of which formed part of Indonesia and was known by it as Kalimantan. At the time of Malaya's independence, the Anglo-Malaysian Defence Agreement had been signed, which, in return for allowing British, Australian and New Zealand forces to be stationed in the country, committed Britain to the defence of the area, subject to consultation at the time. The formation of Malaysia was seen by Macmillan and Sandys, who in 1962 added the responsibilities of the Colonial Office to those of the Commonwealth Relations Office, as yet another means of divesting Britain of its direct responsibilities in the hope that not only would subversive movements be defused, but that the new amalgam of territories would be capable of looking after its own security, other than from a direct threat by a major external power such as

---

*Although 30 years have passed, the final report has not been made available in the Public Records Office, but is held back for 50 years. A summary, however, is given in a brief to the Foreign Secretary dated 15 March 1960 which has been released (PRO FO371/152133) from which these quotations are taken. Preliminary 1959 papers relating to it were released as PRO CAB134/1934 and 1935.

China or the Soviet Union. SEATO existed for that, and Britain would need to retain her forces and bases in the area to meet her commitment to that alliance. By then the Americans had committed forces to Vietnam, but as yet only in small numbers – 2,600 in January, rising to 5,500 by June 1962. Their attitude to Britain's military presence outside the NATO area had changed significantly since Suez. They were only too eager to find partners to share the White Man's Burden in containing the spread of communism in the developing world. Playing the role of world policeman east of Suez was therefore seen as another way of cooperating with the USA in defending interests which, in general, we had in common, although at times commercial rivalry intervened.

But this attempt to divest Britain of direct responsibility in the Far East rapidly involved her in a greater military commitment, just as it was later to do in Aden. The fellow-travelling President Soekarno of Indonesia saw the prospective removal of British rule in northern Borneo as an opportunity to extend his dominion to the three territories. The Sultan of Brunei, whose small territory embraced the profitable Shell Company oilfield at Seria, saw no advantage in being absorbed into Malaysia. Soekarno lent his support to a rebellion in December 1962 against the Sultan, which was put down promptly and effectively by the rapid deployment of British and Gurkha troops from Singapore on the orders of the newly appointed joint-service Commander-in-Chief, Admiral Luce. When the rebellion failed, Soekarno developed it into a general campaign against the absorption of the three territories into Malaysia. When the latter became established in September 1963, Britain officially handed over responsibility for the conduct of operations to the Malaysian government (virtually the government of Malaya*), while in fact continuing to direct and provide the resources for the campaign, which continued until August 1966.

The Borneo campaign served many useful purposes for many different people. It justified the Chiefs of Staff in their belief in the priority given to maintaining a capability east of Suez; in the value of bases near to likely areas of operation; and in the provision of 'balanced forces' capable of dealing with eventualities which nobody had foreseen. 'The need to provide for the unforeseen' was one of their favourite themes. Mountbatten was particularly pleased as it appeared to justify his emphasis on integrated joint-service operations, including joint-service Commanders-in-Chief overseas, and

*Singapore broke away from Malaysia in August 1965. Brunei never joined.

his pet project, the commando carrier, although the marines and their helicopters, both of which proved invaluable, once deployed ashore, remained there and never operated from their ship. To the army it justified the retention of a number of infantry battalions which the NATO commitment cast doubt on, and the retention of Gurkhas above the figure of 10,000 agreed with Nepal at the time of India's independence and maintained above it while the emergency lasted in Malaya. To the Labour administration, which took over in 1964, it provided an opportunity to show that it supported the armed forces as resolutely as did their opponents, and a reason, although a thin one, for refusing to take a direct part, as Australia and New Zealand did, in supporting the Americans in Vietnam.

While events developed satisfactorily in Borneo, albeit at the expense of the hopes of both governments that defence expenditure would be reduced, the use of Aden as a base for protecting the oil supplies in the Gulf was causing trouble. The town of Aden, many of the workers in which came from the Yemen, had practically nothing in common with the sheikhdoms of the hinterland, but the Colonial Office had persuaded some of the latter to come together in a loose federation, into which it was hoped that Aden would some-how be incorporated. A blow was dealt to these hopes in 1962 when, on the death of the aged ruler of the Yemen, his son was overthrown by a military coup supported by Nasser. The leader of the coup, Colonel Sallal, then proceeded to subvert the neighbouring tribes and Aden itself. Trouble brewed throughout 1963, culminating in a tribal revolt in the Radfan, which involved a brigade of British troops in operations lasting two months, just before the brigade in Kenya was transferred to the brand-new base built for it at Little Aden. That coincided with a decision, taken in July 1964, when Alec Douglas-Home had succeeded Macmillan as Prime Minister, that 'South Arabia' would be granted independence in 1968, although Britain intended that the base at Little Aden would be maintained thereafter. Aden was not to be free of trouble until that date, when the base had to be abandoned, together with the unfortunate sheikhs who had been promised its protection.

The Sandys reforms rested on the hope that a combination of air transport and new technologies would reduce the cost in money and manpower of overseas commitments. National Service did come to an end, although postponed as a result of renewed anxieties in Europe – the last National Serviceman left the army in 1964 – but the army complained loud and long about 'overstretch' with soldiers separated from their families for long periods and subjected to frequent moves. As a result, both recruiting and retention were at a low ebb. Emphasis on the east-of-Suez role had not only increased expenditure on air transport and on island bases to act as staging posts and means of avoiding political obstacles to overflying other countries, but had also justified a modernization of amphibious capability. Some admirals had resisted this on the same grounds as they had the commando carrier: that the expense in money and manpower was considerable, but that it contributed nothing to the exercise of sea-power to assert command of the seas. Another argument was that it would compete against the development of 'afloat support', the auxiliary fleet of Royal Naval supply and maintenance ships which would free the fleet from dependence on fixed bases. A compromise was reached by which the navy built and manned two assault ships (Landing Ships Dock), from which Royal Marines could sail out their own craft, while the army built a fleet of Landing Ships Logistic, to be manned by merchant seamen, which would deliver men, equipment and stores to the beaches after the assault. Both came in useful in a series of evacuations and were first to be used in their proper role in the Falkland Islands in 1982, by which time the LSLs had been transferred to the Royal Navy.

All this cost money, but it was nothing to what was being committed to future aircraft. The TSR2 was still in embryo and had been joined by other projects: the P1127 transonic VTOL★ and the supersonic model, the P1154, the former intended as an interceptor-fighter for the navy, the latter as a successor to the Hunter as a fighter-bomber for the RAF. Watkinson hoped that one type would suit both services, and this did eventually happen when the P1154 was cancelled after a great deal of money had been spent on it, and some of its features transferred to the P1127's final version known as the Harrier, which initially went only to the RAF to give close support to the army. Another expensive Hawker-Siddeley project was the HS681 STOL† tactical transport aircraft. A long-overdue replacement for the aged Shackleton long-range maritime reconnaissance aircraft for Coastal Command was being considered. The February 1963 Defence White Paper (Cmnd 1936) wrote up the TSR2 in glowing terms. Having stated that the V-bomber force was 'only now reaching its final peak' equipped with Blue Steel, it said that the TSR2's 'exceptional all round performance will make it fully capable of playing a part in the strategic as well as the tactical

★Vertical Take-off and Landing.
†Short Take-off and Landing.

nuclear role, not only before the introduction of the Polaris submarines but also, when required, to supplement the Polaris force'. The paper also took a very different line from those produced in the days of Sandys when it spoke about fighter aircraft. Admitting that the threat to the United Kingdom came predominantly from missiles, it said that 'a substantial fighter force would be maintained' to prevent enemy reconnaissance, investigate unauthorized intrusions into our airspace and deter or prevent the enemy from jamming our warning system by intercepting the jamming aircraft. Some squadrons would also be available to provide air cover for operations overseas. The warning to enable the V-bombers to take off before their bases were attacked by missiles would come from the Ballistic Missile Early Warning station at Fylingdales, due to start operating in that year.

Army equipment projects were not so expensive to develop, but production costs were high in relation to their predecessors' and numbers were, of course, much greater than those of navy and air force equipments. A major re-equipment programme took place during this period covering all arms, remedying a situation in which the army's contribution to NATO was much less up-to-date than many others', especially the Americans and the Germans. It included the introduction of the Chieftain tank to replace the 20-year-old Centurion and the conversion of all artillery to armoured self-propelled models.

All this meant that defence expenditure, estimated at £1,721m for 1962/63 and £1,837m for the following year, was no longer falling but rising, although still held at 7 per cent of GNP. Total manpower had fallen at the end of 1962 to close on Sandys' target of 375,000, the army having come down to 175,000, of whom 5,000 were National Servicemen. Hope of getting better value for money and manpower rested in the major reorganization of the defence departments announced in March 1963 and due to be implemented on 1 April 1964. Its design owed everything to Mountbatten, its implementation to the determination of Macmillan. In December 1959 Macmillan proposed to Mountbatten that, when his normal three-year tenure of the post of Chief of the Defence Staff would come to an end in April 1962, it should be extended for a further two years to give him time to see through the reorganization which Macmillan was determined to introduce. Mountbatten refused, but after his wife, Edwina, died in February 1960, he changed his mind and a year later was officially told that it had been approved. Soon after Thorneycroft's appointment as Minister of Defence, Mountbatten, without consulting anybody else, produced a paper outlining his proposals to abolish the separate service departments and absorb them into one integrated Ministry of Defence, organized on functional, not separate service, lines. Having used this to brief Macmillan and Thorneycroft and obtained their support, he prepared a more formal paper which he discussed only with the Permanent Under-Secretary of the Ministry, Sir Rob Scott, before submitting it officially in October 1962 to Thorneycroft, who received it with caution, aware that it would arouse strong opposition. At a shooting week-end at Broadlands in November, Mountbatten discussed it with Macmillan and suggested that, to defuse opposition, some *éminence grise* should be invited to consider the matter, but no decision was taken. Macmillan then called a meeting at which only he, Thorneycroft, Mountbatten, Rob Scott, Solly Zuckerman and the Cabinet Secretary, Burke Trend, were present. It was agreed that the proposals would be made known to the Service Secretaries of State and their Chiefs of Staff, the latter having already received copies informally from Mountbatten. As expected, fierce opposition was expressed by them and by several retired Chiefs of Staff, including Slessor. Of the serving ones, the Chief of the Air Staff, Pike, was most adamant. The First Sea Lord, Caspar John, favoured reform, but was careful not to endorse proposals as radical as Mountbatten's. The CIGS, Richard Hull, was opposed, although not as violently as Pike, guessing that he might be Mountbatten's successor, the army not yet having held the post. There was much talk of the danger of creating a situation similar to that in Germany under Hitler, when the latter's supreme headquarters, OKW,* had by-passed the army headquarters, OKH,† with results which were believed to have been one of the main causes of the German defeat in Russia. Some of the violence of the air staff's objection came from sensitivity to any threat to the sacred independence of the Royal Air Force, established in the teeth of opposition from the navy and the army in the 1920s.

The reaction persuaded Macmillan to revert to Mountbatten's suggestion of an *éminence grise*. With some difficulty Lord Ismay was persuaded to act the part, provided that all the work was done, as it was, by General Sir Ian Jacob. They had worked together with great distinction in the secretariat which served Winston Churchill in his capacity as Minister of Defence in the Second World War and

*Oberkommando des Wehrmachts.
†Oberkommando des Heeres.

could be relied on both to favour a more effective central organization for defence and to respect the hallowed ritual and sensitivities of the Chiefs of Staff. Their report was completed before the end of February 1963 and suggested three options: (a) some modifications to the existing system, which was clearly not favoured; (c) a fully integrated and functional Ministry as Mountbatten had proposed – it should be the eventual goal; (b) a compromise, which the authors preferred, of a single Ministry, to which the separate service departments would be subordinate, all to be housed together in one building. Mountbatten was disappointed, but foresaw that co-location and other pressures would lead to further changes in the direction of his final goal, as step by step it did. The separate Secretaries of State and their Chiefs of Staff accepted it with varying degrees of resignation or approval, laying emphasis on the reservations, such as preservation of the right* of the Chiefs of Staff, together or separately, to have access to the Prime Minister and the principle that the Chief of the Defence Staff had no right to give his own advice to the Minister, unless the Chiefs of Staff as a body were not in agreement with each other. The application of this principle, if the CDS disagreed with his colleagues united against him, as had been the case over the reorganization, was not clear. Thorneycroft suggested that, in order to see the new organization through its initial stages, Mountbatten's tenure should be further extended to 1965, although advised against it by Rob Scott on the grounds that it would only arouse further opposition. He persisted and, with the Prime Minister, Douglas-Home's, agreement, the extension was approved. For the same reason, Macmillan, in October 1963, had suggested to Mountbatten that he should replace Thorneycroft as Minister, but Mountbatten sensibly refused. The new organization, therefore, came into force, in the building on the river side of Whitehall originally designed to house the Air Ministry and the Board of Trade, on 1 April 1964.

The election was held in October 1964 and resulted in a Labour victory, Harold Wilson appointing Denis Healey as Secretary of State of this huge new department, which controlled almost as many civil servants – 406,000 – as it did men and women in the armed forces. In the eight years since Suez, there had been four different Ministers of Defence, two of them, Watkinson and Thorneycroft, having been entirely ignorant of defence matters before being appointed. Healey had served on active operations in the army in the

*Of uncertain origin.

70

Second World War and had become a defence expert, specializing in matters of nuclear weapon policy. He was to remain Defence Secretary for six consecutive years, during which he imprinted his strong personality on every aspect of the life of the armed forces. Although determined to exert his authority as Secretary of State, he made no immediate attempt to press forward the sort of functional integration which Mountbatten favoured. He did change the functions of his junior ministers, one for personnel and administration and the other for equipment matters, retaining initially separate service parliamentary under-secretaries. He also introduced methods of assessing financial and manpower effort on a functional basis, and a greater degree of coordination and 'cross-servicing' between the three armed forces, but he did not attempt to integrate them on the model that Canada had already introduced. In theory the Defence Council was the top body which made the major decisions, but in practice it seldom, if ever, met. The Defence Secretary made his decisions on the basis of advice from the Chiefs of Staff, the Permanent Under-Secretary and the Chief Scientist, major matters being referred by him to the Defence and Overseas Policy Committee of the Cabinet, presided over by the Prime Minister, which the Chiefs of Staff attended.

Healey's remit from Wilson was to reduce the expenditure which Douglas-Home's Conservative administration had planned for his department by £400m a year, bringing it down from 7 to 5 per cent of GNP. The Conservatives' last Defence White Paper (Cmnd 2270. February 1964) had forecast £1,998.5m for 1964/65. After allowing for expenditure by the central part of the Ministry of Defence, and the Ministry of Aviation, the Ministry of Public Building and Works and the Atomic Energy Authority on behalf of defence, amounting in all to £473m, the balance was almost equally divided between the three services at around £500m each. Manpower (UK male adult) at the end of 1964 would total 87,700 for the navy, 173,500 for the army, of whom 2,600 were still National Servicemen, and 130,400 for the RAF. For all three services, women totalled 17,600 and boys 21,000. The army employed 27,800 locally enlisted soldiers overseas, including some 14,000 Gurkhas, the navy 2,100, mostly Chinese as cooks and laundrymen, and the air force 1,000.

There was no scope for immediate economies by reductions in manpower. The army was still struggling to reach its authorized figure of 180,000 (to which it had been reduced) and was fully committed in Aden and Borneo. The axe would have to fall on equipment projects which had not yet reached the production stage.

71

Healey was appalled at the mess he discovered in the aircraft field. Over the previous 13 years of Conservative administration, 26 major projects, costing £300m, had been cancelled and current ones were escalating in cost and behind schedule. The answer he received from the airmen, when he asked them for advice, was to buy American. There were not many regrets when he dropped the HS681 in favour of the American C130 Hercules transport aircraft, which would be cheaper and enter service earlier to replace the Hastings and Beverley. It did not meet the STOL specification of the HS681, but was to prove an invaluable workhorse for many years to come. Nor did the purchase of the Phantom fighter cause much concern, although, unlike the P1154, it would not be VTOL. Anxiety about vulnerability of airfields to nuclear and missile attack had led the air staff to demand the ability to use short runways or none at all, and this had been one of the factors leading to staff requirements which the industry found it very difficult and expensive to meet. They were, therefore, angry that the RAF then accepted US aircraft which would not have met those demanding requirements. They protested that, had the specifications been relaxed to those which the US aircraft actually met, they could have produced acceptable aircraft in time and at competitive cost. Another casualty of this process was the Anglo-French variable geometry aircraft, seen as a successor to the TSR2, from which the French withdrew in 1967. Had the government been prepared to accept the Phantom as produced in the USA, Healey would have been able to save more money. The decision to fit it with a British engine, the Rolls-Royce Spey, and with British avionics, which would not only benefit British industry but also improve the aircraft's endurance and operational performance, added 40 per cent to its unit cost. Controversy arose over Healey's decision in February 1965 to drop the TSR2, for which an order of 120 was planned, in favour of the American variable geometry F1–11, the former's development cost having escalated alarmingly to £750m. He faced serious opposition in Cabinet both from those, like the Prime Minister and Roy Jenkins, Minister of Aviation, who disliked yet another US purchase, because of its effect on industry and the balance of payments, and from those who wished to drop the TSR2 without replacement. Having with difficulty persuaded the RAF to accept its cancellation by the promise of the F1–11 instead, Healey stuck to his guns, but only 50 were to be ordered. As already explained, the P1127 was kept in the programme as a fighter-bomber for the close support of the army and plans were put in hand to adapt the Comet, Britain's first jet passenger aircraft, to replace the Shackleton for long-range maritime reconnaissance, to be known as the Nimrod and to have a long life in that role.

The controversy over the aircraft programme was mild in comparison with the row that broke out when Healey turned his attention to the navy. In 1963 the Royal Navy had four aircraft-carriers, two of which would normally be east of Suez at all times. All were old and would not be able to operate future modern aircraft. Only one new carrier of that capability had been ordered, known as CVA–01. The cost of new carriers, the aircraft for them, and all the other ships needed to escort them against aircraft and submarine attack, would be very large. Even if that cost were met, manning problems would prevent the navy from having more than three in service. Allowing for periodic refits, that would mean that only one carrier could be permanently maintained east of Suez and at times that would have to be the almost obsolete HMS *Hermes*, which could only operate 8 strike and 12 fighter aircraft. Maintaining a fleet of three carriers would cost £170m a year. Healey commissioned a number of studies of the problem, as a result of which the air staff, represented by the very able and equally charming Chief of the Air Staff, Sir Charles Elworthy, and his Assistant, Air Vice Marshal Peter Fletcher, both of them with university law degrees, persuaded him that air cover and support for any naval or amphibious operations in which we were likely to be involved could be provided from land-based aircraft. Elworthy was supported by Hull, Chief of the Defence Staff. But neither the First Sea Lord, Admiral Sir David Luce, nor his Minister, Christopher Mayhew, could accept that. Mayhew argued that, if the carrier force were not to be modernized, the commitments which required it east of Suez should be abandoned. When Healey stuck to his decision to cancel CVA–01, both Luce and Mayhew resigned, Luce replaced by Sir Varyl Begg, who, unlike Luce, was not an aviator, but a gunnery expert.

Healey's first Defence White Paper (Cmnd 2592. February 1965) was a good deal longer than any of its predecessors, but took much the same line as they did. After complaining that he had inherited forces which were 'seriously over-stretched and in some cases under-equipped', he maintained that his predecessor's programme had estimated an increase in expenditure in one year of 8.7 per cent in cash and 5.5 per cent in real terms. Illustrating the remarkable increases in the unit cost of different types of new equipment over that which they replaced, the paper was just as dismissive of the likelihood of a major war in Europe as Sandys had been and gave just as much emphasis to the east-of-Suez role as had Watkinson and Thorneycroft. 'Deliberate aggression, even on a limited scale, is unlikely in Europe. But there is always the risk arising out of miscalculation or misunderstanding.' The 'overwhelming US nuclear strike force' deterred the former: the conventional forces of NATO were designed to counter the latter before it could escalate to major war. 'In the unlikely event of failure' the use of nuclear weapons would 'cause such destruction that it is impossible to conceive of a land campaign in Europe lasting for many days'. It was 'pointless to tie up resources for a prolonged land campaign following a nuclear exchange'. When the paper turned to consider the issues outside the NATO area, it opened with a statement of doubtful historical validity, clearly a sideswipe at the Suez affair: 'Experience has shown that it is neither wise nor economical to use military force to seek to protect national economic interests in the modern world.' Our forces were not trying to hold on to overseas territories, but to help them forward to independence, and were maintaining interests, that we shared with others, in peace and stability. Britain's contribution in this respect was 'paramount in many areas East of Suez'. We had obligations there to allies and fellow members of the Commonwealth, to fulfil which we maintained bases at Aden and Singapore. Our presence was 'a substantial contribution to international peacekeeping'. The pious hope was expressed that allies would share the burden – pious indeed when the USA was fully committed in Vietnam.

No mention was made of the independence of Britain's nuclear force. Considerable space was devoted to Healey's alternative to McNamara's Multilateral Nuclear Force, dubbed 'Atlantic Nuclear Force'.

It would be concentrated and controlled under conditions which would both meet the legitimate requirements of the non-nuclear members to play their part and remove any incentive for the dissemination of nuclear weapons. We are proposing that the Atlantic Nuclear Force should consist of the British V-bombers (except those required for commitments outside the NATO area); the four British Polaris submarines; at least an equal number of US Polaris submarines; some kind of mix-manned and jointly armed element or elements in which the existing non-nuclear powers could take part; and any force which France may desire to subscribe. The British forces would be wholly committed for as long as the Alliance continued. The US, the UK and any other participating country which so wished would have a veto over the release of the weapons of the force.

This in the event never materialized. It satisfied neither the desire of the Americans, that they should have complete control, nor that of the French, that they should be truly independent, nor of the non-nuclear members of NATO who saw it for the bit of window-dressing that it was. The one sentence in the paper on this subject with which everybody could agree was that 'The strategic concept needs revision.'

The economies that Healey had been directed to achieve were not yet reflected in the figures. The previous year's estimate of £1,998.5 was confirmed and the estimate for 1965/66 was £2,120.5m, over the magic figure of £2,000m which the previous administration had set as a *ne plus ultra*. The actual out-turn was £2,105m, which represented an increase of £23m at constant prices, the percentage of GNP remaining at 5.9. The manpower figures were increased to 393,000 UK adult male, the RAF male strength having fallen to 123,400, while the Royal Navy, including the Royal Marines, increased to 92,300 and the army to 177,200, its target having been raised to 181,000 on the transfer to it from the RAF of responsibility for airfield repair and construction in the field.

Having started to clear up the mess left by his predecessor, as he chose to represent it, Healey was now all set to develop his own policy, which would have to be implemented within a limit of expenditure of £2,000m at 1964 prices. Like his predecessors, he saw the way to do this as through a basic reliance on the nuclear weapon to deter a war in Europe, and providing only sufficient conventional forces to deal with some temporary aberration, while gradually reducing commitments elsewhere which were undertaken in order to meet not so much our own national economic interests as our general world-wide responsibilities, especially to the Commonwealth. A respectable performance in both was essential to maintain the general support and goodwill of the USA, which, although regarded by many in the Labour Party as an unwelcome necessity, Healey recognized as essential.

5

HEALEY HEADS WEST: 1966–1970

THE LINE TAKEN in the 1965 Defence White Paper about commitments east of Suez did not go unchallenged, either within the Labour Party and the government itself, or outside it. A wide spectrum of opinion held that the protection by military force of our interests, whether regarded as national or part of the general White Man's Burden, was outdated and counterproductive. A significant element of the government's supporters thought that way; the Liberal Party proclaimed it as their policy, and, to the dismay of a large section of his party, the Conservative Shadow Defence Minister, Enoch Powell, took that line at their October 1965 party conference and even received a standing ovation when he had done so. There were also those among the military who went some way with it, on the grounds of the danger of being saddled with a commitment if it was not backed by the resources that would make it possible to meet it effectively. It could lead to being sucked into a military campaign which escalated beyond the limit set either by one's interest or the resources that could be made available, as appeared to be happening to the Americans in Vietnam.

But pressure from the Americans and the Commonwealth, and a general desire to accept responsibilities towards both, demonstrating that a Labour government was just as much to be relied on to support Britain's standing in the world as a Conservative one, persuaded Wilson to remain wedded to the concept, reinforced by Michael Stewart at the Foreign Office and Healey and the Chiefs of Staff, that our obligations in that area must be backed by a military presence.

The February 1966 Defence White Paper (Cmnd 2901), published in the month before Wilson went to the country in a General Election which returned him with an increased majority of 97, made this clear, although hedging it with some qualifications. 'We must be ready to continue living in a world in which the United Nations has not yet assumed responsibility for keeping the peace, and the arms race has not yet halted' was perhaps a reminder that not only were the Americans engaged in Vietnam and ourselves in Borneo, but that the latest Indo-Pakistan war had only just come to an end, not through any influence exerted by Britain or the Commonwealth, but by the mediation of the Soviet Union. However the paper went on to speak of the 'unacceptable strain' that would be imposed by trying to maintain all existing commitments. While we should retain a major military capability outside Europe, it would be subject to certain general limitations: we would not undertake major military operations except in cooperation with allies; we would not accept an obligation to provide another country with military assistance unless it was prepared to provide us with the facilities we would need to make such assistance effective in time; and no attempt would be made to maintain defence facilities in an independent country against its wishes. The second condition was a dig at Kuwait, which had shocked Healey by taking that line. There were to be reductions in the Mediterranean, both in Cyprus, where the RAF still remained at Nicosia airfield outside the Sovereign Base Areas, and in Malta. The latter had become independent in September 1964, but its Prime Minister, Dom Mintoff, reacted strongly against reductions in the naval presence which could adversely affect employment in the island. The historic post of Commander-in-Chief Mediterranean, which had also been a NATO command appointment, was abolished. The paper announced the decision that when 'South Arabia' became independent in 1968, forces would be withdrawn from Aden: a 'small increase' in the forces stationed in the Gulf would then make it possible for us to meet our obligations there. Pride of place was given to the Far East with the statement:

It is in the Far East and Southern Asia that the greatest danger to peace may lie in the next decade, and some of our partners in the Commonwealth may be directly threatened. We believe it is right that Britain should continue to maintain a military presence in this area. Its effectiveness will turn largely on the arrangements we can make with our Commonwealth partners and other allies in the coming years. As soon as conditions permit, we shall make some reductions in the forces which we keep in the area. We have important facilities in Malaysia and Singapore, as have our Australian and New Zealand partners. These we plan to retain for as long as the Governments of Malaysia and Singapore agree that we should do so in acceptable conditions. Against the day when it may no longer be possible for us to use these facilities

77

freely, we have begun to discuss with the Government of Australia the practical possibilities of our having military facilities in that country if necessary.

The paper then explained the decisions about the phasing out of the aircraft-carrier force and stated:

Our plan is that, in the future, aircraft operating from land bases should take over the strike-reconnaissance and air defence functions of the carrier on the reduced scale which we envisage that our commitments will require after the mid-1970s. Close anti-submarine protection will be given by helicopters operating from ships other than carriers. Airborne Early Warning aircraft will continue to be operated from existing carriers and subsequently from land bases. Strike capability against enemy ships will be provided by Surface-to-Surface Guided Missiles.

By this time it was clear that it would not be long before 'confrontation' in Borneo came to an end. In October 1965 a coup against Soekarno, engineered by army officers led by General Soeharto, had taken place and, although a state of confusion reigned until Soeharto finally replaced Soekarno on 12 March 1966, it was clear that the latter's days were numbered when Healey visited Australia on his way round the world in February 1966. He explained to Harold Holt's government that, once confrontation was over, Britain would reduce her forces in the Far East to, he hoped, about half their current strength, but that 'we intend to remain, and shall remain, fully capable of carrying out all the commitments we have at the present time, including those in the Far East, the Middle East, and in Africa and other parts of the world. We do intend to remain in the military sense a world power.'* He told them that, in spite of the phasing out of the carrier force, land-based air support could be provided as a result of the development of a number of island staging posts. One had already been acquired south of the Gulf on the barren island of Masirah, leased from the Sultan of Muscat and Oman, and one at Gan in the Maldives. The plan to acquire one at Aldabra, one of the Seychelle islands north of Madagascar, was being hotly opposed by environmentalists, but was still being relied on to provide a link between these and Ascension Island in the South Atlantic. The aim was to free the RAF from dependence on other countries,

*Denis Healey, *The Time of My Life*. London, 1989, p. 292.

who might not be favourably inclined, for staging, refuelling and overflying facilities.

Healey met with a cool response to his proposal that a base of some sort should be established in Western Australia to cater for the day when we might wish to leave Singapore. The Australians pointed out that there was no sign that Malaysia or Singapore wished either Britain or Australia and New Zealand to remove their forces from their countries; that the British government had stated that they would be maintained there as long as the countries wished, and that to start preparations for a base in Western Australia would undermine that assurance. There could also be local objections. In spite of mounting pressure within the Labour Party, the British government stuck to its policy right up to the financial crisis of July 1966. On a visit to Canberra at the end of June, Michael Stewart said: 'We have neither the wish nor the intention to abandon the world east of Suez', and as late as 12 July Healey told journalists in Hong Kong that Britain would stay in Singapore and Malaysia as long as she was wanted on acceptable conditions.

A week later Wilson announced £100m cuts in government expenditure, of which defence was expected to take a large share, the official end of confrontation in Borneo following a few weeks later. Air Chief Marshal Sir John Grandy, the joint-service Commander-in-Chief Far East, had already been warned to plan on a withdrawal of all troops from Borneo within six months, leaving only a small Gurkha garrison in Brunei, and a subsequent reduction of forces in Malaysia and Singapore, leaving, as far as the land forces were concerned, only the British contribution to the Commonwealth Brigade in Malaya and the Royal Marine Commando Brigade in Singapore. This would reduce the UK-recruited element of his forces by 8,000 men. More controversial was the proposal to revert to the plan, which had been mooted before the Borneo campaign, to reduce the Gurkhas from the 15,000 to which they had been expanded to the 10,000 which was the figure agreed when the Indian Army broke up on independence in 1947. The Ministry of Defence began yet another review, working to a target below £2,000m at 1964 prices, while behind the scenes Wilson and Healey were seriously considering the possibility of a total withdrawal from east of Suez, as political pressures grew for defence to take a larger share of the economies demanded by the precarious financial position.*

*Harold Wilson, *The Labour Government 1964–70*. London, 1971, p. 297.

No major new decisions, however, were announced in the February 1967 Defence White Paper (Cmnd 3203). It stated:

Our aim is that Britain should not again have to undertake operations on this scale [that of the Borneo campaign] outside Europe. The purpose of our diplomacy is to foster developments which will enable the local peoples to live at peace without the presence of external forces. But, provided that they are needed and welcome, the continuing presence of British forces can help in the meantime to create the environment, in which local governments are able to establish the political and economic basis for peace and stability. There can also be no certainty – so long as threats to stability remain – that those forces will not be required to give help to friendly governments, or to play a part in a United Nations peacekeeping force, as they have done in recent years.

We are continuing our discussions with the Australian government about the possibility of having new facilities in Australia. We are also examining what benefits we should get from a new staging airfield in the British Indian Ocean Territory. These arrangements would offer us greater flexibility in our future defence planning, particularly in relation to the Far East.

However by then Healey had come to the conclusion that, as long as we maintained forces in South East Asia, we had to plan to reinforce them in emergency, and that the resources to cover both stationing and allowance for reinforcement could not be provided within the financial limits to which he was being forced to work. He therefore decided that a withdrawal from Malaysia and Singapore was the only answer, and that our obligations in that area, at least as far as Australia and New Zealand were concerned, should be met by a much smaller base for the navy and some marines in Western Australia. The target date for final withdrawal should be 1975–76. This provisional plan was explained in secrecy by George Brown, who had replaced Stewart as Foreign Secretary in August 1966, in the margins of a SEATO meeting in Washington in April 1967 to his colleagues Dean Rusk, the US Secretary of State, Paul Hasluck, Australian Minister of External Affairs, and Keith Holyoake, who doubled that post with the Premiership of New Zealand. While accepting the need for reductions, all strongly urged Brown not to make a public announcement of the decision to withdraw, certainly not as long as the Vietnam War lasted. There would certainly be no enthusiasm for a British withdrawal from Singapore to Australia while the latter still had soldiers fighting in Vietnam.

Immediately after that, Healey visited Singapore and Malaysia to assess the impact of a faster rundown of forces than that which he had announced after the end of confrontation – 10,000 in one year. He proposed withdrawal of a further 10,000 by April 1968, leaving a total, in all three services, of 30,000. When he revealed the intention to withdraw altogether to Tunku Abdul Rahman in Kuala Lumpur and Lee Kuan Yew in Singapore, they both urged him not to announce it publicly and followed that by visits to London with the same plea, which was backed by the Foreign Office and the Ministry of Defence. The Cabinet was divided on the issue, the Chancellor of the Exchequer, Roy Jenkins, supported by left-wing Ministers including Richard Crossman and Barbara Castle, demanding a firm date to be fixed and announced.

While this issue was being hotly debated, two other events affected it: one the situation in Hong Kong, the other that in the Middle East. The former was suffering from the effects of the Cultural Revolution in China. After the Portuguese authorities in Macao had given way to pressure from the Red Guards, trouble spread to Hong Kong, where there were serious riots in May 1967, necessitating reinforcement of the garrison from Singapore. In June and July police posts on the frontier were attacked by Red Guards and had to be rescued and then replaced by soldiers. These events lent strength to the argument that, far from being reduced, as the British government had hoped, the garrison should be increased when it could no longer be reinforced from Singapore. It was eventually to provide the solution to the controversy about the future of the Gurkhas. At the same time, the Commander-in-Chief Far East's* attention was drawn in the opposite direction. He had been warned that the provisional date for South Arabia's independence was 1 January 1968 and that for six months thereafter he would have to keep an aircraft-carrier and a Royal Marine Commando afloat off Aden to provide air support for the newly independent Federation or to help rescue British residents, if the situation turned sour. Meanwhile, in mid-May, tension built up round Israel, as Nasser demanded the withdrawal of the United Nations peacekeeping force from Sinai and declared a blockade of the Straits of Tiran. While Israel's neighbours mobilized, Jordan allowed an Iraqi division to enter her territory and link up with Syrian forces. Wilson planned to send a naval force

*The author.

81

from off Aden through the Red Sea to break the blockade, but neither the USA nor the French showed any enthusiasm for the idea. Nothing came of it and it was overtaken by the outbreak of the Six-Day Arab–Israel war on 5 June, the presence of the aircraft-carrier off Aden leading to the false accusation that its aircraft had flown sorties in support of Israel.

These reminders of British commitments east of Suez immediately preceded the Supplementary Statement on Defence in July (Cmnd 3357) which described itself as 'ending the process of defence review'. It reminded readers of the words of the February paper, which had stated the government's policy as being 'to foster developments which will enable the local people to live at peace without the presence of external forces' and thus to allow our forces to be withdrawn from the Middle and Far East. The rate at which this could take place could not be predicted; it depended on the impact it would have on the countries concerned and on the policies of our allies. The decision to withdraw from South Arabia and Aden in January 1968 was confirmed. In the Far East, the forces in Singapore and Malaysia would have been halved by 1970–71 and would thereafter consist largely of naval and air forces. 'We cannot plan the period beyond 1970–71 in the same detail', it continued.

The reductions over the next few years will be considerable: we are determined that they will take place in an orderly manner, which will enable our Commonwealth partners to adjust their plans, and will allow Singapore and Malaysia to make the necessary economic transition as smoothly as possible. We plan to withdraw altogether from our bases in Singapore and Malaysia in the middle 1970s; the precise timing of our eventual withdrawal will depend on progress made in achieving a new basis for stability in South East Asia and in resolving other problems in the Far East.

When pressed in the House of Commons by Edward Heath as to what he meant by 'the mid-1970s', Wilson replied, 'between 1973 and 1977'. Having declared that 'air power will be as indispensable to the fleet of tomorrow as it is today', the statement announced that the aircraft-carriers *Ark Royal* and *Eagle* would continue in service until then, *Victorious* being phased out in 1969 and *Hermes* in 1971. The army was to be reduced by 17 battalion-sized combat units, the increase in the Gulf being small. Apart from the withdrawal from Aden, there would also be further reductions in Malta and Cyprus.

The garrison in Hong Kong would be 'maintained' and, while 'some Gurkhas' would remain in Malaysia, the main reductions would take place there and in Singapore. Most of the RAF reductions would come from the Far East, Malta and Aden, from which four squadrons would be redeployed to the Gulf. All this was expected to make it possible to stick to the target of remaining below £2,000m a year at 1964 prices. The budget for 1970/71 was expected to be £1,900m, £200m below the February estimate, and by the mid-1970s should be £1,800m. At 1967 prices these figures would be £2,200m and £2,100m. The actual out-turns were much higher – £2,462 and £2,799m at 1970 prices.

By this time the situation in Aden and South Arabia had sharply deteriorated. The choice by the Sultans of the shaky South Arabian Federation of the first Arab officer to succeed the British commander of their army was disputed by some of the officers, leading to a mutiny, the suppression of which by other Arab officers sparked off rumours of British intervention. This quickly spread to Aden itself, where mutineers ambushed and killed a British officer. This led to further incidents and finally, after some hesitation, to the occupation of the whole Crater area of the town by British troops. From then on, the Federation collapsed and near-chaos ruled while fruitless attempts were made by the United Nations and others to bring together the different factions contending for power. The rapidly worsening situation led to the decision to bring forward the evacuation and to cancel the guarantee to the Federal Sultans to provide air support thereafter, their army, and indeed their Federation itself, having disintegrated. Supported by most of the Far East Fleet, which reinforced the garrison with a Royal Marine commando, the final evacuation took place without incident in the last week of November 1967, the responsibility of government having been handed over to the communist extremist faction, the National Liberation Front, which had progressively defeated its rivals.

While suffering this humiliating cold war defeat, Wilson's administration faced yet another financial crisis, which forced the devaluation of sterling on 18 November. More cuts in public expenditure were imposed, including a further £100m from defence, which Healey at first said he could find without altering the decisions announced in July. But the Chiefs of Staff, fed up with the whole process, dug in their heels and protested that no further cuts in the forces or the resources to support them could be entertained unless there were corresponding cuts in commitments. There they parted company with the Foreign and Commonwealth Relations Offices, which believed that a presence of some sort could be maintained at lower force levels. The Chiefs found themselves hoist with their own petard when, in a further review of policy, the government accepted a wholesale abandonment of military commitments east of Suez, including most significantly in the Persian Gulf. Various dates for final withdrawal from Malaysia and Singapore were discussed, 31 March 1973 being succeeded by the same date in March 1972, and then a year earlier being decided on. After that date no 'special capability' would be maintained to undertake operations east of Suez. These decisions were arrived at in mid-December and were to be announced when Parliament returned from the Christmas recess. George Brown set off for Washington to break the news to Dean Rusk, as a result of which President Johnson attempted in vain to deflect Wilson, while Brown's unfortunate junior Minister, Goronwy Roberts, was despatched to tell the sultans, emirs and sheikhs of the Gulf that the assurance he had personally given them only two months before was to be withdrawn. George Thomson, the Commonwealth Relations Secretary of State, was sent to explain this abandonment of promises to Malaysia, Singapore, New Zealand and Australia, where John Gorton had only just taken over as Prime Minister after Harold Holt had been drowned when bathing. Not surprisingly Thomson had a frosty reception, especially in Australia and Singapore, Lee Kuan Yew immediately flying off to London to protest personally to Wilson. His reward was a postponement of the planned date of final withdrawal to 31 December 1971. These missions were graced with the name of consultations, but the recipients recognized them for what they were – unilateral decisions made without prior consultation – and objected all the more because of that.

The principal decisions were announced, accompanied by a Defence White Paper (Cmnd 3540), on 16 January 1968. It stated that they were based on

the fundamental principle that reductions in capability . . . must be accompanied by reductions in the tasks imposed by the commitments that we require the Services to undertake. We have no intention of allowing a repetition of the situation which existed in 1964 when, because of the lack of balance between military tasks and resources, our forces were seriously overstretched.

The paper went on to say that in future our forces would be concentrated in Europe and the North Atlantic; and that we would accelerate the withdrawal from Malaysia and Singapore so that it would be completed by the end of 1971, when we should also have withdrawn from the Persian Gulf, the carrier force being then finally phased out. The Gurkhas would be further reduced to 6,000, and no general capability would be maintained for operations outside Europe, although 'we shall, however, retain a general capability based in Europe, including the United Kingdom, which can be deployed overseas as, in our judgement, circumstances demand, and can support United Nations operations as necessary.' That capability would be smaller by the cancellation of the order for F1–11s. As a result of these decisions, there would be other reductions in new naval construction and cuts in RAF Transport Command. At home there would be major reorganizations of the United Kingdom Command organization of all three services. The Royal Navy's would be reduced to the headquarters of Commander-in-Chief Western Fleet, responsible for combat ships, and Commander-in-Chief Home for shore establishments. All army combat formations and units in the United Kingdom were to come under Strategic Command, while the geographical commands were to be reduced by the amalgamation of Southern and Eastern. RAF Bomber, Fighter, Coastal and Signal Commands were to be amalgamated into Strike Command, while Transport, Flying Training and Technical Training Commands were to be amalgamated into Support Command. The Ministry of Defence was to be reduced. These measures were expected to reduce expenditure, after making allowance for changes in accounting procedures, by £58m at constant prices below the 1967/68 total; by £110m below the 1969/70 estimate, and by some £210–£260m a year by 1972/73.

The practical consequences of these decisions were announced in a Supplementary Statement on Defence Policy in July (Cmnd 3701). In general they entailed not so much further reductions in the size of the forces below that planned as a result of the 1967 decisions as a more rapid rundown to the final level, which involved a reduction in overall manpower of 75,000. It was intended that the burden of future reductions would fall on headquarters, logistic and training establishments, to be achieved by a further rationalization or integration of them between the three services. As the carriers were phased out, all the navy's Buccaneers and Phantoms, with their crews, would be transferred to the RAF, which would lose a total of 20 stations by the mid-1970s. By 1970 the implementation of some of these measures would have reduced the percentage of GNP taken up by defence expenditure from 6 to 5½. The reduction in real terms between 1967/68 and 1968/69 had been £111m, and between 1968/69 and 1969/70 would be £68m. The government forecast that by 1972/73 it would be reduced to 'a little under 5 per cent'.

As everybody juggled with the figures, Healey was engaged in two balancing acts. The first has been described: that between those who wished Britain to maintain its presence and responsibilities east of Suez and those who, for a variety of reasons, some financial, some ideological, some practical, were determined that they should be given up. The second tightrope test involved defence policy in Europe. As has already been explained, Healey followed the example of his Conservative predecessors in relying on nuclear weapons as its basis, although there were significant elements in his party – some in government – who were strongly opposed to it. The first test came over the future of the Polaris submarine programme. At a crucial meeting at Chequers in November 1965, Healey, supported by Wilson and Patrick Gordon Walker, the Foreign Secretary, persuaded his Cabinet colleagues that Macmillan had obtained an excellent bargain at Nassau and that, if the number of vessels planned were reduced from five to four, the running costs would amount to only £4m a year, 2 per cent of the defence budget. There was no strong opposition from the admirals to this reduction in number, although it would mean that, when one vessel was undergoing a refit, it would not always be possible to keep two at sea, regarded then as the minimum to ensure the full credibility of an independent deterrent force. They accepted it because they had doubts about devoting that amount of manpower to the force at the expense of other elements of the Fleet. A year after that decision, the Americans revealed that the Soviet Union was developing an Anti-Ballistic Missile system to defend Moscow and that they were going to replace Polaris by a larger missile, Poseidon. In September 1967 they announced that it was to carry MIRVs* in order to defeat ABM systems and that they themselves were going to develop one to deal with a nuclear threat less than that from the Soviet Union, for instance from China.

The implication of this was that a system like the British Polaris would not be credible against the Soviet Union. Voices were raised on both sides: that we should drop Polaris before it had come into service and switch to Poseidon, modifying the vessels under construction; or that we should abandon the idea of maintaining a strategic nuclear strike force altogether. The easy way out was taken:

*Multiple Independently-targeted Re-entry Vehicles

to continue with Polaris and instruct the warhead designers to try and find some way of making it penetrate the Soviet ABM system, known as Galosh. During the rest of Harold Wilson's administration, the issue ceased to be very controversial. The peak of the anti-nuclear movement, aroused by the development of the megaton weapon, had passed, and the professional protesters turned their attention instead to the American involvement in Vietnam. Playing down the independent aspect of the Polaris force and emphasizing its NATO role helped to allay some potential opposition. Healey's project of an Atlantic Nuclear Force played a part in this.

There were two other issues, apart from the basic one of the balance between nuclear and conventional forces, that affected British defence policy in Europe at this time, and both were linked to de Gaulle. The first was his decision in March 1966 to remove France from the military organization of the North Atlantic Alliance, and to demand the withdrawal from French territory of all its installations and the forces of fellow-members. The second was Wilson's decision to make another attempt to join the European Economic Community. Both of these events made it more than ever necessary that Britain should be seen, both by the Americans and by its fellow European members of NATO, to set a good example within the Alliance.

In doing this, Healey found that he had to walk the tightrope between McNamara's pressure for an increase in conventional forces, so that early resort to nuclear weapons could be avoided, and the general European, particularly German, insistence that there must be no 'decoupling' of the threat of US strategic nuclear attack on the Soviet Union from an incursion of Soviet or Warsaw Pact armies across the Iron Curtain, or the Inner German Border to give it its official name. Pressure to reduce defence expenditure lent emphasis to the latter. Healey's own view was that, as long as US forces were stationed in Germany and were supported by US nuclear weapons, there was no real danger of a deliberate Soviet invasion of Western Europe. The function of the Alliance's conventional forces was to cater for some miscalculation by the Soviet Union which did not involve prolonged operations. This was superficially the same as, but significantly different from, the concept of the NATO command organization, dominated by the Americans. They defined them as needed to force a pause, during which political pressure would be brought to bear under the threat that nuclear weapons would be used if the aggressor did not desist and return to base. From the American point of view, the longer the pause before they had to face the risk of nuclear retaliation on their cities, the better. If nuclear weapons had to be used, they hoped that they might be limited to targets in the battlefield area and behind it, although McNamara himself believed that, once they were used, escalation could not be controlled. The Europeans, not unnaturally, were not in favour of a nuclear war limited to their countries, nor were they inclined to make provision for an extended period of conventional warfare. They had almost all skimped on the logistic backing needed for this, preferring to devote what money they were prepared to spend on the men and equipment to provide front-line units. They were the outward and visible sign, to friend and foe alike, of their contribution to the Alliance, and it was also hoped that, when it came to the crunch, the Americans would open their supply depots to them, in spite of the latter's insistence, for that very reason, that logistics was a national, not an Alliance, responsibility.

It was not easy to reconcile these conflicting views, and, indeed, they never were reconciled. But, after de Gaulle's dramatic move, a serious attempt was made to undertake a major review of policy and strategy under the chairmanship of the Belgian Minister, Pierre Harmel, emphasis in the former being laid as much on détente as on deterrence. Healey played a major part in the review, being already familiar with many of his European colleagues and others who had been concerned with these matters, as he himself had been before he took office. He made his views clear in the February 1966 Defence White Paper, in which he 'urged the Alliance to abandon military preparations which rested on the assumption that a general war in Europe might last for several months. Once nuclear weapons were employed, unless the aggressor quickly decided to stop fighting, the conflict would quickly escalate to a general nuclear exchange.' At the same time NATO, he suggested, must maintain enough conventional forces to deal with small-scale conflicts in European theatres without resort to nuclear weapons. The number of army formations for this was 'probably sufficient', but more air support for conventional operations was needed. This could be provided by a reduction in the number of long-range strategic bombers maintained in addition to those provided by the USA. In implementing this, Healey was making a virtue out of necessity, as he had to get rid of the Valiant V-bombers because of metal fatigue. The paper stated that 'as things now stand, we think it right to maintain our ground forces in Germany at about their existing level until satisfactory arms control arrangements have been agreed in Europe, provided, however, that some means is found for meeting the foreign exchange cost.'

French departure from the NATO military organization (although not from the Alliance) made it easier to tackle nuclear questions. European NATO members were prepared to man nuclear delivery systems – aircraft, missiles and guns – with American warheads on a dual-key basis, but they wished to have a say in determining the policy affecting their use and the guidelines given to military commanders as a basis for training and planning their use in war. Healey was instrumental in obtaining NATO Council agreement in December 1966 to establish a Nuclear Defence Affairs Committee and a Nuclear Planning Group to meet this demand, which it did in subsequent years to a limited degree. It put an end to ideas of a Multilateral or Atlantic Nuclear Force and to the sort of Nuclear Standing Group of the nuclear powers which de Gaulle had demanded.

The February 1967 White Paper injected some political realism at the expense of military sense into the revision of NATO strategy which had been set in hand.

It has been apparent for some years [it stated] that none of the NATO governments is willing to pay for the forces which SACEUR would need to carry out his mission as hitherto defined. Uncertainty about the wartime role of French forces further reduces the strength which NATO can rely on. At their meeting in July 1966, the NATO Defence Ministers finally agreed to instruct their military advisers to revise NATO strategy in the light of the forces which governments would undertake to make available on a rolling five-year programme, while retaining the commitment to the forward defence of the NATO area.

In other words: 'Never mind the threat: do your best with what you've got; but you cannot change the plan to defend every inch of territory!' The paper also reported that no progress had been made on the foreign exchange issue. Healey threatened to remove one brigade and a squadron of aircraft back to the United Kingdom unless this was resolved by 1 July. It was not, and the moves took place at the end of the year. They were expected to save £4.5m a year, but did not do so; and the foreign exchange cost of the forces in Germany increased as a result of the devaluation of sterling in November. The February 1968 White Paper noted this and remarked that further discussions on this issue with Germany were in train.

That paper claimed that a major step forward in NATO defence planning had taken place. The new strategic concept recognized, first, that the assessment of the threat should take into account the political intentions of the Warsaw Pact as well as its military strength: second, that the Alliance should receive timely, possibly prolonged, warning of any change in the political situation that might make war in Europe more likely; and finally that NATO strategies should be based on the forces that member countries were prepared to provide. A sop to the Americans had been agreement that 'adjustments should be made, particularly in the air forces, with the object of extending the conventional phase of hostilities should war break out; this would give more time in which any decision to use nuclear weapons could be taken.'

Healey's hope that he had weaned NATO away from too great an emphasis on conventional forces received a shock in August 1968, when Soviet forces entered Czechoslovakia to force Dubček to abandon his attempts at liberalizing the political and economic life of the country. NATO's alarm bells rang and the Americans pressed for a strengthening of conventional forces, only a month after Wilson's government had announced major reductions in the services. Healey's response was to promise to make available to NATO the amphibious forces, when they had been withdrawn from the Far East, and parachute troops, whose principal potential commitment had been in the Middle East. The following August was to see another commitment for conventional forces arise, the extent and duration of which was certainly not foreseen at the time: the commitment of British troops to reinforce and, for a time, virtually to replace the police in Northern Ireland.

Healey's attitude to NATO strategy had its effects in two other areas: the volunteer reserves and civil defence. The Sandys reforms had relegated most of the Territorial Army to home defence, but had not fundamentally reformed it or the other forms of reserve. The liability of National Servicemen to be called up into the Territorial Army after the end of their service, although never implemented, had helped to preserve a far larger number of units than could be manned at a viable strength by volunteers or could be adequately equipped. The concept of a separate army, which could not be ready for operations until after a period of mobilization and training, was irrelevant to current NATO strategy; nor did defence against troops landed in the United Kingdom from the air or sea make sense in that context. What the regular army needed was an organization which could expand it from its peacetime strength into immediate readiness for war. This should include a body which could be called upon for eventualities short of a major war. Reforms to provide this entailed a major reduction in the number of units and a change in attitude to the relation between the Territorial and the regular army and its other reserves, notably the Army Emergency Reserve. Healey's proposals to merge the army's reserves into one, to be called the Territorial and Army Volunteer Reserve, involving not only a major reduction in the number of units and their drill halls, scattered all over the country, but also of the County Associations which administered them, met with strong opposition from the traditional Territorial Army establishment, led by its Council, supported by the Conservative Party. But Healey persevered, and in 1966 the act was passed which established the new reserve. It included authority for 8,600 'Ever Readies' and a further 42,000 who could be called out when 'warlike operations are in preparation or in progress'. A further 23,000 were authorized as T & AVR III for purely home defence, including help to Civil Defence. This sop to the Council, which allowed it to keep in existence a number of units for which full military equipment could not be provided, was disbanded in 1968, having attracted few volunteers.

The creation of T&AVR III coincided with a lessening of the emphasis which the previous Conservative administration had placed on Civil Defence, which was a corollary of greater reliance on nuclear weapons. The 1966 White Paper announced that Civil Defence preparations would be 'restricted to those which would be likely to contribute significantly to national survival', but did not make clear what they might be. In 1968 the government appeared to have come to the conclusion that little could in fact be done, and announced that Civil Defence preparations would be 'placed on a care and maintenance basis'.

Healey's last Defence White Paper, that of 1970, struck a rather different note from its predecessors, reflecting NATO's policy of 'flexible response'. The paper described it as:

> designed to provide a wider and more flexible range of response appropriate to the nature of the threat. It recognizes that, while NATO must be ready to use nuclear weapons if necessary, this must not be the only response which the Alliance can make to any of the threats which it might have to face, and that steps must

therefore be taken to maximize the capability of NATO's forces in conventional conflicts.

The paper said that, as part of a NATO study of remedial measures to compensate for the withdrawal of Canadian land and air forces in Europe, it had been suggested that the units which Britain had recently removed in order to save foreign exchange should be returned to Germany and that discussions were being held with the Federal Republic to see whether satisfactory arrangements could be agreed. They were, and the brigade and other units returned towards the end of the year, their retention in England while being expected to train in Germany having caused considerable practical problems. The paper said that 'we look forward to the 1970s as an era of negotiations between the opposing alliances', welcoming the beginning of talks between the USA and the USSR on the limitation of strategic arms, while NATO continued the study of mutual arms reduction. The United Kingdom had put forward a draft convention on the prohibition of bacteriological warfare and on preventing nuclear weapons being placed on the sea-bed. The government welcomed the move towards the entry into force of the nuclear Non-Proliferation Treaty.

One of Healey's achievements at this time was the formation of the Eurogroup within NATO. This established meetings of the Defence Ministers of the European members of the Alliance so that they could coordinate a European view before meeting their American and Canadian colleagues in a NATO meeting. The French refused to join on the grounds that it formed part of the military organization. One of Healey's principal objects in setting it up was to try and achieve a greater cooperation in arms procurement within Europe, including decisions on buying American equipment, one of the advantages of which would be a greater degree of standardization. The absence of the French detracted significantly from his concept. By the time of the General Election of October 1970 Healey had achieved a great deal and had set in motion moves towards a greater degree of rationalization of inter-service matters, particularly in administration, which, although not approaching the degree of integration which Mountbatten had envisaged, were to be carried forward, step by step and rather gingerly, by his successors. This, ironically, came at a time when the withdrawal from east of Suez meant that it was less likely that the British navy, army and air force would be engaged together in the same operation. Under NATO command, it was more likely that each service would be more closely involved in operations with the same service of other members of the Alliance than it would be with other services of its own nation. This was particularly true in the case of cooperation between the army and the Royal Navy. Different elements of the RAF, mostly based in the United Kingdom, would be involved with the Royal Navy, and, mostly based in Germany, with the army.

6

TORIES MARK TIME: 1971–1974

HAVING SEVERELY CRITICIZED Wilson's Labour administration for 'scuttling' from east of Suez, for inflicting savage cuts on the armed forces, for trifling with the nation's security, and for undermining Britain's standing in the world, Edward Heath's new Conservative government had to appear to do something to put Labour's policy in reverse. All they did, in fact, was to apply the brakes and make some cosmetic indications of an intention to engage reverse gear, while actually moving into neutral. Lord Carrington, Healey's successor as Defence Secretary, was a pragmatist with considerable experience of defence matters. He had begun his career as a regular officer in the Grenadier Guards, and had served with distinction in command of a tank company in the Second World War. He had been Parliamentary Secretary to three successive Ministers of Defence – Harold Macmillan, Selwyn Lloyd and Walter Monckton – and First Lord of the Admiralty until Alec Douglas-Home succeeded Macmillan in 1963, when he became Leader of the House of Lords. His own extensive contacts with the armed forces, combined with his down-to-earth commonsense, encouraged him to adopt a policy of granting the services as far as possible a period of calm in which to adjust to the changes imposed on them, many of which had not yet been put into effect. As he wrote in his memoirs: 'There was no question of completely putting the clock back; we accepted much of the situation as we found it, although we had been, in Opposition, very sceptical of it.'*

This policy was outlined in the Supplementary Statement on Defence Policy published in October 1970 (Cmnd 4521).

The Government is determined [it stated] to restore Britain's security to the high place it must take among national priorities,

---

*Reflect On Things Past. London, 1988, p. 218.

94

and to make good as far as possible the damage of successive defence reviews. There are three objectives:

(1) To enable Britain to resume, within her resources, a proper share of responsibility for the preservation of peace and stability in the world;

(2) to improve the capabilities of the Armed Forces, to overcome their manpower difficulties, and to enhance their role in the community;

(3) to establish and maintain a sound financial basis on which to develop and carry out defence policy and plans in the years ahead.

Like its predecessors, the government was to find it difficult to reconcile (1) and (2) with (3). The paper went on to describe the practical consequences of its policy. In the Far East, 'The Government believe that total withdrawal would have weakened the security of Malaysia and Singapore, and that a continuing British military presence on the spot will be valuable in helping to preserve confidence in the area.' It was proposed that a Five-Power (Britain, Australia, New Zealand, Malaysia and Singapore) defence arrangement should replace the Anglo-Malaysian Defence Agreement. Britain would keep five frigates or destroyers on station east of Suez, including Hong Kong; contribute an infantry battalion, with some helicopters, to the Commonwealth Brigade to be stationed in Singapore; and keep a detachment of Nimrod Long-Range Maritime Patrol aircraft in the area. This was estimated to cost between £5m and £10m a year. The Royal Navy would be able to keep the aircraft-carrier *Ark Royal* in service 'until the late 1970s'. By that time, not only would other ships have been fitted with the Exocet anti-ship missile, but what were described as 'the new cruisers' would be 'starting to become available'. These were the navy's successful device to circumvent Healey's abolition of the fixed-wing carrier. They called them 'through-deck cruisers' and said that their function was to combine acting as command ships and serving as carriers of helicopters for anti-submarine operations. They argued that this would be a more efficient method than distributing single helicopters to smaller ships. But, in order to protect the fleet from observation by enemy long-range maritime patrol aircraft, for example the Soviet Bear, they wanted also to be able to operate from them a small number of VTOL aircraft. The helicopter requirement justified a flight deck, a hangar beneath it and a lift to bring the aircraft up to it. At this stage Carrington was not prepared to go further than to state that these 'new cruisers' would be 'capable of operating V/STOL aircraft if further study shows that their provision would be effective and give value for money'. He remained sceptical about them, as did the First Sea Lord's non-naval colleagues in the Chiefs of Staff Committee, and suspected that it was a dodge by which the navy could get back into the aircraft-carrier business. The maritime version of the Harrier was not finally given the go-ahead until after the Labour Party had returned to power in 1974, when Roy Mason persuaded his Cabinet colleagues to approve it, largely in order to continue providing employment at Hawker-Siddeley, while the negotiations to concentrate the aircraft industry into British Aerospace were not yet concluded.

For the army, the paper stated that: 'the Government would have preferred to cancel the second phase of the reduction of major army units. But, after carefully reviewing the manpower situation, it reluctantly concluded that there was no alternative to proceeding with the rundown,' but it went on to announce some cosmetic changes which saved one infantry battalion* from disbandment, while six, which were to have been amalgamated or disbanded, were retained as companies. It was explained that 'they will be a nucleus for potential expansion in the future. These changes have enabled the names of famous regiments, if they so wished, to be retained.' In the event four† were returned to battalion strength in 1972 to help meet the demand for infantry in Northern Ireland, the manpower situation having by then improved. The same paper announced that the Brigade of Gurkhas would remain at a strength of four or five battalions, and that there would be some increases in the T&AVR.

The manpower situation was serious. The overall strength of the forces had fallen 2,000 below the target of 375,000 which Sandys had originally set. The paper stated that this was 18,300, or nearly 5 per cent, below the numbers needed to meet the programme set by the previous administration. The annual intake of male recruits had fallen from 40,000 in 1966/67 to 32,000 in 1967/68 and 28,000 in 1968/69. It had risen in 1969/70 to 34,000, but this was still 12,000 (or 25 per cent) short of what the forces needed to make up the previous shortfall. In spite of some relaxation, the government hoped to hold defence expenditure at very much the same level as had been forecast in their predecessors' 1969 Public Expenditure

*The Glosters.
†2nd Scots Guards, Royal Hampshires, Argyll & Sutherland Highlanders, 3rd Royal Green Jackets.

Survey and claimed that their programme would actually cost less than their predecessors' would have done.

Carrington's hopes of achieving this were pinned on the equipment field. He was convinced that better value for money could be obtained if, first, procurement was centralized and made more efficient; second, development was organized internationally, so that production runs would be longer; third, if arms sales were more vigorously promoted; and, finally, if the services were forced to accept simpler equipment, instead of demanding the ideal. As far as the organization for this in the Ministry of Defence was concerned, he achieved a major step forward in obtaining Derek Rayner from Marks and Spencer to conduct a study, which resulted in the recommendation for a unified Procurement Executive, and then in persuading him to be its first head.

But reorganization within the Ministry of Defence would not by itself be enough. Although the number of different firms competing for business in the aircraft, missile and electronic fields had been significantly reduced over the past decade, there was still greater capacity, both for development and for production, than could be filled by the much smaller equipment orders that the future size and shape of the forces would generate. Even if arms sales overseas were markedly increased, the existence of several rival firms, each maintaining heavy overheads, was a significant factor in pushing up costs, particularly when the Ministry of Defence placed contracts, as it did, on a cost-plus basis. Furthermore it made negotiation of international collaboration projects more difficult. Carrington attempted without success to persuade the remaining aircraft companies to merge. It was left to the succeeding Labour government to force them together to form British Aerospace.

Anglo-French collaboration in this field, although it had its failures, had produced some good results, notably the Jaguar tactical strike aircraft. The joint helicopter programme, although successful, did not turn out to be all that joint. Of the three models, the Puma for the RAF and the Lynx and the Gazelle for the army, only the Lynx was of British design and the French took hardly any of them, producing, and marketing for export, a near-equivalent of their own. The aborted Anglo-French variable geometry aircraft was replaced by the Multi-Role Combat Aircraft project, which they would not join; but Britain, Germany and Italy agreed at this time to go ahead without them to develop the Tornado, of which only Britain eventually took the air-defence version.

Heath's government made no changes to the decisions which

Wilson's had made in the nuclear field. They did not attempt to resuscitate the idea of a fifth Polaris submarine, partly on the grounds of cost, partly because, by the time it came into service, the Polaris system might be out of date. A switch to *Poseidon*, favoured by the navy, was considered but rejected on a number of grounds, including having to accept yet another American system, just as Britain was once more engaged in an attempt, this time successful, to enter the European Economic Community; the difficulty of developing a MIRV system of our own; and cost – perhaps as much as £500m, although the Royal Navy originally estimated it at half that figure.

By this time the warhead designers at Aldermaston had come up with a proposal based on a project called Antelope, which the Americans had discarded in favour of MIRVs. It was christened Chevaline. The 1972 agreement between the USA and the Soviet Union to limit ABM systems made it appear adequate to meet the criterion that it should be able to penetrate the defences of Moscow, and it was expected to cost significantly less than a switch to Poseidon. A disadvantage was that the additional weight of the warhead reduced the range and, therefore, very significantly the area of ocean in which the Polaris submarines could operate within range of Moscow. In the event its cost, concealed for a long time from public gaze, escalated to such an extent that it might well have proved cheaper to have switched to Poseidon. At this stage the government did no more than authorize further development. They did, however, go further than their predecessors in initiating a study of what should succeed the Polaris submarine force, whose vessels were expected to reach the end of their life in the mid-1990s. This raised the hopes of the air staff that the prestigious task of manning Britain's independent deterrent might return to the RAF with some modernized form of missile launched from aircraft, thus justifying a replacement for the V-bombers. They pinned their hopes on the abandonment of insistence on the Moscow criterion, but were disappointed when the study, headed by the Ministry of Defence's Chief Scientist, Sir Hermann Bondi, came firmly down in favour of another submarine-launched ballistic missile.

A further nuclear matter which caused concern to the government at this time was the Strategic Arms Limitation Talks (SALT) between the USA and the USSR. They feared that the Americans might accept a clause limiting their freedom to transfer weapon systems or relevant technologies to other nations. Such a clause was included in Article IX of the ABM Treaty, to which the other members of NATO did not object, as they did not envisage developing ABM systems themselves; but representation to the US government resulted in a rider that this article did 'not set a precedent for whatever provision may be considered' by a future treaty on offensive arms. The Polaris programme was on schedule both in time and in cost, so that the government's nuclear policy was not going to cause financial problems. Initially, partly as a result of Heath's annoyance at American support for Pakistan in the December 1971 Indo-Pakistan war which led to the formation of Bangladesh, and partly connected with entry into the European Economic Community, there had been talk of preferring nuclear cooperation with France to continuing it with the USA; but, when tentative talks with the French started, it soon became clear that there was little common ground, and almost no advantage to be gained, by an attempt at cooperation which would prejudice the very valuable connection with the Americans.

Carrington's emphasis on arms sales fitted in with the government's policy towards the Middle East. Surprisingly perhaps, they did not reverse the Labour administration's decision to remove British forces from the Gulf. They could have done, as they had not yet left, and there would have been no great political or financial problems involved in leaving them there. Instead, it was decided to rely on the equivalent of 'The Nixon Doctrine', which the Americans were attempting to apply further east. Local countries were to be encouraged to assume responsibility for their own security, internal and external, by the purchase of arms and the attachment of British training teams, as well, in some cases, as employing British service or ex-service personnel in their armed forces. As almost all the countries of the area, large or small, were oil-rich, they could afford to do this. Britain would benefit in three ways: from the direct saving in defence expenditure; from the cash-flow, particularly into the defence industry, which should also result in lowering the price of arms to Britain's own armed forces; and also, it was hoped, from the provision of stability and protection from anti-Western influences in an area of great strategic importance to us. Iran was to be one of the major pillars of this framework, Oman and the Gulf states minor ones. British forces were accordingly withdrawn in 1971.

The retention of defence facilities in Malta, which had become independent in 1964, led to a seemingly endless argument with its Prime Minister, Dom Mintoff, about compensation for the loss of employment caused by the reduction that had taken place, in the form of payment by the British government for retaining certain defence facilities. Healey had refused to revise the current defence agreement upwards in Malta's favour, but Heath's government made a more generous offer in the hope that it would help the leader of the rival party, Borg Olivier, to win the election in Malta due in June 1971. Unfortunately he failed by one vote, and Dom Mintoff was returned to embark on eight months of drama-ridden negotiations, in which the Italian government and NATO became involved. A NATO package was finally agreed on 26 March 1972, after Mintoff had demanded that all British forces should leave and Carrington had called his bluff. The agreement gave Britain the right in peace and war to station forces and use facilities in Malta for the defence purposes of the United Kingdom and of NATO. These included the port and harbour facilities, naval and air force headquarters, barracks and the use of Luqa airfield. The forces that had been withdrawn returned to the islands.

Much of Carrington's attention during his time as Defence Secretary, and almost all that of the army, was centred on Northern Ireland. When British troops had first been committed to action in support of the police in August 1969, they had generally been welcomed by the Catholic population as saviours from the heavy-handed, and they believed biased, attention of the Royal Ulster Constabulary and their reserve, the 'B Specials'. But in spite of – perhaps because of – changes introduced by the Labour government, which included the disbandment of the 'B Specials' and their replacement by a local army reserve, the Ulster Defence Regiment, and the assumption by the army of many of the tasks carried out normally by the RUC, the Catholic population, influenced by the IRA, turned against the British army's presence. The IRA, then divided into two factions, the Officials and the Provisionals, the former inclined to political and the latter to 'military' action, saw the appearance of its traditional enemy, the British army, particularly in the guise of a defender of the Catholics against the Protestants, both as a threat to its influence and future, and as an opportunity to re-establish itself in its traditional role.

From the time that Heath's administration took over, the situation deteriorated and appeared increasingly to slip out of the control of the Prime Minister of Northern Ireland, James Chichester-Clark,* and the Chief Constable of the RUC, Graham Shillington. Lieutenant-General Sir Ian Freeland, commanding the troops, was in an invidious position, subject to the authority of the government at Westminster, while the responsibility for law, order and the political

*Later Lord Moyola.

decisions that affected them, lay in the hands of Stormont. One of the factors that influenced Heath's policy was the extreme reluctance of his Cabinet to escape from this unsatisfactory situation by assuming direct control of affairs themselves. The issue was brought to a head in 1971, after Chichester-Clark had been succeeded by a more dynamic and politically astute Protestant politician, Brian Faulkner. The crunch came over the annual Apprentice Boys' March in Londonderry in August. Pressure from the extreme Protestant faction, headed by the so-called Reverend Ian Paisley, urged Faulkner to demand, successfully, the introduction of internment of suspected members of the IRA. The incompetence of the RUC in their selection of the prospective internees, and the unfortunate introduction of methods of interrogation of those picked up, based on those used by the Chinese on our own troops captured in Korea, combined with other incidents were exploited by the IRA to swing the bulk of the Catholic population, willingly or as a result of intimidation, to its support. Much worse, it influenced the government in Dublin to support their protests. The result was a further deterioration in the security situation, involving an increase in the strength of British troops deployed in the province, many of them on rotation from Germany.

A decisive event occurred on Sunday 30 January 1972 during a major demonstration in Londonderry, organized by the Northern Ireland Civil Rights Association. Whatever its original, purely political aims, it had by this time become a front organization for the IRA. Marches had been banned and the streets bordering the Catholic housing area had been reduced almost to ruins by hooligans. The demonstration was a flagrant breach of the law, and Faulkner's Security Council – himself, the General, then Sir Harry Tuzo, and the Chief Constable – decided that force must be used to prevent the march from entering the Protestant area and that those who appeared the ringleaders should be arrested. In doing this, the soldiers, believing they had been fired on, returned fire, killing 13 people and wounding an equal number. This caused an uproar, the event being christened 'Bloody Sunday'. It put paid to the slender burgeoning hope that a political solution to the troubles could be found.

More significantly, it convinced Heath, Carrington and Maudling, who, as Home Secretary, held responsibility at Westminster for the affairs of Northern Ireland, that they could no longer accept a situation in which the government at Westminster was held responsible for events, while the decisions were made at Stormont. In

101

March 1972 Heath proposed to Faulkner that the responsibility for law and order in Northern Ireland should pass from Stormont to Westminster, and, when Faulkner refused to accept that, Heath declared that Westminster would assume total responsibility for all aspects of government in the province. The Stormont parliament and government ceased to have any authority. To give effect to this, a Northern Ireland Office was created, of which William Whitelaw was appointed Secretary of State.

Hope that this would improve matters was not fulfilled, in spite of a short period of ceasefire declared by the Official IRA on 29 May and by the Provisionals a month later. Inter-factional quarrels led to the latter resuming action in July, culminating in the explosion of 20 bombs in Belfast on the 21st, killing ten and injuring 130 civilians, mostly in the bus station. This created an atmosphere favourable to taking drastic action to eliminate the 'No-Go' areas which had evolved in Catholic enclaves of Londonderry and Belfast. A major military operation was prepared for this, Operation Motorman, for which the strength of the army in Northern Ireland was raised to 21,000. It took place on 31 July and was entirely successful without a shot being fired, but did not solve any problems other than restoring the presence of the security forces in the 'No-Go' areas. It marked the peak of the army's involvement in operations in the province. After the failure of Whitelaw's major political initiative, following the Sunningdale Conference in December 1973, caused to a significant degree by the General Election of February 1974 following so soon after the devolution of power to the newly-formed Northern Ireland Executive and Assembly, led by Faulkner, the army gradually handed back to the RUC the prime responsibility for enforcing the law and maintaining order. The strain on the army's manpower had been considerable, units from Great Britain and from Germany, a high proportion of other arms acting as infantry, spending four months at a time in the province, while a few units and many individuals served on longer tours of two to three years.

The combination of challenge and publicity, much of it favourable, which this brought to the army, allied to pay reform for all three services, designed to introduce comparability with civilian jobs, helped for a time to improve the manpower situation. In 1970/71 38,900 adult males had joined, bringing the overall total for all three services to 351,000, of whom 166,000 were in the army. In the following year 46,300 were recruited, raising the total to 353,700 (170,800 in the army), but it fell again in 1972/73 to 39,100. A more difficult problem was the retention of skilled men at a time when the demand for them in industry was keen.

The disruption to training, readiness for war and other aspects of military efficiency, resulting from the constant turnover of army units between Germany and Northern Ireland, caused concern in NATO circles. It came at a time when SACEUR was much concerned with the improvement in quality, particularly in modern equipment, of the Soviet and Warsaw Pact forces, while the equipment of many of NATO's forces was not being kept up to date. Hitherto the Alliance had tended to rest on the assumption that, although greatly inferior in quantity, it enjoyed a significant technological edge, but in many different weapon systems this was ceasing to be true. Under pressure from the Americans, the European members of NATO instituted a European Defence Improvement Programme. The British contribution to this, according to the February 1972 Defence White Paper (Cmnd 4891), was, for the navy, an acceleration of orders for two Type 42 destroyers, four Type 21 frigates and a number of support vessels and small craft; for the army, the restoration of four infantry companies to battalion strength (actually done for Northern Ireland reasons); and for the air force, orders for additional Buccaneer and Nimrod aircraft. The Americans hoped that the programme would lead to greater European purchases of American equipment, the end of the Vietnam war in January 1973 having left the US defence industry in the lurch. The Pentagon exerted strong pressure on the European members of NATO to achieve a greater standardization of weapons within the Alliance in the hope of giving support to this. They were not very successful, Carrington and his European colleagues, notably Helmut Schmidt, showing greater enthusiasm for developing European cooperation in arms procurement. They, in turn, were not significantly successful in that either, although the Tornado project progressed slowly. Attempts at joint production of tanks and artillery foundered partly on the rival ambitions of the national procurement authorities and their suppliers, partly on the real difficulty of coordinating the timing of replacement of existing equipment, which was subject to domestic financial considerations, and partly on technical failures. On the sidelines the Americans and the French did their best to ensure that they were not excluded from the market.

The general result of all these factors was to disappoint Carrington's hope that greater efficiency in the field of arms procurement would make it possible for him to hold defence expenditure at the level which the Wilson administration had planned. In 1971/72 the estimate was £2,545m; in 1972/73 £2,854m, 5½ per cent of GNP; in 1973/74 £3,365m, 5¾ per cent of GNP, a 5.6 per cent increase in real terms over the previous year and £523m above the Public Expenditure Survey's forecast, £350m of it being due to pay and price increases. In the aftermath of the 1973 Yom Kippur Arab–Israel war and the economic difficulties caused by the dramatic rise in oil prices which resulted from it, this was too much for the Chancellor of the Exchequer, Anthony Barber, who demanded a reduction to 4½ per cent of GNP, to be achieved within one year. At a tense meeting at Chequers with Heath and Barber, Carrington won agreement to a stay of execution, on condition that an inter-departmental review, including the Treasury, should report to the Cabinet what the effect would be of reductions to different percentages of GNP. The machinery to give effect to this was established and had just begun its work, when, as a result of the miners' strike, Heath decided to go to the country in the General Election of February 1974. His decision proved to be a serious political misjudgement, Labour being returned with a majority of only five seats over the Conservatives, another 37 going to small parties, 14 to the Liberals, 7 to the Scottish Nationalists and 11 to the Ulster Unionists.

7

LABOUR CUTS AGAIN: 1974–1979

IN OPPOSITION, AND during the election campaign, the Labour Party was committed to a reduction of defence expenditure, as a percentage of GNP, to the level of that of our major European allies in NATO – about 4 per cent. At its 1973 party conference Harold Wilson and Healey had successfully resisted pressure to accept a target of reduction by £1,000m a year. When Wilson took office, he was persuaded by the Cabinet Secretary, Sir John Hunt,* that a review designed to meet this commitment should be entrusted to the machinery which had recently been established for the same purpose by Heath. This was accepted by Roy Mason, the newly appointed Defence Secretary, and the Chiefs of Staff, although it meant that the review, before its conclusions were presented to the Defence and Overseas Policy Committee of the Cabinet, would not, as had hitherto been the case, be carried out within the Ministry of Defence with the advice of the Foreign Office. By directly involving both the Foreign Office and the Treasury from the start at a lower level, and by inserting the hitherto unused Defence and Overseas Policy Official Committee before the final review was presented to the Cabinet Committee, many of the issues which might have divided the latter were ironed out beforehand. The Official Committee was chaired by the Cabinet Secretary and included the Permanent Under-Secretaries of the Treasury, the Foreign Office and the Ministry of Defence, the Chief of the Defence Staff,† and the formidable inquisitor heading the Cabinet Policy Review Staff, Lord Rothschild.

The principal challenge to the Defence Ministry was that of its traditional ogre, the Chancellor of the Exchequer, Denis Healey, over whose bushy eyebrows it was impossible to pull the main

---

*Later Lord Hunt of Tanworth.
†The author.

product of his native Yorkshire – wool. As was to be expected, the Treasury immediately demanded to know what the effect on defence would be of reductions to 5, 4½ and 4 per cent of GNP in (a) five and (b) ten years. The Chiefs of Staff glanced this bowling to leg, bitter experience having taught them that that approach led to the production of 'shopping lists', all the items on which were then hailed by Treasury officials, and some in the Defence Ministry, as therefore expendable.

Instead, the Chiefs of Staff retaliated, first, with an agreed statement of priorities; and then, based on it, an assessment of the 'critical level of forces' to meet them, in fact bearing in mind an approximate target of achieving a reduction to 4½ per cent of GNP within ten years on the Treasury assumption of an average increase in GNP of 3 per cent per annum. By concentrating on that, they managed to divert attention from all the other permutations of GNP percentage and time limit. They agreed to place an equal priority on (a) the current effort devoted to a British strategic nuclear force, (b) the defence of the United Kingdom, which was not defined, and (c) that contribution to both the Supreme Commands of NATO which our allies, particularly the USA and Germany , would regard as 'critical' to confidence that we were playing our proper part in the Alliance. Within NATO, a continued commitment to SACLANT's* forces and to the Central and Northern sectors of SACEUR's command was regarded as 'critical', but economies could be achieved by withdrawal of support to his Southern sector in the Mediterranean. Both army and naval contributions there were already small, neither making much military sense. The air force contribution was more significant, including LRMP and bomber aircraft based in Malta and bomber and fighter squadrons in Cyprus. Other overseas commitments were classed as a lower priority, all but the most politically sensitive, like Hong Kong and Gibraltar, regarded as expendable.

While the question as to whether forces should be maintained in Cyprus at all was under discussion, a crisis arose there following the coup against Makarios in July, initiated by the Greek government of colonels. While the Archbishop escaped into British protection, Turkey, ironically, considering their views about him, demanded restoration of the status quo. When we refused to intervene or grant her facilities to do so, she invaded the island in two stages and occupied the northern part of it, while we reinforced the United Nations Force with troops from our Sovereign Base Areas and

*Supreme Allied Commander, Atlantic.

with aircraft flown from England. James Callaghan, the Foreign Secretary, felt greatly frustrated at finding his freedom of action restricted and his hand weakened by the need to consider the safety of the large number of service families who lived outside the base areas. The whole affair influenced him and others to consider favourably the idea of abandoning our bases on the island.

The government accepted the recommendations of the review after it had passed through the Official Committee, with the exception of some of the overseas commitments suggested as expendable, the latter having to be retained within the financial and manpower limits which had assumed their abandonment. In general it would result in a reduction to 4½ per cent of GNP by 1985, on the assumption of a 3 per cent annual increase in the latter. Although it would represent a reduction in real cash terms from the Conservatives' forecast (the latter had been based on 5½ per cent of a GNP assumed to rise at 3½ per cent per annum), there would in fact continue to be a rise in expenditure in real terms for a few years before it began to fall. This was concealed by the government, who always referred to how much it would save compared to the Conservative forecast.

The 'critical' level of forces was accepted, largely on the grounds that, in our precarious economic state, we could not afford to antagonize the Americans or the Germans by making any drastic reduction in our force contributions to NATO. This was contested by Denis Healey, who argued that greater reductions were needed and could be achieved without damage to NATO, if only the strategy were revised. He warned that, unless this were done, the whole exercise would have to be repeated in a few years' time, but he failed to persuade his Cabinet colleagues. It was decided that we should withdraw from Malta within five years and from Cyprus also; remove the Gurkha battalion from Brunei* and reduce the garrison of Hong Kong, insisting that the government of the colony should pay 75 per cent of the cost of what was left there; and that the minimum provision should be made for those awkward relics of Empire, the Falkland Islands and Belize. The remaining forces in Singapore would also be withdrawn, as would the RAF staging posts on the islands of Gan and Masirah and the naval radio station in Mauritius.†

*This decision was reversed in 1979, the Sultan paying the full cost of its retention.
†Facilities to replace the latter were being established in the British Indian Ocean Territory of Diego Garcia, which had been separated from the administration of Mauritius before the latter's independence in 1968. The Americans had been granted the right to establish much more important facilities there.

107

We would no longer declare specific forces to the Central (CENTO) and South East Asia (SEATO) Treaty Organizations, although we would remain members, as we would of the Five-Power Defence Arrangements with Malaysia, Singapore, Australia and New Zealand. Negotiation to end the agreement with South Africa to use naval facilities at Simonstown would be initiated.

The general effect on the navy would be a reduction by one-seventh in the numbers of destroyers, frigates and mine counter-measure vessels, one-quarter in conventional submarines and one-third in afloat support. Plans to replace the two assault ships, *Fearless* and *Intrepid*, would be cancelled. Refitting would be concentrated in the Royal Dockyards. The Royal Marines would be reduced by one-seventh, losing a commando.

The army's equipment programme would be substantially modified, abandoning cooperation with Germany and Italy in the development of the RS80 long-range rocket artillery. There would be no reduction in the strength of the army in Germany, except in the context of the MBFR (Mutual and Balanced Force Reductions) negotiations with the Warsaw Pact in Vienna. It was assumed that, under that umbrella, it would be possible to reduce by 5,000 men, but this was not revealed to the public or our allies.

The main reduction in the RAF would be in transport aircraft, which would be progressively cut by half, while the future planned helicopter force would be reduced by one-quarter. Twelve RAF stations in the United Kingdom would be closed and there would be some reduction in the RAF Regiment. These measures would reduce the strength of the services by 35,000 men and 30,000 directly employed civilians. They were estimated to save £300m in 1975/76, about £500m a year by 1978/79 and some £750m in 1983/84, a total of £4,700m below the estimates inherited from the Conservatives.

The Cabinet agreed the programme shortly before the General Election held in October 1974, which returned the Labour Party to power with a majority of 43 over the Conservatives, but of only three over all other parties, the Liberals holding 13, the Scottish Nationalists 11 and the Ulster Unionists 10 seats. The Defence Review decisions were confirmed, but, before they were announced, consultations were held with the Americans and Germans. As a result of representations by the former, the decision to abandon the bases in Cyprus was reversed, and that of withdrawing from Masirah was delayed to allow the Americans to negotiate its use by them with the Sultan of Oman, but no compensating increase of money or manpower was allowed.

Mason announced the results of the review in the House of Commons on 21 November, NATO being briefed on them on the same day. The latter was told that, at that stage, they were proposals which were subject to change in the light of NATO's views, provided that it did not add to the cost, two months being allotted for consultation. They were not changed in any significant detail, and were finalized in the March 1975 Defence White Paper (Cmnd 5976). It began with reference to nuclear matters:

> The Polaris force, which Britain will continue to make available to the Alliance, provides a unique European contribution to NATO's strategic nuclear capability out of all proportion to the small fraction of the defence budget which it costs to maintain. We shall maintain its effectiveness. We do not intend to move to a new generation of strategic nuclear weapons. We shall also maintain our tactical nuclear capability, in accordance with NATO strategy.

'Maintaining its effectiveness' was a hidden allusion to the Chevaline programme which the government had decided to continue to support in spite of technical problems and escalating costs.

The paper then reviewed non-NATO commitments, pointing out that to give them all up would only save £150m a year. It confirmed that forces would be maintained in Hong Kong, Gibraltar, Belize and the Falklands, and that all forces would be withdrawn from Malaysia and Singapore by April 1976, except for a small contribution (manning a radar at Penang) to the Malaysia–Singapore Integrated Air Defence System, to which Australia contributed. The withdrawal from Cyprus of fighter, bomber and transport squadrons 'to be replaced by smaller numbers of aircraft on detachment from the United Kingdom' was explained away as being 'in order to ease the severe accommodation problems that have arisen within the Sovereign Base Areas since the events of the last year', a reference to the decision to restrict the number of service families living outside the perimeter of the bases. The Canberra bombers and Nimrod maritime patrol aircraft in Malta, like the Vulcan bombers in Cyprus, assigned to CENTO, would be withdrawn by 1979. Within the RAF as a whole, more Jaguars would replace Phantoms in the strike/attack and reconnaissance roles, the Phantoms replacing the Lightnings as defensive fighters. The planned purchase of 385 Tornados would be maintained, but the rate of delivery reduced. Nimrod LRMP strength would be reduced by a quarter, as a result of withdrawal from the Mediterranean, and that of transport aircraft reduced from 115 to 57 by phasing out all Comets, Britannias and Andovers and reducing the number of VC10s and Hercules from 66 to 47.

The army had been engaged in a tortuous exercise not so much to reduce strength as to devise a method by which it could cope with the shortfall in manpower caused by difficulties in retention and in recruitment, which had been affected by the raising of the school-leaving age. At that time about half its entry came in as juniors, at the age of 15. Only 25,800 men had been recruited for all three services in 1973/74. The Army Board was determined to avoid yet another round of disbandments or amalgamations, and came up with a scheme to abolish brigade headquarters, form smaller divisions in Germany and call brigades elsewhere by another name – Field Forces. The purpose of this 'restructuring', as it was called, was explained as designed 'to maintain as far as possible present combat capability while reducing the overall number of men'. Its principles were said to be:

a. The elimination of a level of command and extension of the span of command at formation and unit level.
b. Economy through the pooling of certain specialist functions, for example the concentration in specialist units of transport vehicles.
c. An improvement of the man/weapon ratio.
d. Closer integration of the T&AVR with the Regular Army.

There would be some reorganization of home commands and the inclusion of some Territorial Army units with regular ones in the same formation in the United Kingdom.

Reorganization of the British Corps in Germany on these lines was due to be completed in 1979. It would result in the formation of what the 1977 White Paper (Cmnd 6735) described as 'four new-style armoured divisions, each smaller than the three which exist at present, an artillery division and a new formation (5th Field Force) which will take over the reinforcing role of 39th Infantry Brigade (the brigade permanently stationed in Northern Ireland).' It was originally intended that there would be no intermediate level of command between the divisional headquarters and battle-groups, each of which would consist of 'four company-sized sub-units of armour and infantry', the supporting arms being concentrated under divisional command. Exercises to test the new organization in 1976

110

proved this unsatisfactory, and an intermediate level of command was reintroduced, similar to the Combat Command concept in the US Army's armoured divisions in the Second World War – not a permanently organized formation, but an *ad hoc* grouping. It was explained that 'each new armoured division would be given the capability of deploying when required two tactical command posts to exercise direct command of the battle-groups. They will be known as Task Force Headquarters, and, when they are deployed, will be headed by brigadiers who in peacetime will also be garrison commanders.' This ill-considered scheme, very similar to the French army's organization, proved unpopular with Britain's NATO allies, making cooperation with them more difficult. Task Force headquarters were made permanent in 1980 and restored as brigades in the following year.

These changes produced an estimate (at 1974 survey prices, before making allowance for pay and price increases amounting to £848m) of £3,700m, 25 per cent of which went to the navy, 34 per cent to the army and 31 per cent to the air force. The forecast for subsequent years, at 1974 prices, was £3,800m from 1976/77 to 1978/79 and £3,790m a year from then until 1983/84. This was claimed to achieve a reduction of £4,700m from the Conservatives' ten-year long-term costing. The strength of the armed forces had been reduced to 325,900 men and 14,200 women, the army's male strength standing at 160,000. This total was further reduced to 319,200 men in the following year, although that of the army rose by 1,000 and women in all three services by 200. Healey did not relax his pressure on the defence budget, reducing the defence review targets by a total of £170m over three years in the 1974 public expenditure survey and making a further cut of £168m (at 1976 prices) in the 1976/77 target in his 1975 budget. He returned to the attack in the 1975 public expenditure review, demanding that defence should find £1,200m over the three years to 1979/80 out of a total public expenditure cut of £2,000–£3,000m. A settlement was finally reached at about half the figure, but 1976 saw the battle resumed, Callaghan having succeeded Wilson as Prime Minister in April. In July Callaghan announced that £1,000m was to be cut from the public expenditure forecast for 1977/78, and in December he went further and announced another reduction of £1,000m for that year and £1,500m for 1978/79. The defence contribution was to be £100m to each of the 1977/78 cuts and £230m in 1978/79. This was to be achieved to a large degree by cancellation and deferment of projects in the equipment programme, the hope being expressed that reductions in front-line contributions to NATO could be kept to the minimum. Mason hoped that economies might also flow from the Management Review which, on Wilson's insistence, had been instituted within the Ministry of Defence, but they were not significant. The military once again succeeded in resisting pressure from the politicians and civil servants for reduction in their power and influence within the Ministry and for further integration between the three services. One casualty was the four-star post of Chief of Personnel and Logistics, whose responsibilities were transferred to the Vice-Chief of the Defence Staff.

In spite of both the anti-nuclear element within the Labour Party and Healey's belief that a radical reappraisal of NATO strategy was needed, neither of these attitudes was reflected in official defence policy. The 1976 White Paper (Cmnd 6432) spelled this out in terms which were to be repeated with hardly any real change in every one of its successors, until the revolutionary change in Soviet policy at the end of the following decade rendered it obsolete. The paper described NATO strategy in these words:

NATO's conventional forces deter, and would defend against, conventional attacks. They deter because they could repel a limited incursion upon NATO territory, and because they would provide a stalwart first defence against a major conventional attack on Western Europe. A strong conventional defence of the kind which NATO forces offer would keep the nuclear threshold high. At least, it would delay the moment when NATO might need to use nuclear weapons and so make time for diplomatic attempts to end the conflict. At best, it would demonstrate to the enemy that he had underestimated NATO's resolve, and cause him to withdraw.

Theatre nuclear forces are indispensable to NATO for two reasons. First, they deter the Warsaw Pact from using its own theatre nuclear forces. Secondly, they represent a link between NATO's conventional and strategic nuclear forces, and they increase the range of options open to the Alliance should its conventional defence prove inadequate. Without such weapons NATO might be faced with the choice of accepting the annexation of part of its territory or of initiating strategic nuclear war.

Strategic nuclear forces constitute the ultimate deterrent. Without them NATO's other forces would not present a credible deterrent to the Warsaw Pact, with its strategic nuclear arsenal.

Thus they help to deter attack at any level, and would also deter attempts to escalate a conflict should one begin.

To this was added the sentence: 'The Polaris submarines *Renown*, *Repulse*, *Resolution* and *Revenge* between them provide a continuous patrol as our contribution to NATO's strategic deterrent.' There was no mention in any of the Labour administration's White Papers of the role of the force as an *independent* British deterrent.

A new NATO role had also been found for the RAF's Strike Command, when it was accepted as one of SACEUR's subordinate commands under the title of UKAIR. When first mooted, this had caused difficulties with the navy and SACLANT's command, as elements of Strike Command's forces, notably refuelling tankers and early warning aircraft, supported forces operating under SACLANT's command also. The naval Buccaneers to be transferred to the RAF when the last fixed-wing carrier, *Ark Royal*, went out of service 'in the late 1970s', would further complicate matters. The issue was resolved by retaining under national command those aircraft which operated in support of both Supreme Commanders. The problem of a replacement for the RAF's aged Shackleton and the navy's equally old Gannet early warning aircraft proved a contentious issue. A project existed to equip some Nimrods, becoming surplus from the Defence Review, with British-developed electronics for the purpose. This project was still at an early stage when the Americans proposed that NATO should have an integrated AWACS (airborne warning and control system) equipped with the Boeing E3A, which the US Air Force had developed from the commercial 707 aircraft. After careful consideration, and in spite of doubts about its suitability both for detecting ships at sea and for dealing with the dense concentration of aircraft tracks expected in the Central Region of NATO's European Command, the Chiefs of Staff concluded that, provided it was subscribed to by all the NATO nations and was large enough in total numbers to cover the whole area, in particular the Eastern Atlantic and the air approaches to the United Kingdom, it would be cheaper, available earlier and in some respects more effective. They therefore recommended that it be adopted and that its main base should be in Britain. After long and difficult negotiations, as a result of which it appeared that only the USA and Britain were prepared to participate, the Treasury refused to support it and the Ministry of Defence reverted to the Nimrod project. However that was dogged by difficulties and delays in development, which increased the cost, so that, in 1986, it was dropped and a straight purchase of the Boeing AWACS made. The Treasury had wasted a lot of money.

At the meeting of NATO Defence Ministers in December 1976, the Americans pressed hard for a greater effort to strengthen European conventional forces in the light of the improvement both in quality and quantity of Soviet and Warsaw Pact forces. In May 1977 they agreed to aim at a 3 per cent per annum increase in defence expenditure, and a NATO summit meeting in London that month agreed in principle to establish a long-term defence programme, for which studies in ten priority fields would recommend action. Britain's short-term contribution to this was not impressive: the retention of a Royal Marine commando which was due for disbandment and the restoration of the commando carrier, HMS *Bulwark*, to operational status; an increase in the army's stock of anti-armour missiles; and a reduction in the planned rundown of manpower by 1,900 men 'to compensate for the effects of continuing emergency commitments, especially in Northern Ireland'. There were in fact no other emergency commitments, support to the Sultan of Oman against the incursion into the Dhofar having come successfully to an end in 1977, unless the maintenance of a garrison in Belize was considered as such. The air force contribution was a build-up of stocks of weapons of various kinds.

American pressure for a greater European effort in the conventional field was accompanied by emphasis on the need for standardization. Their forceful Defence Secretary, James Schlesinger, claimed that greater standardization of arms procurement could save European members of NATO 15 per cent of their defence expenditure, which could then be devoted to improvement in quality or quantity or both. The influences behind this emphasis were partly pressure from prominent members of Congress, including Senator Sam Nunn, to reduce US forces stationed in Europe, or planned to reinforce it in emergency, unless the European members of the Alliance did more in their own defence and did not rely so heavily on the first use of American nuclear weapons; and partly pressure from the US defence industry, hard hit by the end of the Vietnam war. Standardization in American eyes almost invariably meant adopting American equipment either by direct purchase or by production under licence. This pressure was unwelcome to the European arms industry and the governments which sponsored it, and Schlesinger was disinclined to accept the argument that European governments were more likely to spend money on defence which brought employment to their own people rather than purchases from

114

the USA. In 1975 Roy Mason was chairman of the Eurogroup, the grouping of European members of NATO, and became an enthusiastic supporter of the concept of a Two-Way Street in arms procurement, a deal by which, in attempting to improve standardization, European adoption of American-developed equipment would be balanced by US acceptance of European projects. An American study, the Callaghan report, had just favoured it. The French, having excluded themselves from Eurogroup, were much concerned that they would be shut out of such a deal, smarting under the rejection of their entry in the competition for an aircraft to re-equip the Belgian, Dutch, Danish and Norwegian air forces in favour of the American Northrop F16. This had left the French aircraft industry with little on its military order books, while Britain, Germany and Italy had the Tornado production programme ahead of them. As their sensibilities prevented them from joining Eurogroup, a new organization was set up, known as the Independent Programme Group, consisting of the Eurogroup plus France, to achieve the same end. It was to have very limited success, Congressional hold on when and where the US armed forces purchased their needs proving one of the principal obstacles to American adoption of European arms. One later success story, which owed nothing to any of these groups, was the adoption by the US Marine Corps of a version of the Harrier, manufactured in the USA by McDonnell Douglas.

In spite of the NATO commitment to a 3 per cent increase, the defence budget for 1978/79 was reduced by £230m (at 1976 prices) from its original target, in accordance with the decision taken in December 1976. This was £267m at 1977 survey prices and brought defence expenditure down from 5.1 to 4.9 per cent of GNP, compared with 5.5 in the USA, 3.9 in France, 3.4 in Germany and 2.5 per cent in Italy. About half of the saving came from the equipment programme and one-fifth from works and accommodation stores. The estimate for 1978/79 totalled £6,919m, including £633m for pay and price increases since 1977. Although recruiting was fairly satisfactory at 40,000, including 2,300 women, the army and the RAF were losing a high proportion of officers and skilled men over and above those being made redundant. The strength of all three services in 1977 was 330,500, including women, of which the army accounted for 161,500 men and 5,800 women.

A significant event for the navy in 1977, apart from the Jubilee Review at Spithead, was the launch of the first of the 'through-deck cruisers', HMS *Invincible*. It was now called an 'anti-submarine cruiser', although its status as a mini-aircraft carrier had been recognized when Mason finally gave the go-ahead to the maritime version of the Harrier in 1976, before he was transferred to the Northern Ireland Office, handing over as Defence Secretary to Fred Mulley. In 1979 it was announced that *Invincible* would enter service in 1980; her sister ship, *Illustrious*, had been launched in 1978 and an order had been placed for a third, to be named *Ark Royal*. Their primary task was described as to act as command ships for anti-submarine warfare forces: 'They will deploy the Sea King anti-submarine helicopter and will also carry the Sea Dart missile system and Sea Harrier aircraft, which will enable them to contribute to air defence and anti-surface ship operations.'

It was natural for a Labour administration to lay stress on disarmament and arms control measures, and the Defence White Papers of 1978 (Cmnd 7099) and 1979 (Cmnd 7474) gave prominence to both, although unable to report much progress or claim realistically that Britain had been able to contribute much. The SALT II talks between the USA and the Soviet Union continued, and the 1979 paper stated that 'the Government looks forward to the satisfactory conclusion of the negotiations and an early ratification of the Agreement by both sides.' Behind the scenes there had been fears, as in the case of SALT I, that the Americans might agree to a clause that would prevent Britain developing a long-range missile to be launched from aircraft, which could prolong the life of the Vulcan and make it possible to regard the Tornado as a long-range bomber also. The 1979 paper stated that the government 'continued to attach great importance to a successful outcome of the MBFR talks' in Vienna and 'regretted that the CSCE (Conference on Security and Cooperation in Europe) follow-up meeting in Belgrade in March 1978 had failed to agree on any development of the military confidence-building measures which had been agreed at the original conference in Helsinki in 1975. It optimistically expressed the hope that agreement between the USA, the Soviet Union and Britain on a Comprehensive Nuclear Test Ban would 'be reached very soon'. It never was. Finally it reiterated 'the Government's objective of general and complete disarmament under strict and effective international control'. Until that had been achieved, however, 'a substantial defence effort remains necessary; and, indeed, is a precondition of successful political action.'

This was Labour's last Defence White Paper, as Callaghan went to the country in May 1979 and lost the election. The Conservatives, led by Margaret Thatcher, were returned with a majority of 71 over Labour – 339 to 268 – and 44 over all other parties. By that time the pay of service personnel had slipped well behind that of their civilian counterparts, leading to further loss of some of the best trained men and causing increasing resentment at all levels. The estimate for 1979/80 was for £8,558m, equal in real terms to the public expenditure survey target of £7,182m at 1978 survey prices and equal also to just under 4¾ per cent of the estimated GNP for the year at market prices. This was claimed to represent an increase of 3 per cent in real terms over the previous year's expenditure, and therefore to meet the commitment to NATO.

8

NUCLEAR FURORE

MARGARET THATCHER'S CONSERVATIVE administration came to power at a time when nuclear weapons were becoming an emotive issue to a degree which they had not been since the years immediately following the development of the megaton bomb. There were a number of reasons for this, other than those directly concerned with nuclear weapon systems themselves, notably the ever-increasing number of weapons in the hands of the superpowers and the development of new weapons and means of delivery. One was the absence of any other major issue to occupy what one might call the professional protesting class. The Vietnam war had come to an end, and the internal struggle in Rhodesia was soon to do so. There was always apartheid in South Africa, but that was rather old hat, and the environment had not yet seriously raised its green head. Another non-nuclear reason was a genuine fear that war might break out between the superpowers. The revolution in Iran, followed by the Iraqi attack on that country and the Soviet intervention in Afghanistan, heightened tension, raising anxiety when the hawkish Ronald Reagan won the Presidential election in 1980. Global war seemed less of a remote possibility than it had been at any time since the Cuban affair in 1962. This fertile ground was exploited by the Soviet Union to foster international objections to new nuclear weapon systems being developed within NATO, while itself actively engaged in modernizing and adding to its own nuclear arsenal.

NATO's stance was not helped by the sorry story of the Enhanced Radiation Weapon, popularly known as the neutron bomb. The Americans had begun to develop this in 1974 as a tactical warhead to be delivered by artillery or short-range missiles, such as Lance, enhancing the radiation from its explosion without increasing the blast effect for a given kilotonnage. It would therefore be more effective than existing warheads in killing soldiers who were protected from blast, such as tank crews or infantry well dug-in, and cause no more 'collateral damage' to the terrain or to buildings. An

American press leak in 1977 described it as a horror weapon which killed people while preserving property. The only real objection to it lay behind one of the reasons for developing it: that it could encourage a return to the idea that tactical nuclear weapons could be regarded as conventional, and that their use would not run the risk of enemy retaliation at a higher nuclear level, one of the fallacies that had always been inherent in NATO's policy of flexible response. It was supposed to be taken care of by 'escalation dominance'. That meant that NATO must always have a superior nuclear system at each level, which would deter the enemy from escalating from one level to another – a sure recipe for an infinity of systems, sometimes referred to as 'the seamless robe'.

NATO Defence Ministers had not been briefed on the new weapon and President Carter himself was none too keen on it. The Ministers were neither prepared to welcome it nor to refuse it. Carter at first took the line that, if the Europeans wanted it, he would put it into production, but would not force it on the Alliance, the most sensitive member being Germany, where they would be stationed and on whose territory they were likely to be used. The Europeans took the line that the decision was the President's, and that, if he regarded it as important that US troops, and their own which manned nuclear delivery systems on a dual-key basis, should have it, they would not object. Helmut Schmidt, the German Chancellor, faced considerable political opposition, including that of his Foreign Minister, Herr Genscher, and had just brought his colleagues round to accepting that formula when, without consultation, Carter in March 1978 decided against production. This put the Germans in a very awkward position, Genscher flying to Washington and persuading Carter to reverse his decision and keep the project on ice as a bargaining chip in arms control negotiations. Faces were saved, but they were pretty red ones.

The Soviet Union exploited this affair to foment objections to the introduction of any new systems (except of course their own). They used it to counter what NATO called 'Theatre Nuclear Modernization', and particularly the introduction of longer-range land-based missiles which could reach targets within the Soviet Union from bases in Western Europe, known as INF – Intermediate-range Nuclear Forces. In a lecture in London in 1977 Helmut Schmidt had urged that NATO should have an answer to the SS20 missile which the Soviet Union was deploying in increasing numbers. It was mobile, had MIRVed warheads, and from bases in the Soviet Union could reach targets all over Western Europe. Schmidt feared

119

that a situation was arising in which the Soviet Union could threaten Western Europe with nuclear attack, while feeling itself secure against it, because the only weapon systems, other than aircraft against which it had efficient defences, that threatened its territory were ballistic missiles in submarines or based in the USA, the use of which was regarded as strategic and therefore automatically risking retaliation against targets in America. He did not apparently consider the counter-argument that copying the Soviet Union might encourage the Americans to think that a nuclear war might be limited to Europe.

With some initial reluctance the US government offered two systems to meet Schmidt's demand: the first a longer-range version of the Pershing missile, which was already based in Germany, but could not from there reach targets in the Soviet Union itself; and the Tomahawk Ground-Launched Cruise Missile (GLCM). It was an air-breathing missile, a modern version of the German wartime V–1. It had initially been developed as a decoy to confuse enemy radars so that the USAF's B52 bombers could have some hope of penetrating Soviet air defences. The enthusiasts for it then suggested that it would be wasteful for it not to have a warhead. The next step was to equip it with a computerized route which could be checked by its own radar, and to give it a terminal guidance system to recognize its target. Its advantage was cheapness, missile for missile, compared with a ballistic one: its principal disadvantage that it should be possible to develop defences against it, although that would absorb a great deal of effort.

At a NATO meeting in December 1979 it was agreed that 464 of these cruise missiles and 108 Pershing IIs would be deployed in Europe, Britain agreeing to receive 160 of the former, to be based on two airfields which were reserved for wartime use by the USAF, Greenham Common near Newbury in Berkshire and Molesworth in Suffolk. All the Pershing IIs were to be in Germany and, when Belgium and Holland refused to take any cruise missiles, as did Denmark and Norway who had never agreed to allow nuclear weapons to be based in their countries in peacetime, the balance of these missiles was split between Germany and Italy.

These systems, while arousing considerable domestic opposition from anti-nuclear movements, soon became a major issue in arms control negotiations. At the time of its decision to deploy them, NATO offered to negotiate with the Soviet Union a mutual limitation in the number of missiles of this type. In 1981 President Reagan offered the 'zero option', which NATO accepted with some misgivings. It would involve no deployment by NATO of the new missiles, provided that the Soviet Union eliminated all SS20s and there were agreed safeguards against the replacement of the missiles by ones of similar characteristics. The Soviet reply was to accept a NATO zero, but to insist that, as they faced other threats, they must retain their SS20s, although not the full number they had planned. Not surprisingly, NATO rejected this. In 1983 the USA proposed the interim solution of parity in missile warheads (the SS20 carried three) as a first step towards the zero option, but the Soviet Union argued that parity already existed between their systems which could reach Western European targets and NATO systems, based in Europe, which could reach the Soviet Union, including the British and French ballistic missile submarines. Hoping that domestic objections would in any case prevent deployment of the new NATO systems, they broke off negotiations in November 1983.

When Gorbachev came to power in 1985, negotiations covering all nuclear systems were resumed, the US government proposing a 50 per cent cut in the strategic delivery systems of both sides and elimination of INF systems. In January 1986 Gorbachev made the dramatic proposal of elimination of all nuclear weapons by the year 2000, and six months later he offered 30 per cent cuts in strategic systems on certain conditions. In September, in reply to a US proposal made in February, he tentatively suggested an agreement to limit INF missile warheads to 100 on each side. This was followed by the meeting between him and Reagan at Reykjavik in October 1986, which had not been intended as a serious arms control negotiation. However, provisional agreement was reached by the two leaders on 50 per cent cuts in strategic systems, leading to equal ceilings of 1,600 strategic nuclear delivery vehicles and 6,000 warheads. Gorbachev suggested the elimination of all strategic systems within ten years, to which Reagan responded with a proposal to link the elimination of all offensive ballistic missile systems to an undertaking not to withdraw from the ABM Treaty for ten years. A provisional agreement was reached to remove all INF from Europe, the Soviet Union retaining 100 SS20s in Soviet Asia and the Americans the same number of equivalent missiles in the USA. The Soviet negotiators tried to impose conditions on the latter, but finally gave way, and, after proposals for total elimination of what were called Short-Range and Long-Range Intermediate systems had been made by both sides, an agreement to do so was signed on 8 December 1987. NATO hailed it as an example of negotiating from strength.

From time to time Mrs Thatcher had been worried that Ronald Reagan was giving away too much and throughout was concerned to seek assurances that on no account should the British ballistic missile submarine force or its warheads become entangled in the negotiations.

The anti-nuclear lobby – and others – were concerned that the American cruise missiles in Britain might be fired without the prior knowledge or permission of the British government, provoking nuclear retaliation from the Soviet Union. The situation was no different from that of the USAF nuclear-capable aircraft which had been based here since the days of Attlee's administration. Since then the formula had always been that their use would 'naturally be the subject of consultation between the two Governments at the time'. It is believed that there was in fact no formal written agreement on the matter, and both authorities were always careful to avoid committing themselves to stating that the British government could exercise a veto. That would have reduced their value as a deterrent – which is what it was all supposed to be about. Some people, including the SDLP leader, David Owen, called for a dual-key agreement, similar to that applying to delivery systems manned by British personnel, of which the warheads were American; but that in reality would have involved a veto.

The revival of the anti-nuclear movement, aggravated at Greenham Common by becoming mixed up with feminist, back-to-nature and green movements, as well as by the fact that the airfield had been built during the Second World War on common land, did not provide an atmosphere favourable to the government's decision to proceed with a replacement for the Polaris submarine system. It was inevitable that a Conservative administration, and certainly one headed by Margaret Thatcher, would do so, although it was not inevitable that the solution would be another ballistic missile submarine. The Chief of the Defence Staff, Marshal of the Royal Air Force Sir Neil Cameron, favoured a cruise missile, launched from an aircraft or from the ground, or at sea from a submarine or surface ship – perhaps a combination of these methods. But thorough discussion of all the options confirmed the conclusion reached by Sir Hermann Bondi's committee in the early 1970s: that a submarine equipped with an American ballistic missile was the best answer from both the operational and the financial aspects.

The decision was taken early in 1980 and agreement with the USA confirmed in July in an exchange of letters between Mrs Thatcher and President Carter,* which reiterated the conditions of the Nassau agreement of 1963: that the force would be 'assigned to NATO like the Polaris force; and, except when the United Kingdom Government may decide that supreme national interests are at stake, the successor force will be used for the purposes of international defence of the Western alliance in all circumstances.' In his reply, Jimmy Carter confirmed 'that the US attaches significant importance to the nuclear deterrent capability of the United Kingdom and to close cooperation between our two Governments in maintaining and modernizing that capability', and viewed 'as important your statement that the Polaris successor force will be assigned to NATO and that your objective is to take advantage of the economies made possible by our cooperation to reinforce your efforts to upgrade the United Kingdom's conventional forces'.

A Defence Open Government Document (80/23) published that month under the signature of Francis Pym, the Defence Secretary, gave a full explanation of the rationale for maintaining such a force and of why the Trident I (C4) submarine ballistic missile, carrying eight MIRVs, was chosen. Pym had revealed the existence of the Chevaline warhead for Polaris for the first time a short while before. The argument he used for the existence of the force was that of the 'second centre of decision'. Emphasizing its independence was liable to suggest that Britain could not rely on the USA to use its nuclear weapons in the defence of Europe or that we should only use ours if Britain itself were directly threatened. The 'second centre of decision' argument could be seen as combining independence with commitment to NATO. Its 'unique contribution' to the Alliance lay, it was argued, in the additional uncertainty it would create in the minds of the Soviet authorities. This was the key paragraph of the paper:

> The decision to use United States nuclear weapons in the defence of Europe, with all the risk to the United States homeland this would entail, would be enormously grave. A Soviet leadership – perhaps much changed in character from today's, perhaps also operating amid the pressures of turbulent internal or external circumstances – might believe that it could impose its will on Europe by military force without becoming involved in strategic nuclear war with the United States. Modernized US nuclear forces

*Cmnd 7979.

123

in Europe help guard against such misconception; but an independent capability fully under European control provides a key element of insurance. A nuclear decision would of course be no less agonizing for the United Kingdom than for the United States. But it would be the decision of a separate and independent power, and a power whose survival in freedom would be directly and immediately threatened by aggression in Europe . . . An adversary assessing the consequences of possible aggression in Europe would have to regard a Western defence containing these [the British and French] powerful independent elements as a harder one to predict, and a more dangerous one to assail, than one in which nuclear retaliatory power rested in United States hands alone.

Having justified the Polaris and its successor force, the paper went on to relate it to other British nuclear weapons with the following far-fetched argument which appeared to overlook the existence of American systems assigned to NATO or to assume that Britain could be engaged in a private nuclear war on its own:

British nuclear forces include both strategic and lower-level components. If we had only the latter they could not serve the key 'second-centre' deterrent purpose, since the threat of their use would not be credible. An aggressor faced with an armoury comprising only non-strategic nuclear weapons would know that he could if necessary use strategic nuclear weapons to overbear it without risking strategic retaliation upon himself; and since he would know that his opponent too must realize this, he could be confident that the non-strategic weapons were most unlikely to be used. The harsh logic of deterrence requires that the nuclear decision-maker should have the evident power to take his resistance all the way to the strategic level if the aggressor will not desist. If Britain's nuclear contribution to NATO is to fulfil its distinctive role in deterrence, it must include an effective strategic element.

This argument was turned round and used in the opposite direction to justify the provision of British nuclear weapons below the strategic level, notably by Admiral of the Fleet Sir Terence Lewin,* Chief of the Defence Staff from 1979 to 1982. He maintained that

*Later Lord Lewin.

an independent strategic deterrent would not be credible without them, because nobody would think that Britain would use its ultimate nuclear weapon, unless it had used lower-level ones first – the 'last resort' argument.

Having provided convincing arguments for the rejection of other systems, the paper explained why 16 missiles per boat – the same as Polaris – had been chosen, and why, in spite of five boats being preferred, a provisional decision to plan on only four had been accepted at an overall cost of some £4,500–£5,000m (at 1980 prices) spread over about 15 years, absorbing some 3 per cent of the defence budget over the period. At that stage no mention was made as to whether the boats would carry the maximum number of eight warheads per missile. In 1987, after the decision to change to the D5 missile had been taken, it was announced that there would be eight warheads per missile, but that that was 'far less than the full capacity of D5'. It represented an increase in the number of warheads that two boats on patrol could fire from 96 in the Polaris force to 256 for its successor. This was explained as being necessary to provide for possible improvements in the Soviet Anti-Ballistic Missile system covering Moscow.

Pym's use of the 'second centre of decision' argument was not novel; it had been used by both previous Labour administrations. It was undoubtedly a weak one; but others were weaker or more embarrassing. There was clearly no need to add to the very large number of American weapons, many of the delivery vehicles of which were manned by other members of NATO – all the British army ones for instance. If the Polaris force, and its successor, were regarded as solely a Theatre Nuclear Force assigned to SACEUR, and therefore a supplement to the US Navy's Poseidon submarines assigned to his support, there was no need for one, certainly not two, of its boats to be capable of firing at Moscow 24 hours of the day and 365 days a year: indeed, no need for them to be capable of penetrating the ABM defences of Moscow at all. That could be left to more sophisticated American systems, and targets which were not protected by ABM systems could be allotted to the British submarines. So there would then be no need for Chevaline, let alone MIRVs, or for four or five boats. The justification for such a reduced force would then be to show that Britain was a staunch supporter of NATO's nuclear strategy.

In the election campaign of 1983, both Mrs Thatcher and Michael Heseltine, then Defence Secretary, in response to accusations that Britain might be responsible for initiating a nuclear war – a reasonable deduction from the 'second centre of decision' argument – emphasized that the Polaris and Trident forces were 'a weapon of last resort'. That tended to undermine the concept that the Soviet Union must be brought to believe that, although she might think that the USA would hesitate to use nuclear weapons for fear that, by escalation, it could result in Soviet megaton weapons landing on American cities, Britain, because she was part of Europe, would not hesitate, regardless of the consequences. Pym, in a speech on one occasion, had maintained that Britain would indeed be prepared to sacrifice herself for the sake of her Western European allies, a sentiment rather foreign to Mrs Thatcher. The reality was what it had always been since Attlee's day. It was not related to deterrence as much as to Britain's standing as a world or European power, and especially in relation to the USA. The idea that it gave Britain a special influence on US nuclear policy or in nuclear arms control negotiations had long been shown up as false. The two arguments for an independent British nuclear force which had most validity – or, more correctly, least invalidity – were that Britain might find herself in conflict with a secondary nuclear power, such as Argentina or Libya, if they developed or acquired nuclear weapons, and that it was politically undesirable to leave France as the only European nation with its own nuclear weapons.

The decision having been taken and announced, opposition, other than that to having British nuclear weapons at all, centred on the great increase in the number of warheads and on the cost, the latter being incurred at a time when the defence budget would be carrying a heavy load in the production of new aircraft, notably the Tornado. In the event, the Trident submarine programme, like its predecessor, kept more or less within planned limits of cost and time. This was largely due to the fact that, in both programmes, the missiles themselves and the nuclear propulsion plants of the boats were already developed and proven. In March 1982 the decision was taken to fit the Trident II D5 missile instead of the Trident I C4. The reason for the change, apart from the increase in range and 'throw-weight' and greater accuracy, was that the US government had decided to replace all its existing ballistic submarines, carrying the Trident I, by the *Ohio* class, carrying the D5, earlier than had previously been envisaged. By the time that the British boats would be in service, the C4 missile would be being phased out of the US Navy. The extra cost of this was estimated as £390m (at September 1980 prices), bringing the total of the D5 force, at those prices, to £5,990m. At that time the dollar stood at 2.36 to the pound. By

September 1981 it was 1.78, raising the total cost estimate to £7,500m at September 1981 prices. This was partly offset by the decision that the missiles should be serviced in the USA, with the Americans' own missiles, instead of having to provide facilities to do so at the base in the Clyde. At 1984/85 prices, with the dollar at 1.38 to the pound, this was estimated to save £700m, bringing the total cost of the programme to £9,300m, 55 per cent of which it was expected would be spent in Britain. The decision to change the missile coincided with one to change the propulsion system to a more modern pressurized water reactor. Initially it had been intended to fit the same one as in the Royal Navy's hunter-killer submarines. The change from PWR 1 to PWR 2 was expected to increase operational availability, as well as reducing noise, and was used as an argument for the final decision to restrict the force to four boats. The contract for the first boat, HMS *Vanguard*, was placed with Vickers Shipbuilding and the keel laid at Barrow-in-Furness in September 1986, and that for the second, HMS *Victorious*, followed soon after. The order for the third was placed in 1989. They were expected to enter service in the mid-1990s. The Chevaline development programme, at a cost of over £1,000m, was completed with a test firing in 1982 and all the Polaris missiles were equipped with it by 1985.

With a Conservative administration firmly ensconced in power, there seemed to be no threat to this programme, apart from pressure from the anti-nuclear movement. The Labour Party was divided on the issue and finally devised a formula – it could hardly be called a policy – which envisaged that Britain's independent nuclear force would be traded away in return for a Soviet undertaking to reduce its arsenal. As Gorbachev made a series of proposals for reduction of that arsenal which went far beyond the equivalent of Britain's force, it was not a very meaningful device. The one serious threat came from an unexpected direction: from President Reagan in the speech he made on 23 March 1983, in which he declared his support of the Strategic Defense Initiative (SDI). Inspired by the enthusiasm of the nuclear weapon design scientists at the Lawrence Livermore National Laboratory, with whom he had had contact when Governor of California, he stated that current technology had attained a level of sophistication where it was reasonable to begin the effort so that 'free people could live securely in the knowledge that their security did not rest upon the threat of instant US retaliation to deter a Soviet attack: that we could intercept and destroy strategic ballistic missiles before they reached our own soil or that of our allies.' He called on the scientific community 'to give us the means of rendering these nuclear weapons impotent and obsolete', a phrase that became known as 'The President's Vision'.

> Tonight [he said], consistent with our obligations under the ABM Treaty and recognizing the need for close consultation with our allies, I am taking an important first step. I am directing a comprehensive and intensive effort to define a long-term research and development program to begin to achieve an ultimate goal of eliminating the threat posed by strategic nuclear missiles. This would pave the way for arms-control measures to eliminate the weapons themselves. We seek neither military nor political advantage. Our only purpose – one all people share – is to search for ways to reduce the danger of nuclear war.

This speech initiated a long period of intense controversy. There were doubts about whether it was scientifically or technically possible, even at enormous expense; and about whether testing, let alone deploying it, would be compatible with the ABM Treaty. The reaction of the Soviet Union, which was immediately adverse, could lead to a great increase in its offensive capability in order to saturate any defence system, to the development of a counter-measure to render it ineffective or to its own development of a Strategic Defence, or a combination of all three. Although Reagan spoke of a system which would destroy missiles before they reached 'our own soil or that of our allies', nobody thought the latter likely to be achievable. The result might be to protect the American continent, while leaving Europe open to Soviet nuclear attack. It was not clear whether The President's Vision envisaged the abolition only of strategic nuclear systems, or just ballistic missile systems, or all nuclear weapons. The Europeans were highly suspicious of the proposal, whatever it was intended to mean. Whether the Vision was realized in full or in part, it posed a clear threat, particularly if the Soviet Union followed suit, to the credibility of small strategic nuclear forces like the British and the French. In meetings with the President in December 1984 and November 1986, Mrs Thatcher hammered out agreement on the following statement:

> The SDI Research programme which is permitted by the ABM Treaty should continue:
> – The US and Western aim is not to achieve superiority, but to maintain balance, taking account of Soviet developments.

- SDI-related deployment would, in view of treaty obligations, have to be a matter for negotiation.
- The overall aim is to enhance, and not to undermine deterrence.
- East–West negotiation should aim to achieve security with reduced levels of offensive systems on both sides.
- These matters should continue to be subject to close consultation within the Alliance.

The Soviet Union for years tried to make abandonment of SDI a prior condition for agreement on reduction in strategic nuclear systems, while the USA replied with a demand for the destruction of the large phased-array radar at Krasnoyarsk in Siberia, which it claimed to be a breach of the ABM Treaty. It was not until after the dramatic events in Berlin in November 1989 that this issue was cleared out of the way, the Soviet authorities agreeing to dismantle the radar, which they admitted had been a breach. By that time, with Reagan's departure from the scene, and in a totally changed relationship between the USA and the USSR, it was clear that the US Congress was not going to fund SDI to any high degree. The success of the Patriot anti-missile missile, a by-product of SDI research, in the Gulf War in 1991, however, reawakened interest in the project.

Meanwhile Britain's Trident programme went ahead as if nothing had happened. It was not the only British nuclear programme. The RAF were to be given a new weapon to replace their old free-fall bombs in the form of a tactical air-to-surface missile (TASM) to be fitted to Tornado. From time to time a Defence White Paper would remind its readers what a wide variety of aircraft, both fixed and rotary-wing, maintained a nuclear capability, including Buccaneers, Sea Harriers and a variety of naval helicopters, while nuclear depth-charges could be dropped by Nimrod LRMP aircraft. The army's nuclear artillery and Lance missiles were equipped to fire US warheads under the dual-key system. Few thought they would ever be given authority to fire them in war.

9

WAY FORWARD TO THE FALKLANDS: 1979–1983

COMING TO POWER in 1979, Margaret Thatcher's administration faced the same dilemma as had previous Conservative governments succeeding Labour ones. It was committed to reducing government expenditure both for its own sake and as a means of reducing taxation; but, in opposition, the Conservatives had castigated Labour for cutting defence, demoralizing the armed forces and putting the security of the nation at risk. The two attitudes did not run easily together. The government was committed by its predecessor to the NATO 3 per cent increase in defence spending in real terms, as well as by its commitment in the Trident agreement to improve conventional forces assigned to the Alliance; and its own inclination was to give greater emphasis than had its predecessor to defence activity elsewhere. One of its first steps was to improve the pay of the armed forces, accepting in full the recommendation of the Armed Forces Pay Review Body for an average increase of 32 per cent to restore comparability with equivalents in civilian life. This had an immediate effect in improving recruitment and retention. The strength of the regular armed forces on 1 April 1979 was 299,700 men and 15,300 women, of whom 270,400 of the former and 13,600 of the latter were trained. In the year that followed recruiting improved from 43,000 to 49,000, which was enough to maintain those figures, but not to improve on them, although it was expected to do so by 1 April 1981. The April 1980 Defence White Paper (Cmnd 7826), which set a new pattern in giving much more information than before in two volumes, appropriately coloured blue, expressed concern about the future manpower situation in these terms:

The maximum requirement for trained personnel in the mid-1980s will be 20,000 greater than the present trained strength. To close the gap will require a sustained improvement in both recruiting and retention over the next four to five years. Recruitment will be more difficult from 1982 onwards because there will be a declining number of young men entering the 16–19 age-range from which the Services normally recruit. The Services currently recruit some 8½ per cent of men entering this age group but will need to recruit about 11½ per cent by the end of the 1980s. This will be a formidable task. Failure could undermine our ability to carry out major defence tasks. The Government must therefore make the best use of existing resources and exploit additional sources of manpower, including the reserves, to the full.

This concern about manpower suggested making more use of women, which all three services were considering, but not to the extent, at that stage, of sending members of the Women's Royal Naval Service (WRNS) to sea or posting women in any service to combat duties. The question of whether or not they should be armed for their own protection was hinted at and dismissed in the 1980 paper, the point being made that this was done in some other NATO countries. Having said that the government believed 'that for the present there can be no question of the Women's Services engaging in combat or being armed for any duties other than in exercises, emergency or war', the paper went on to state that 'within this general limitation, however, we are considering how far it would now be desirable to go.' The 1981 paper (Cmnd 8212) carried the subject further, stating:

The Government has announced that some members of the WRAC and the WRAF will be trained in the use of arms for defensive purposes. This step was taken only after the deepest consideration and after weighing public views, including the comments made in Parliament and outside on the ideas in last year's Statement. Most of those who commented believed that the arming of Servicewomen on a limited scale was sensible, timely and should go ahead. The decision now taken does not mean that women are to be employed in combat units; it remains the Government's policy that they should not be. But in the Army women do certain jobs in which at present they have to be guarded by armed men, and if the women themselves can be armed these men can be freed for other tasks. In the Royal Air Force women trained in the use of arms can now be employed in the defence of air stations. As last year's Statement made clear, the options for employing WRNS personnel are not critically dependent on

131

arming them; it remains possible, however, that they will undertake operational duties short of combat.

Considerable emphasis was also given to a greater use of reserve
manpower, some rather exaggerated hopes being placed on it. In
the expectation that it would help recruiting for it, the T&AVR was
renamed the Territorial Army.

These measures produced by 1 April 1982 a rise in total regular
male manpower to 312,200 with a slight increase of female to 15,600.
Over the same period volunteer reserve manpower rose from 67,900
males and 5,600 females to 77,100 males and 7,500 females. The
figures for 'premature release at own request' of regulars had been
reduced from 1,220 to 851 for officers and from 9,695 to 4,158 for
other ranks. The manpower situation at the start of the period had
caused combat units in the army in Germany to be under strength,
some tanks having to be manned with less than a full crew and some
infantry battalions being forced to put one company on a cadre basis.
Some of this was caused by having to bring units up to full strength
for service in Northern Ireland by reinforcing them with men from
other units. About 3,000 men from the British Army of the Rhine
were serving in Northern Ireland in 1980.

The government's emphasis on what the Defence White Papers
called 'Wider Defence Interests' was not accompanied by any significant measures to back it up. The 1980 paper stated that 'The
Government believes that the Services should also be able to operate
effectively outside the NATO area, without diminishing our central
commitment to the Alliance', and announced that it was considering
certain improvements to this end: some extra transport aircraft,
afloat support and logistic backing, and more manpower and equipment for the army's 8th Field Force, which had the dual role of
home defence and preparedness for deployment overseas at short
notice. The 1981 paper repeated this emphasis, saying that the
Soviet threat outside the NATO area, primarily its military activity
in Afghanistan, had led to much discussion in Britain and NATO as
to whether or not we should do more about it, but that the question
had to be considered 'with due respect for realities. Reinstatement
of the former British presence "East of Suez", whatever the arguments for and against it, is no longer either a political or an economic
possibility. What we can do is to ensure that our available resources
are being used as effectively as possible, both in the national interest
and as part of a coherent overall response by the West.' The most
effective step would probably have been to restore the RAF airfield

at Akrotiri in Cyprus to full operational status from that of a staging post and temporary base for aircraft on training exercises, but that would have cost too much in money and manpower and would have competed with another air force demand to which the government attached a new priority, the direct air defence of the United Kingdom.

The increasing reluctance of everyone, in spite of NATO's official doctrine, to contemplate an early resort to the use of nuclear weapons, and indications that the Soviet armed forces were assuming that operations would be kept non-nuclear for as long as possible, led to greater emphasis on air defence against Soviet aircraft. As long as the threat appeared to come from ballistic missiles delivering nuclear warheads, conventional air defence had only a limited value. But, if air operations with conventional weapons were to last for some time, it became more significant, if only to defend the bases of our own nuclear-capable aircraft. The F2 air defence version of the Tornado would not be in service for several more years, but some minor measures were implemented to improve matters. An additional Lightning squadron was formed, Hawk training aircraft were to be fitted with the Sidewinder air-to-air missile, and the missile control system of the Phantom improved. The Sky Flash missile, to be fitted to the Tornado F2, was also to be improved. The government said that it would have liked to have done more, but 'it must be recognised that modern fighters are costly to buy and operate, and they need highly skilled manpower; other claims on defence funds and manpower limit what is possible'.

It was not only direct air defence to which emphasis was given, but also to the direct defence by sea and on land of the home country. Expansion of the Territorial Army was designed to contribute to the latter, and the government considered 'what increase from the pool of uncommitted reserve manpower we would need to supplement the forces assigned to this task and what improvements in equipment the Territorial Army needs to fulfil this role'.

All these improvements, marginal as they might be in military terms, cost money. The position was aggravated by the termination of the German offset agreement, so that overseas expenditure on defence of £1,000m a year had to be met unaided. The estimate for 1979/80 was for £8,001m at 1979 survey prices, a 3½ per cent increase in real terms from the actual expenditure of the previous year. If the agreed 3 per cent increase were to be maintained, this would produce budgets, at 1979 prices, of £8,243m, £8,496m and £8,745m in the three subsequent years. In 1979 Britain rated second only to the USA in the percentage of GDP spent on defence – 4.9 compared to France at 4.0 and Germany at 3.3, although the actual expenditure of both the latter was higher.

Something clearly had to be done about this, and Mrs Thatcher did not think that Francis Pym was the man to do it. Her choice fell on John Nott, who was transferred from being Secretary of State for Trade early in 1981, while Pym became Leader of the House of Commons. Both had served in the army, Pym with tanks in the 9th Lancers in the Second World War, Nott as a regular officer with the Gurkhas in Malaya from 1952 to 1956, before qualifying at the Bar and pursuing a successful career in merchant banking. Nott quickly came to the conclusion that the Ministry of Defence's ten-year programme was not realistic and could not be funded even within an annual 3 per cent increase in real terms, which in any case could not go on for ever. At the heart of the problem was the escalating cost of equipment, for which all three services were rightly clamouring. Some of the existing materiel was very old and incapable of dealing effectively with the equipment then coming into service not only in the Soviet and Warsaw Pact forces, but also in others, including some in the Middle East. The 1980 paper gave some examples of the cost of individual items and of complete programmes. For instance, one nuclear-powered fleet submarine with all its equipment cost £140m, a Type 42 guided missile destroyer £85m, a Tornado GR1 aircraft £10m, a Puma helicopter £1.5m and one round of a Milan anti-tank missile £7,000. The whole programme for the Sting Ray lightweight torpedo would, at the 1980 estimate, cost £920m, the Sea Eagle air-to-surface anti-ship missile £350m and improvement of the Rapier ground-based air defence missile £320m. At that time 41 per cent of the defence budget was devoted to equipment, of which one-third was spent on research and development (almost all development), one-quarter on production of spares and the remainder on production of new equipment, 40 per cent of all production going into air systems, 33 per cent into sea systems and 20 per cent into land systems, whichever service they were destined for.

Nott himself wrote and signed the introduction to the March 1981 Defence White Paper which foreshadowed his 'The Way Forward' published in June. Having remarked that in the previous year defence expenditure had risen by 5 per cent in real terms at a time when the GDP had actually fallen, making our contribution to NATO, expressed in those terms, significantly higher (5.2 per cent) than that of our principal European allies, he declared that the combination of escalating costs and the development of new techno-logies, by friend and potential foe alike, meant that 'new ways must be found of coping with resource pressures, and we must re-shape our forces to meet the developing threat'. In his key paragraph he wrote:

> Changes cannot happen overnight. The value of the total inven-tory of ships, aircraft, vehicles and weapons – embodying past decisions and technology – available now to our Armed Forces is enormous; and it takes time for changing technology to reach our forces through new equipment. The same is true of changes driven by shifts in the threat, in the mix of our forces and in tactical thinking. Change is overdue, and new programmes are needed to exploit new technology and tactical concepts. But the last five years have not been propitious for change. Successive budgetary pressures have meant cutbacks on procurement, and, given the inevitable constraints of a large investment programme already committed, these cuts have fallen unduly on newer programmes still at an early stage. One consequence is that the capital stock is unbalanced, with too much tied up in weapons platforms – at sea, on land or in the air – and not enough in the weapons and sensors they need to carry. The economic pressures generated by the current recession and the faster industrial deliveries of major equipments have also led to deep cuts in procurement of ammu-nition, fuel and oil, and essential spares, so that activity – training and certain deployments – has been held back too severely. We must re-establish in the long-term programme the right balance between the inevitable resource constraints and our necessary defence requirements.
>
> We need, therefore, to look realistically, and with an open mind, at the way in which our forces fulfil their roles. I shall be considering in the coming months with the Chiefs of Staff, and in consultation with our allies, how technological and other changes can help us fulfil the same basic roles more effectively in the future without the massive increases in real defence expenditure which the escalation of equipment costs might otherwise seem to imply.

The United Kingdom Defence Programme: The Way Forward (Cmnd 8288) was the fruit of that consideration, and reflected the views of the scientists and civil servants in the Ministry more than it did those of the Chiefs of Staff Committee, certainly of its two admirals, Sir Terence Lewin, Chief of the Defence Staff, and Sir Henry Leach,

First Sea Lord and Chief of the Naval Staff. In its introductory paragraphs Nott said:

> Our forces need to be equipped, operated, trained and sustained to the standards imposed by the mounting Soviet effort and the increasing sophistication of weapons. Our current force structure is however too large for us to meet this need within any resource allocation which our people can reasonably be asked to afford . . . The fast-growing power of modern weapons to find targets accurately and hit them hard at long ranges is increasing the vulnerability of major platforms such as aircraft and surface ships. To meet this, and indeed to exploit it, the balance of our investment between platforms and weapons needs to be altered so as to maximise real combat capability . . . Moving in this direction will mean substantial and uncomfortable change in some fields. But the alternative, of keeping rigidly to past patterns, would be a recipe for overstretch, inadequacy and waste – it would leave us the certainty of attempting too much and achieving too little. We cannot go on as we are.

Having dismissed any change in the areas to which Britain made contributions to NATO or in nuclear policy, the operation of the strategic force being described as 'the Royal Navy's first and most vital task of Britain's security', Nott stressed the importance the government attached to 'Defence of the Home Base'. 'We need to do more, not less, in this field,' he wrote. Noting that 'in the mid-1980s the air defence version of Tornado (F2) will enter service and our airborne early warning capability transformed with the advent of the Nimrod in this role,' he announced that the air defence fighter strength would be increased by retaining two squadrons of Phantoms instead of phasing them out when the Tornado F2 entered service; that he was considering switching the production order for the last 20 of the 220 Tornado GRs to F2s; that the number of Hawk trainers equipped with the Sidewinder air-to-air missile would be doubled to 72; and that the tanker force would be increased by modifying VC10s. In the Royal Navy greater emphasis would be placed both on mining our own sea approaches and on mine counter-measures; for the army, further expansion of the Territorial Army from an authorized establishment of 76,000 to 86,000 and an increase in the number of training days for which they could be paid from 38 a year to 42 would be introduced.

Turning to the continental commitment to NATO, he stated

that 'despite all the financial pressures on our defence effort, the Government has decided that this contribution is so important to the Alliance's military posture and its political cohesion that it must be maintained.' The British Army of the Rhine would be kept at 55,000 men, but not increased to 56,000 as had been planned. Its equipment would be substantially improved, including replacement of the ageing Chieftain tank by four regiments' worth of Challengers, available as an offshoot of the Iranian revolution, having originally been ordered by the Shah for his army. The RAF in Germany would receive more Harriers of the model (AV8B) being developed for the US Marine Corps, 60 of them to be bought. We would 'not be able to afford any direct and early replacement for the Jaguar force in Germany and at home'. Discussions, however, would proceed with potential partners on future combat aircraft.

The heart of the paper, and its sting, lay in what was said about 'Maritime Tasks'. After stating that 'the power of maritime air systems and submarines in tactical offensive operations is especially apt in our forward geographical situation', he went on to say that:

> If we are to maintain and improve these capabilities, we cannot at the same time sustain a surface fleet of the full present size, with its heavy overheads and continue to equip it with ships of the costly specification needed for protection in independent operations against the most modern Soviet air-launched and sea-launched missiles and submarines. Nevertheless there will remain a wide range of tasks for which surface ships are uniquely suited; and we must therefore retain a large and versatile ocean-going fleet.

The result would be 'a rather smaller but modern fleet with less heavy overheads (which) will give better value for defence resources'. The nuclear-powered hunter-killer submarine fleet would be increased from 12 to 17 boats; the third carrier, *Ark Royal*, would be completed as planned, but in the long term only two would be retained. The older carrier, *Hermes*, would be phased out as soon as the second, *Illustrious*, was operational. 'We intend to make particular use of the new carriers, with Sea Harriers and helicopters, in out-of-area deployment'; the practice of sending 'a substantial naval task group' on long voyages 'in the South Atlantic, Caribbean, Indian Ocean and further east' would be resumed. It was subsequently decided to offer HMS *Invincible* for sale to Australia. No more Type 42 air defence destroyers would be ordered, and the total of 59 destroyers

137

and frigates declared to NATO (although only 51 were reported as such in the 1981 White Paper) would be reduced to 'about 50'.

As a result of these decisions, naval manpower would be reduced by 8,000–10,000 by 1986; the naval base and Royal Dockyard at Chatham would be closed by 1984; there would be a significant reduction in the dockyard work at Portsmouth, and the effect on Gibraltar would be discussed with the colony's government. A new status for the dockyards, the Royal Ordnance Factories and Defence Research establishments was under consideration. Civilian employment in the United Kingdom by the Ministry of Defence had already been reduced by 20,000 to 228,000 and the new decisions would involve a further 15–20,000, with the hope that the total number employed would later fall to 'significantly below 200,000'. The final paragraph summed it up as follows:

In its review work the Government has confronted complex choices, with no easy or painless solutions available. To go on simply as before, or with all plans and aspirations unabated, is not an option; change is necessary. The Government has taken hard decisions. These reflect our resolve to give defence the resources Britain's security demands; but equal resolve to see that those resources, which the nation cannot spare without much penalty elsewhere, are put to work in accordance with realistic, unsentimental and up-to-date judgement of what will be most relevant and effective in future years.

In financial terms, the result was expected to be a continued real increase of 3 per cent per annum up to 1985/86, by which time it would be 21 per cent higher in constant prices than it had been when the Conservatives came to power. It was accepted that this might well mean that it would represent an even higher percentage of GDP. In future the Ministry, in common with other government departments, would not be allowed to spend beyond its estimate to allow for pay and price increases during the financial year, but was to be held to a cash limit. That was set at £11,535m for 1981/82, subsequently increased by £82m to cover a pay increase for the armed forces, and £300m 'to reflect the importance attached to defence', the total being adjusted for various reasons to £319m, the estimate for 1982/83, made before the Falklands War, being £14,091m. What it would have been had Nott not wielded his axe was not disclosed.

The changes announced in 'The Way Forward' were followed by

organizational changes within the Ministry, which edged it further towards Mountbatten's ideal pattern. One Minister of State, in addition to the Secretary of State, and three Parliamentary Secretaries, each responsible for one of the services, were replaced by two Ministers of State, one responsible for the armed forces, the other for equipment procurement. It was intended to 'increase the Secretary of State's ability to delegate functional responsibility to his Ministers; to emphasize the defence, as opposed to the single-service, responsibilities of the Department; to strengthen political direction throughout the Department' – a concept anathema to the military, and not altogether welcome to the civil servants – and 'to allow for greater Ministerial control of the defence procurement process at an earlier stage than in the past', which, given the influence of political lobbying, was not generally considered to increase the efficiency or objectivity of the defence procurement machinery.

A change which Mountbatten would have welcomed was to give the Chief of the Defence Staff greater authority over his single-service colleagues, described in the 1982 Defence White Paper (Cmnd 8251) as giving him 'a rather stronger voice, while maintaining the authority of the single-Service Chiefs of Staff. The Chiefs of Staff Committee will now be the forum in which the Chief of the Defence Staff seeks the views of his single-Service colleagues: the central Defence Staffs will be accountable to him.' Hitherto, military advice to the Secretary of State was meant to come from the Committee as a corporate body, and the purists maintained that the Chief of the Defence Staff could only give his own personal advice to the Defence Secretary if the Chiefs of Staff as a body were not in agreement. This change was intended to place the responsibility for deciding what advice to give on the CDS, who would arrive at it by a combination of consulting the Chiefs of the Staff and the Central Defence Staff. The latter was already responsible to him rather than to the Chiefs of Staff as a body, the Chiefs of Staff secretariat being the exception. The difference it would make would depend very largely on personalities. 'These changes,' the paper stated, 'reflect the increasing importance in defence affairs of resource allocation and balance of investment questions. In such areas Ministers look to the Chief of the Defence Staff for independent and timely advice on military priorities across all our defence commitments and programmes.' One significant change was that, in future, only the CDS would attend meetings of the Defence and Overseas Policy Committee of the Cabinet. Hitherto all the Chiefs had done so, although they seldom spoke. Mrs Thatcher is said to have found their presence unnecessary and annoying. The announcement, however, stressed that the right of the single-service Chiefs of Staff of access to Ministers, and the constitution and responsibilities of the Service Boards were unchanged.

The new regime was soon put to the test. Admiral Lewin was on an official visit to New Zealand when, following the landing of some Argentine scrap merchants, escorted by marines, on South Georgia, the Argentine Admiral Allara's fleet set sail from Buenos Aires on 27 March 1982 with 700 marines. From a European Summit meeting in Brussels, Mrs Thatcher gave John Nott authority to send three nuclear-powered hunter-killer submarines to the Falklands, but it was not until the evening of 31 March that definite intelligence was received that a major Argentine force was approaching the Falklands and had orders to land there on 2 April. Nott sought an urgent meeting with the Prime Minister, to which neither the acting CDS, Air Chief Marshal Sir Michael Beetham, Chief of the Air Staff, nor his colleague Admiral Sir Henry Leach, was invited. General Sir Edwin Bramall, the CGS, was visiting troops in Northern Ireland. But Leach, when he got to hear of it, went there of his own accord and suggested that, although nothing could be done to reinforce the 79 Royal Marines there and the 22 who had been despatched in the ice-patrol ship, HMS *Endurance*, to South Georgia – double the normal garrison, as a relief was in progress – a 'retrieval force' could be sailed within a few days, consisting of the Royal Marine Commando Brigade with the two assault-landing-ships, *Fearless* and *Intrepid*, supported by the old light fleet carrier *Hermes* and the new *Invincible*, with a suitable escort of destroyers and frigates. The force would take three weeks to get there and its maintenance in the area, 8,000 miles away, would pose a formidable problem and would involve 'taking up' merchant shipping. The use as a staging post of the British Ascension Island in the South Pacific would be essential.

Leach's proposal was formally agreed next day, Beetham warning that the force could face an adverse air situation on arrival from the land-based Argentine air force and navy, the latter having recently acquired some French Super-Étendard aircraft and five Exocet missiles to be fired from them. Bramall also expressed doubt that the Royal Marine force alone, with its three commandos, would be strong enough to 'retrieve' the islands. A parachute battalion, a battery of Rapier anti-aircraft missiles and two troops of light tanks from the army were therefore added to the force, which was to be supported by the maximum number of helicopters and aircraft that could be deployed. A period of intense activity followed before the force, under the command of Rear-Admiral 'Sandy' Woodward, sailed from Portsmouth on 6 April, some of the escorts joining from Gibraltar, and reached Ascension Island on 17 April, the first submarine entering Falkland Islands waters on the 12th, when a Maritime Exclusion Zone was declared.

There were still hopes that hostilities could be avoided and that the diplomatic shuttle, vigorously pursued by the American Secretary of State and former NATO SACEUR, Alexander Haig, would achieve a peaceful solution. The United Nations Secretary-General, Señor Perez de Cuellar, was pursuing a parallel and sometimes conflicting course. The British Ambassador to the United Nations, Sir Antony Parsons, had achieved a major diplomatic victory at the start with a Security Council resolution demanding an immediate cessation of hostilities and immediate withdrawal of Argentine forces from the Falkland Islands, and calling on the governments of Argentina and the United Kingdom to seek a diplomatic solution. Mrs Thatcher was determined not to accept any such solution which did not include Argentine withdrawal or threw doubt on British sovereignty.

Far from showing any willingness to withdraw, the Argentine Junta had reinforced the eastern island to a strength, by this time, of 13,000 men. It was therefore decided to reinforce the Royal Marine Commando Brigade with another parachute battalion, a battery of field artillery, the parachute engineer squadron and more helicopters, but they could not sail before 26 April. This would bring the landing force to a strength of 7,000, the crews of 20 warships, eight amphibious landing-ships and nearly 40 other ships of the Royal Fleet Auxiliary and Merchant Navy bringing the total up to 15,000. Admiral Sir John Fieldhouse, Commander-in-Chief Fleet, with his headquarters at Northwood in the western suburbs of London, was in overall command of the whole operation, under the orders of the Chief of the Defence Staff. His land force adviser was Major-General Jeremy Moore, Commander of Royal Marine Commando Forces. When they both flew to Ascension Island to confer with Admiral Woodward and Brigadier Julian Thompson, Commander of the Royal Marine Commando Brigade, on 18 April, Fieldhouse came to the conclusion that, although Thompson's brigade should be able to succeed in landing, more troops would be needed to achieve a rapid victory – a long-drawn-out operation would pose very serious problems – and that more helicopters would be needed to move and supply them. On 25 April this was agreed and 5th Infantry Brigade was allotted to him. Two of its units, 2nd and 3rd Parachute Battalions, had already joined the commando

141

brigade, and its commander, Brigadier Antony Wilson, was given 2nd Scots Guards and 1st Welsh Guards to replace them and join his 1st/7th Gurkhas. Moore was appointed Land Force Commander, but remained as adviser to Fieldhouse until he sailed, on 12 May, with the 5th Brigade in the cruise liner *Queen Elizabeth II*, which had been requisitioned to carry them. The container ship, *Atlantic Conveyor*, had already been taken up to carry more RAF Harriers and helicopters, and sailed on 25 April. Moore's place as land force adviser to Fieldhouse was then taken by the army Lieutenant-General Sir Richard Trant.

The plan at this stage was for Woodward to sail his carriers to the Falklands area and spend two weeks engaging the Argentine navy and air force and softening up the garrison by naval gunfire. He hoped that in this period he would meet and defeat the Argentine fleet before he had to carry out an amphibious operation. Meanwhile a force of Royal Marines and SAS, transported by destroyer, would recapture South Georgia. The sinking of the Argentine cruiser, *General Belgrano*, by the Royal Navy submarine *Conqueror* on 1 May and that of HMS *Sheffield* by the Argentine navy aircraft, equipped with Exocet, three days later, removed any doubt there had been that a landing on the Falkland Islands would be needed to 'retrieve' them.

The firm decision to proceed with this was taken by the War Cabinet on 8 May, by which time the amphibious shipping, carrying 3rd Commando Brigade, had left Ascension Island to join Woodward's fleet 200 miles north-east of the Falklands on 18 May, planning to land at San Carlos, at the northern end of the Falkland Sound between the two main islands, on the night of 19/20 May. Whitehall insisted on a 24-hour postponement, not being prepared to risk keeping three battalions on the liner *Canberra* until transferring to landing-craft. 19 May was spent transferring two of them, one each to *Fearless* and *Intrepid*, both of which already carried one commando. The landings went smoothly against hardly any opposition, but it was not long before, as Beetham had forecast, ships off-shore were under constant attack by Argentine aircraft, flying from the mainland. After their first clash with the Sea Harriers based on Woodward's carriers early in the month, the Argentine air force never challenged them again and confined their attacks to ships and targets on land. The impressive performance of the Sea Harriers in air-to-air fighting came as a surprise to almost everyone, except their own pilots.

Losses of ships at sea off the landing area caused Woodward to insist that their loads must be put ashore and that they be withdrawn from the danger area, causing disruption to the logistic plan, aggravated by the loss of the *Atlantic Conveyor* carrying the heavy-lift helicopters. This delayed Thompson's preparations to advance towards Port Stanley itself, and he came under pressure from London to get a move on, the Prime Minister fearing that some diplomatic compromise might prevent a decisive victory. Once he had landed, Thompson ceased to be under Woodward's command and was directly subordinate to Fieldhouse, from whom the order to respond to this pressure came, until Moore came ashore. At this time Moore was at sea in the liner *Queen Elizabeth* and out of communication until he landed on 30 May, by which time Thompson's troops had 'yomped' their way on foot to contact the outer defences of Port Stanley. The attack was launched on the nights of 11/12 and 12/13 June, by which time Wilson's 5th Brigade had joined Thompson after his Welsh Guards had suffered a severe blow when the landing-ship, *Sir Galahad*, carrying them, was hit and set on fire by Argentine aircraft. The attack was a brilliant feat of arms and achieved a rapid victory at a cost of 250 dead, of whom 141 were due to attack by aircraft and only 56 in attacks on Argentine army defences. The navy had four ships sunk and many more damaged: they would have lost more if many of the Argentine air force bombs had not failed to explode. Ten fixed-wing aircraft and 24 helicopters were lost. The Argentines lost 746 men killed, of whom 368 were in the *General Belgrano*: over 1,000 were wounded or fell sick and nearly 13,000 were captured or surrendered.

Postmortems were soon put in hand, the most important of which was a committee of Privy Councillors, headed by Lord Franks, the remit of which was: 'To review the way in which the responsibilities of Government in relation to the Falkland Islands and their Dependencies were discharged in the period leading up to the Argentine invasion of the Falkland Islands on 2 April 1982, taking account of all such factors as are relevant.' It was given access to all secret material and reported in January 1983 (Cmnd 8787). The committee was sympathetic to the dilemma in which successive governments had been placed. Argentina had never wavered from her view that sovereignty must be ceded, and that cooperation should be a step towards that end. Part of the cooperation was that after the Falkland Islands Company had withdrawn its shipping service to Uruguay as uneconomic, Argentina provided an air service between Port Stanley and the mainland and supplied the Islands with petroleum fuels. The islanders never wavered from their opposition to a transfer of sovereignty, even in the form of a lease-back or a condominium, and became more confirmed than ever in that attitude when the military Junta came to power in 1976, intensified when General Galtieri succeeded General Viola in 1981. Successive British governments would have liked to have found a formula which could have made it possible for the standard of living of the 1,800 islanders to have been raised by access to the educational, health and other social and economic facilities of Argentina, which the far larger number of Argentinians of British descent enjoyed; but they knew that any attempt to force an arrangement on the islanders against their will would be frustrated by an effective lobby of all parties in both Houses of Parliament. The only solution that the Foreign Office could suggest was lease-back, preceded by a campaign of education aimed at persuading the islanders and their lobby that it would be in their interest. But Lord Carrington, the Foreign Secretary, judged that it would not only not succeed, but would be counterproductive. The committee did not dispute this, but criticized him for not insisting that the Defence and Overseas Policy Committee of the Cabinet should consider the subject, which they did not do between January 1981 and 1 April 1982, the eve of the Argentine invasion.

The committee firmly rejected the accusation that the government had had previous warning, or could have had it. It did, however, make two criticisms of the Ministry of Defence: that it had not reacted to the Prime Minister's comment on a telegram from the British Ambassador in Buenos Aires on 3 March, reporting the Argentine communiqué on talks with Richard Luce in New York, which included the clause 'Argentina reserves [the right] to terminate [negotiations] and to choose freely the procedure which best accords with her interests'. Mrs Thatcher's comment was: 'We must make contingency plans', but none were made. The other criticism was of John Nott's refusal, supported by the Prime Minister, to agree to Lord Carrington's repeated request that the decision, announced as part of 'The Way Forward' in June 1981, to withdraw the naval ice-patrol ship HMS *Endurance* from service at the end of the 1981/82 Antarctic summer and not to replace her should be reversed. Although her only armament was a 20-mm Oerlikon gun and two helicopters, the decision appeared to indicate that Britain was not prepared to defend by force of arms her claims to sovereignty over the Falklands and other islands in the area. It certainly reinforced that view, which the Argentine Admiral Anaya, head of the navy, had gained in his previous post as naval attaché in London.

It raised strong protests from the Falkland Islands Council. *Endurance* was still on station when the invasion took place.

The committee appreciated the dilemma which the government faced over precautionary military measures when the Argentine position hardened as the month of March went by and the intelligence assessment, although still regarding a major military operation to invade or occupy some part of the Falklands as unlikely, was not prepared to dismiss it. To have despatched reinforcements, even purely naval ones, could have precipitated Argentine military action, and they could always get there first and could have wrong-footed Britain in international eyes, particularly at the United Nations. It also sympathized with the decision of the previous government not to agree to Lord Shackleton's recommendation to construct an airfield capable of taking long-range jet aircraft. No diversion airfield would be available, unless Argentina agreed to the use of one in her country; it would make an Argentine airborne invasion easier; its construction would take some years and was likely to exacerbate relations with Argentina; and it had the disadvantage from the point of view of the Chiefs of Staff that, if troops and aircraft were flown there to demonstrate, in some tense situation, that Britain was determined to defend the islands, they could not be withdrawn without giving the opposite impression. Lord Carrington explained this problem, when he resigned as Foreign Secretary after the invasion, to be succeeded by Francis Pym.

The Ministry of Defence's own postmortem, entitled 'The Falklands Campaign: The Lessons' (Cmnd 8758. December 1982) was largely an essay in self-congratulation. It confirmed some announcements previously made: that in future two carriers would remain available, resulting in the retention of three (allowing for one in refit), so that the sale of *Invincible* to Australia was cancelled; that, in addition to the replacement of all ships lost in action, the destroyer/frigate force would be kept at about 55, instead of being reduced to 50; that the restrictions imposed on all three services on expenditure for training would be removed; and that more aircraft of various kinds would be ordered and maintained for both the Royal Navy and the Royal Air Force. It had already been decided to keep in service the assault ships, *Fearless* and *Intrepid*, and *Endurance* was to soldier on, although nearing the end of her life. A strategic airfield was to be built near Port Stanley, and a defence force of all three services maintained there to ensure that there could be no repetition of the Argentine adventure. The paper stressed the handicap under which the navy had operated in having no Airborne Early Warning;

145

the very significant influence of the hunter-killer nuclear sub-marines, which, having sunk the *Belgrano*, kept at bay the Argentine navy, which had no means of dealing with them; the threat which both aircraft and missiles posed to surface ships, and the need to improve defences against them, and realistic training in operating them; the great importance of helicopters to lift men and stores in that type of operation; the importance of having adequate logistic stocks; and dependence on civil shipping, which could be modified for many purposes. The British forces were fortunate in having access to information from American satellites, and in that the Argentines had no similar means of discovering the whereabouts of British ships. The report tactfully did not mention that, if the Argentine invasion had taken place a few months later, not only would HMS *Invincible* and several other ships have been on an extended tour in the Indian Ocean, but the weather conditions in the Falklands would have made the operation a great deal more difficult.

The House of Commons Defence Committee* expressed concern that the infrastructure projects connected with the establishment of the garrison 'should not be open to misinterpretation as a commitment to the establishment of a permanent military presence'. The government's reply (Cmnd 9070, para. 8) said that 'the decision to build the airfield demonstrates our commitment to safeguarding the Islanders' future. The Government hopes the Argentines will draw the proper conclusions and that this will result in a policy character-ised by peaceable intentions rather than belligerence and threats.' The reply did not speculate on what conclusions Argentina might draw if the garrison were ever to be withdrawn or reduced to its pre-war minuscule strength. The airfield was completed in 1985, the garrison based, as far as the army was concerned, on an infantry battalion group.† In the initial stages it outnumbered the total popu-lation of the islands, certainly by a long way that of adult males, thereafter being slightly reduced in size.

The higher direction of the campaign had worked well. At the summit, the Prime Minister presided over a Defence Committee (Falklands), generally known as the War Cabinet, the other mem-bers of which were the Lord President of the Council, William Whitelaw, the Foreign and Defence Secretaries, and the Chairman

---

*3rd Report 1982–83 Session. 14 June 1983. Para. 140. vi.
†Later reduced to a company.

of the Conservative Party, Cecil Parkinson. The Chief of the Defence Staff was always present, and, on certain occasions, notably the final decision to go ahead with the landings, taken on 19 May, all the Chiefs of Staff attended. The latter had met daily – sometimes twice a day – and always before the CDS was due to attend a War Cabinet, so that he was invariably able to give their agreed advice to Ministers. The general exercise of command below that level was helped by the fact that it was primarily a maritime operation and that orders were passed on well-established naval lines from one admiral to another, all three of them having recently served together when Lewin had occupied Fieldhouse's post. The only failure in the command channel was that of keeping Moore on as Fieldhouse's land force adviser after he had been appointed Land Force Commander, and leaving him incommunicado in the *Queen Elizabeth II* from 12 May until he landed on the 30th. Trant should have replaced him on 25 April, or earlier, and he should have been flown to Ascension Island to join Woodward.

10

CREEPING UP TO THE GULF:
1983–1990

In the general Election of May 1983, basking in the glory of the Falklands campaign, Margaret Thatcher was returned to power with a majority of 144 over all other parties, Labour having won only 209 seats. She appointed Michael Heseltine as Defence Secretary, John Nott, his 'Way Forward' having taken a severe knock, leaving political life to return to the City. Heseltine's formula for keeping defence expenditure under control was to pin his hopes on better management within both the Ministry and the services as a whole, on greater competition in arms procurement, and on postponing decisions about expensive equipment matters for as long as he could. The 1983 Defence White Paper (Cmnd 8951) reported that the cash limit set for 1982/83 had been increased from £13,288m to £13,606m to cover the Falklands campaign and that the out-turn was expected to be within it. The budget for 1983/84 stood at £15,973m, including £624m to meet Falklands costs, the cash limit set at £15,036m, a 10 per cent increase from the previous year, making defence the second largest public spending department at 5.1 per cent of GDP, compared to France at 4.1 and Germany at 3.4 per cent. Only Greece (6.9), the USA (6.6) and Turkey (5.3) were higher. Britain was second only to the USA in total and per capita expenditure. The equipment programme absorbed 46 per cent, of which 24 per cent went on research and development, 22 per cent on sea, 16 per cent on land and 32 per cent on air equipment.

Heseltine hoped that his reform of management would keep this under control. It consisted of introducing MINIS (Management Information System for Ministers and Top Management) and in the introduction of 'responsibility budgets', combined with a devolution of managerial responsibility to lower levels. MINIS was intended to record detailed information about the Ministry's activities, costs and performance to provide a basis for Ministers and senior officials to review the work of the department and to decide on future action.

It included studies which could lead to changes in organization and redeployment of manpower and resources. Responsibility would, as far as possible, be delegated to line managers, including that for their own budgets. They were supposed to achieve a specified level of performance in a defined area of activity against a financial budget, but given a degree of freedom as to how to do this, in contrast to the tight financial control from finance branches, manned by civil servants, which had traditionally prevailed. This system was initially applied experimentally to service establishments which could be equated to civil organizations. These were the navy's medical service and its aircraft repair yard; the army's principal vehicle workshop; the RAF's flying training schools; and the Royal Signals Research Establishment. This system was gradually extended in the rest of the decade so that it pervaded almost every aspect of service life, providing a heyday for accountants. It led to such absurdities as military units having to pay each other for the use of their sports facilities, including playing fields. The incident for which Field Marshal Montgomery got into such trouble, when he commanded a brigade in Portsmouth in 1938 – letting a football field to a fair promoter for August Bank Holiday to replenish his garrison welfare fund* – would have received Heseltine's strong approval. Management reform was applied also to the Chiefs of Staff machinery in the most decisive transfer of power from the single-service elements to the centre since Mountbatten's day. The central military staff, serving the Chief of Defence Staff, was to be merged with the Defence Secretariat, serving the Permanent Under-Secretary, into a single Defence Staff responsible to them both 'jointly and severally'. It would absorb significant elements of the single-service staffs, who had been subordinate to their own Chiefs of Staff, leaving the latter with staffs greatly reduced in numbers and in rank. This Defence Staff would 'provide advice for all parts of the Ministry, including as appropriate the Service Chiefs of Staff'. The Chief of Defence Staff would be responsible for the preparation for and conduct of all military operations and not just those involving more than one service. The single-service Chiefs of Staff were told that they should concern themselves primarily with managing their own service, chairing the Executive Committee of their Service Board. They were to aim at streamlining management and delegating authority for day-to-day administration to Commanders-in-Chief, reducing the

---

*Montgomery of Alamein, *Memoirs*. London, 1958, p. 46.

'potential overlap that exists between the formulation of advice on operations, defence policy and resource allocation on the one hand and the management of defence resources on the other'. It had always been one of the principal arguments for the previous organization that only those who had the responsibility for management were in a position to give sound advice about what could or should be done in operations or policy. These changes caused considerable concern on those grounds. They were seen as strengthening the hand of Ministers who, as Nott was seen to have done in 'The Way Forward', overrode military advice from the heads of the armed forces in order to save money. The first CDS to enjoy this increase in authority was Admiral of the Fleet Sir John Fieldhouse*, who had been Commander-in-Chief Fleet and overall commander in the Falklands campaign.

In the 1986 Defence White Paper (Cmnd 9763) Heseltine claimed a significant success for his introduction of greater competition into arms procurement, one of the principal steps in which was to abolish the right of the firm which had received the development contract to obtain the first production order. He claimed that the decision to apply this to the new Warrior armoured personnel carrier had saved about £100m or 12 per cent of the previously estimated cost. He was equally keen on NATO, particularly European, collaboration and wished to introduce more competition into that. The export of Tornados to Oman and Saudi Arabia was hailed as a concrete success in that field, as was European production by Britain, France and Germany of the US Multiple-Launch Rocket System (MLRS), all four countries collaborating in the development of a terminal guidance system for it. A number of other important collaborative projects were in the pipeline, but not yet far up it and with no certainty that they would emerge at the far end. These included the NATO frigate replacement, the European Fighter Aircraft, the EH101 naval anti-submarine warfare helicopter, a NATO helicopter for the 1990s (NH90) and an army battlefield helicopter.

It was on a helicopter issue that Heseltine himself was to crash: the row over whether Britain's only helicopter manufacturer, Westlands, should be allowed to merge with an American firm or, as Heseltine wished, form part of a European consortium. He flounced out of the government over the issue and was succeeded by George Younger, who, as a National Service officer in the Argyll and Sutherland Highlanders, had served in Korea and subsequently in the

*Later Lord Fieldhouse.

regiment's Territorial Army battalion. Heseltine's new management techniques and emphasis on competition had not reduced or held defence expenditure. His last budget, that for 1986/87, was the first to be free of the NATO commitment to an annual increase of 3 per cent in real terms. It was for £18,479m, 5.2 per cent of GDP and higher in real terms than that of France (22,618m US dollars to 20,132m) and of Germany (19,767m): higher than them also in per capita expenditure (401:365:324 US dollars), but it was intended to fall in real terms by 6 per cent over the next three years. The government consistently denied that it intended to carry out yet another defence review, but the 1986 White Paper came close to it in stating:

> We are currently engaged in the annual re-costing of the defence programme to provide an up-to-date framework for Ministerial decisions on expenditure commitments. We shall need to balance the preservation of our present front line numbers against the requirement to invest in expensive new equipment to strengthen further the fighting power of our armed forces in the 1990s and beyond. Some difficult decisions will have to be taken but there will be no need for any change in our main defence posture.

During this period there were significant improvements in the equipment of all three services. The navy's losses in the Falklands were being replaced and HMS *Ark Royal*, the third carrier, entered service in 1986. The number of nuclear-powered hunter-killer submarines had been brought up to 15 and orders placed for four of the new Type 2400 diesel-powered ones. The design of the new Type 23 frigate had been agreed after a fierce argument between those who favoured a short fat one and those who wished to stay with a long thin design. The latter won. The air defence version of the Tornado, the F3, was at last entering service, while delivery of the GR1 strike version continued, as did that of the Harrier GR5 and the Chinook heavy-lift helicopter. The first Challenger tanks had entered service and it was planned to equip eight regiments in Germany with them out of the 12 to which the tank fleet had been increased. Warrior armoured personnel carriers for 13 infantry battalions had been ordered, as had Multiple-Launch Rocket Systems for three artillery regiments. More light anti-aircraft batteries had been equipped with the Rapier missile and a tracked version was being introduced. The infantry were getting a new lighter rifle (SA80) and mortar, and the army's signal communications system was being extensively modernized. These improvements coincided with a change in the operational concept for the defence of West Germany from that of a defensive strategy, relying on the use of tactical nuclear weapons, to more mobile operations involving counter-attacks. This was linked to an American concept of exploiting new technologies to attack targets in the rear of the battlefield, designed to limit the enemy's build-up of reinforcements.

George Younger, therefore, inherited armed forces in significantly better shape than they had been when the Conservatives came to power in 1979. The Falklands had given a boost to recruiting and there were no immediate worries about the manpower situation. Male adult recruiting had risen from 19,342 in 1982/83 to over 30,000 in each of the following three years, maintaining an overall strength of about 308,000 men and 16,000 women in all three services. But, after the General Election in June 1987, as a result of which the Conservatives were returned to power with a majority of 102, Younger had to face a different financial climate, one in which the defence budget was due to decline in real terms, while there was no let-up in the cost escalation of equipment or in the cost of manpower. This coincided with the change in the international atmosphere following Gorbachev's assumption of power in the Soviet Union. There was much talk of 'alternative strategies' which did not depend on nuclear weapons or on offensive-related weapon systems, as tanks were seen to be. It was suggested that purely defensive strategies, based on militias, equipped with light weapons, scattered about the countryside and in urban areas in small bodies, would provide an effective defence at much lower cost than heavily equipped conventional forces in the NATO pattern, and would pose no threat to nations beyond their borders. They would therefore encourage a move towards disarmament in Europe. Such suggestions found no support in NATO and certainly not in British official defence circles.

In this new relaxed atmosphere, the government began to apply its economic ethos to the defence field. Plans were made to privatize the Royal Docklands and sell off the Royal Ordnance Factories, which had already been placed on a trading basis. Vickers bought the one remaining tank factory at Leeds, while 'Royal Ordnance', as the remainder was known, was bought up by British Aerospace, just as the sad story of the Nimrod AEW came to an end. One of the forms which the government's ethos took was that known as 'The Next Steps'. This followed the lines of Heseltine's management reforms. The concept was that, as far as possible, the executive functions of government should be delegated to agencies, headed by a chief executive working within a policy and framework set by the Minister responsible. The 1987 Defence White Paper (Cmnd 344) announced that consideration was being given to bringing together the main Defence Research establishments into one such agency and to turning the Meteorological Office, subordinate to the Ministry of Defence, into another. This came about in 1991.

The new atmosphere, combined with the prospect of the Single European Market in 1992/93, also lent emphasis to a greater degree of cooperation in European arms procurement which was linked to, although not entirely compatible with, more competition in development and production. For some time France had been urging that the almost defunct Western European Union should be given a greater rôle in this field and also serve as a European pillar to balance the overwhelming influence of the USA in NATO. The British government hesitated to back this trend, giving it half-hearted support. A slight boost was given to it at a meeting in Rome in 1984 to celebrate its thirtieth birthday, the Foreign and Defence Ministers agreeing to meet twice, instead of once, a year, and to put a bit more life into it. It was described in the 1985 Defence White Paper (Cmnd 9430) as:

> unique in having an Assembly specifically empowered by the Treaty to discuss matters relating to the defence and security of Europe. It thus provides a forum for European political debate about issues of major concern to us, and makes it easier to achieve a consensus on them. It has an important role in stimulating greater public debate of security issues, and in generating greater public awareness of Alliance policies. It can act as a 'ginger group' giving political impetus to practical work in other groups aimed at improving European defence cooperation, and assists the development of a more unified, and thus stronger, European contribution to the Alliance.

Its activity as a ginger group was not very evident over the next five years, but it continued to feature in Defence White Papers as it had not done previously, partly to emphasize the contribution which the European members of NATO were making to the Alliance in response to criticism by members of the US Congress that they were not doing enough and threats that, if they did not, American troops would be withdrawn.

The WEU proved a convenient political umbrella under which to coordinate the deployment of warships, principally minesweepers, to protect shipping in the Persian Gulf during the Iran–Iraq war, but the actual staff work involved was almost certainly done in the NATO staff of the Commander-in-Chief Channel, one of the NATO hats worn by the British C-in-C Fleet at Northwood. At the WEU meeting at The Hague in October 1987 the Ministers of the seven nations produced what they called a 'Common Platform on European Security Interests', stating: 'We are determined to carry our share of the common defence in both the conventional and the nuclear field, in accordance with the principle of risk- and burden-sharing, which is fundamental to allied cohesion.' There was to be no chickening out of NATO's nuclear strategy under domestic anti-nuclear pressure, which was growing in Germany. It was surprising that the British Ministers agreed to another phrase: 'We remain determined to pursue European integration including security and defence and to make a more effective contribution to the common defence of the West.' In spite of having agreed that, the British government remained extremely cautious about anything which, in giving the WEU more defence responsibility, might prejudice the cohesion of NATO. The Americans viewed any such move with deep suspicion.

1989 was the fortieth anniversary of the signature of the North Atlantic Treaty and much was made of the contribution NATO's resolution over that period had made to the relaxation in East–West relations, demonstrated by the Soviet withdrawal of its troops from Afghanistan in 1988 and Gorbachev's announcement, at the United Nations Assembly meeting in December of that year, of his intention to cut the number of Soviet conventional forces, not only in Europe, but within the Soviet Union also. But British defence policy showed great caution in accepting that any real change in the situation had occurred, basing itself on the principle that no change could be contemplated until agreement had been reached in the Conventional Armed Forces in Europe (CFE) talks which, in Vienna in 1989, replaced the fruitless MBFR talks which had been dragging on for 16 years. NATO's proposal was that the combined total of NATO and Warsaw Pact forces, split equally between the two alliances, should not exceed 40,000 tanks, 33,000 artillery pieces and 56,000 armoured personnel carriers, the limit of each in any one country of either alliance to be 3,200 tanks, 1,700 guns and 6,000 APCs. It was not until the dramatic events towards the end of 1989 occurred, including the breach of the Berlin Wall, that the government was prepared to accept that radical changes were taking place and that NATO, and therefore British, defence policy must change also.

By that time Tom King, who had been Secretary of State for Northern Ireland, had succeeded George Younger as Defence Secretary in the Cabinet reshuffle in July in which John Major replaced Geoffrey Howe at the Foreign Office. King had held a commission in the Somerset Light Infantry in his National Service. The possibility of a 'peace dividend' was not unwelcome to the government. The economic climate was not favourable: the pressure to spend money in other fields – health, education and the general infrastructure of the nation – was growing in anticipation of a general election in 1991. The 1990 Defence White Paper (Cmnd 1022) announced that the actual out-turn of expenditure in the year 1989/90 was £20,630m with cash targets set for the three following years at £21,223m, £22,360m and £23,340m. These figures represented a slight drop in real terms in the first and a recovery in the second and third years. Expenditure had fallen to 4.0 per cent of GDP, which was still higher than that of France (3.7) and Germany (2.9), although in total it was below both and per capita between the two.

Early in 1990 the Ministry of Defence embarked on a study known as 'Options for Change', the preliminary results of which were announced on 25 July. Earlier that month a NATO summit meeting had been held in London, the final communiqué of which had stated: 'As Europe changes, we must profoundly alter the way we think about defence.' King's announcement did not go as far as that, but did propose significant reductions in all three services. The Trident four-boat deterrent force was not affected, and 'in accordance with NATO policy for an appropriate mix of nuclear and conventional forces, based in Europe' a 'sub-strategic force of dual-capable Tornados with a stand-off missile' would be needed. Altogether there would be six squadrons of the strike version of Tornado, deployed partly in Britain and partly in Germany, where the RAF's airfields would be reduced from four to two, on one of which Harriers and helicopters would still be based. They would no longer contribute to the air defence of Germany and all seven air-defence Tornado squadrons would be based in Britain, supplemented by the armed Hawk training aircraft. The two Phantom air defence squadrons would go. The anti-shipping rôle of the Buccaneers would be taken over by the British-based strike Tornados, re-equipped with Sea Eagle missiles.

The navy's three carriers would stay and an amphibious capability would be retained in the longer term, implying replacements for the two assault ships, *Fearless* and *Intrepid*. The destroyer/frigate force would be reduced to about 40 and the submarine fleet, other than the Trident boats, to about 16, of which three-quarters would be nuclear-powered. There would be a small reduction in Nimrod LRMP aircraft. The army in Germany would be reduced by about half, its four divisions reduced to one, which would be reinforced in emergency from Britain to a strength 'of the order of a division'. The contribution would have to be designed to fit into whatever new force structure was developed in NATO's Central Region. At German request, troops would remain in Berlin until Soviet forces were withdrawn from East Germany, although allied responsibility for Berlin ceased on German reunification. The general result of these reductions would, by the mid-1990s, produce a regular army of about 120,000, a navy, including the Royal Marines, of 60,000 and an air force of 75,000, a reduction in manpower of 18 per cent. The number of civilian employees was expected to fall in the same proportion. The decision as to which tank, the Vickers Challenger II or the American General Motors' General Abrams, would be chosen to replace the remaining Chieftains would be deferred until it was clearer how many would be needed. The project to design an entirely new tank, MBT80, preferably on a European cooperative basis, had been abandoned. The German Leopard 2 had been considered and rejected.

Only a week after this announcement and before the impact of it could be assessed, Saddam Hussein invaded Kuwait on 2 August, and on the 8th announced that he had annexed it. On that day the US President, George Bush, announced that US forces, at the request of King Fahd, were being deployed to Saudi Arabia to help in its defence. The United Nations Security Council had by then adopted two resolutions, one condemning the invasion of Kuwait and demanding Iraq's unconditional withdrawal, and, when Iraq refused to comply with that, another imposing extensive mandatory sanctions. The immediate military need was to reinforce the defence of Saudi Arabia and the Gulf states and to impose the sanctions. For the first, the British government's immediate reaction was to provide air forces. A squadron of 12 Tornado F3 air defence fighters, on exercise in Cyprus, was deployed to Dhahran in Saudi Arabia, and a squadron of 12 Jaguar ground-attack aircraft and three LRMP Nimrods with two VC10 tankers to Thumrait in Oman, Royal Marine and army detachments joining a RAF Regiment squadron for their local defence. To meet the second need, a group of three mine counter-measure vessels (MCMVs), with a survey ship to act as a headquarters, set off from Rosyth on the long voyage to join the three destroyers of the Armilla Patrol already in the Gulf. Air Chief Marshal Sir Patrick Hine, C-in-C of RAF Strike Command (also NATO CINCUKAIR), was appointed in overall Joint Service Command, exercising it from his headquarters at High Wycombe to which staff from the other two services were added. His subordinates were an Air Vice-Marshal, already head of a mission to Saudi Arabia, and a Senior Naval Officer Middle East. It was not long before pressure from the USA for larger contributions, supported by Saudi Arabia and the Gulf states, who did not wish to appear totally dependent on the Americans, led to an increase in the British contribution, although not yet to a land force one. A squadron of RAF Tornado GR1 strike aircraft was deployed from Germany to Bahrein after a visit to the Gulf states by Alan Clark, the Defence Minister for Procurement, accompanied by the Vice-Chief of the Defence Staff, General Sir Richard Vincent, and at the end of August a Type 42 air defence destroyer was despatched to join the one already there.

But this did not satisfy the Americans, who were sensitive to the potential problem that, if it came to actual fighting, GIs should not be the only troops killed. Pressure for other nations to contribute land forces increased, and was the principal theme of the US Secretary of State, James Baker, at a NATO Council meeting in Brussels on 10 September. It is believed that Mrs Thatcher, at that time, wished to limit Britain's army contribution to an infantry or parachute battalion, but Baker's plea was for tanks, and the Chief of the General Staff, General Sir John Chapple, persuaded her that an armoured brigade group was the minimum viable tactical entity that should be sent. On 14 September it was announced that 7th Armoured Brigade would be sent from Germany, with two armoured regiments (battalions of tanks – that is, about 100 in total) and one infantry battalion in armoured personnel carriers, with the appropriate support of other arms and services. The tanks would be the new Challengers and the APCs the new Warriors. The media made great play of the brigade's historic link with the original 7th Armoured Division, formed in Egypt in 1940, which had fought in the desert from the beginning to the end of the North African campaign in the Second World War, earning the nickname of the 'Desert Rats'. The brigade had inherited its insignia of a jerboa, which had unfortunately become transformed into a creature more like a kangaroo. Contributions by other European members of NATO were disappointing, only France providing any significant land force, a Foreign Legion light armoured brigade, called a *division léger*, which initially emphasized its independence from the American effort. In contrast to that attitude, the British government agreed that, when 7th Armoured Brigade completed its deployment to the Gulf at the end of October, it would operate under command of the US Marine division on the southern border of Kuwait. By then the RAF had sent an additional Tornado strike squadron to Tabuk in north-western Saudi Arabia with more VC10 tankers and RAF Regiment personnel for their defence, and in November 15 Puma helicopters were sent in US transport aircraft to support 7th Armoured Brigade.

These deployments made a change necessary in the local British command organization, and Lieutenant-General Sir Peter de la Billière, on the point of retirement from command of South East District in England, was sent out in command of all British forces in Saudi Arabia and the Gulf, subordinate to Sir Patrick Hine in the United Kingdom. He did not exercise any operational command. The army and air force contributions were to operate under US 'control', when authorized by de la Billière to do so, while the naval force remained under C-in-C Fleet in the UK for sanctions imposition duties and under US naval coordination if hostilities broke out. General de la Billière located himself and his staff alongside the joint supreme headquarters of the Saudi Arabian C-in-C and General Schwarzkopf, the overall US Commander, an arrangement which worked very smoothly, helped by the fact that de la Billière had on previous occasions worked with both Arab and US forces.

In November the emphasis changed from defence of Saudi Arabia and the Gulf states to preparations for offensive action to evict Iraqi forces from the territory of Kuwait, which it was hoped would persuade Saddam Hussein to comply with the Security Council resolutions. Both American and British plans to prepare for the relief of their troops deployed to the Gulf were cancelled and the planned reliefs became reinforcements. A number of factors influenced this decision. Although sanctions were being effectively imposed, Jordan being the weak link, it was becoming clear that, even if they did achieve their aim, it would take a long time. It appeared doubtful if the remarkable success in forming an international coalition, including Egypt and Syria, would hold together long enough for that: American public opinion, including important Congressional and retired military figures, was becoming divided; and US troops in the Gulf were showing signs of impatience. If military operations had to be undertaken, they should be completed before the hot weather set in and preferably be initiated before the month of Ramadan, which fell in February.

When, therefore, President Bush, on 8 November, committed a further 150,000 troops, including two armoured and two mechanized divisions and a second Marine amphibious group, with substantial air and naval support, Margaret Thatcher and her government decided to increase the British army contribution by adding the 4th Armoured Brigade (an armoured regiment and two mechanized infantry battalions) and a strong artillery brigade, which, together with 7th Armoured Brigade, would form the 1st Armoured Division, commanded by Major-General Rupert Smith. The whole force came from the British Army of the Rhine in Germany, which it virtually stripped of all its Challenger tanks and their spares, as well as most of its Warrior APCs. The units chosen to go were those who had been trained on these equipments and had to be brought up to strength with soldiers from other units who were also trained on them, regardless of regimental or other affiliations.

This reinforcement brought British army strength in the Gulf up to 33,000, more than half that of BAOR, and a total service strength of about 45,000. Deployment of personnel was carried out almost entirely by air, while most of the equipment was shipped in chartered vessels to the extremely well-equipped Saudi Arabian port of Al Jubayl. Logistic support in a distant theatre, where there were no established British military facilities, posed severe problems which were overcome by drawing on the whole of the British army's logistic and administrative resources, as well as on the firms who had manufactured the equipment. In the medical field, this involved the call-up of medical reservists and the deployment of a Territorial Army General Hospital. The artillery brigade consisted of three field and two heavy regiments, one of the latter equipped with the new Multiple-Launch Rocket System, and an air defence regiment – a generous allocation of fire support.

Before the deployment had got far under way, the political crisis over the leadership of the Conservative Party erupted. While the contest was being fought out, one of the arguments put forward by Margaret Thatcher's supporters (including the Chief of the Defence Staff at the time of the Falklands campaign) for keeping her at the helm was that she was an experienced war leader and that the morale of the forces in the Gulf would be adversely affected if she were thrown out. More down-to-earth views about the relative merits of different politicians were expressed by some of the soldiers already there, and, when John Major took her place on 28 November, there were no signs of any weakening in the British government's resolution or in the determination of the men and women in the armed forces to put it to the test if necessary. Deployment of these reinforcements was completed early in January 1991, together with that of two more Tornado squadrons and more helicopters, some naval. The navy also sent two more MCMVs.

On the day after John Major became Prime Minister, a UN Security Council meeting at Ministerial level gave Saddam Hussein until 15 January to comply with UN resolutions, and authorized the use of military force if he did not. A flurry of diplomatic activity as the date approached, including a meeting between James Baker and the Iraqi Foreign Minister, Tariq Aziz, on 9 January in Geneva, and a visit by the UN Secretary-General, Perez de Cuellar, to Saddam Hussein in Baghdad, produced no result. There had been signs of wavering by France at one stage, and neither the Soviet Union nor China appeared keen on military action, but President Bush had strong international backing when he authorized General Schwarz-kopf to initiate military action in the early hours of 17 January 1991. The declared aims of Operation *Desert Storm* were: to secure a complete and unconditional Iraqi withdrawal from Kuwait; to restore its legitimate government; to re-establish international peace and security in the area; and to uphold the authority of the United Nations.

During this period of waiting and build-up, the media, with the help of self-styled experts, including retired senior military figures (not the author), indulged in an orgy of speculation about how operations might develop and their prospects of success. Schwarzkopf's army, although formidable, was significantly out-numbered, notably in tanks, and the Iraqi forces had had ample time in which to develop defensive positions on the borders of Kuwait, including mine-fields, ditches which could be flooded with burning oil, and 'berms' – great banks of sand. They were known to have chemical weapons and were believed to have developed bacteriological ones also and to be developing nuclear ones. Schwarzkopf's strength lay in the number – some 2,400 aircraft – and quality of his air forces, and the sophistication of weapon systems which they and the US Navy could deliver, backed by every facet of electronic warfare and space-based information, communication and navigation systems. His strategy therefore was to destroy the Iraqi air force and Iraq's capability of delivering weapons of any kind by missile, of which the Iraqis had a considerable number. When that had been done, he would switch his air and missile effort against the

Iraqi army, wearing it down until a land offensive could expect a fair chance of success.

The air campaign, involving an average of 2,500 sorties a day, was successful beyond all expectations. It drove the Iraqi air force from the sky, some of them taking refuge in Iran, and inflicted great damage on military installations of all kinds. One of the priority targets, involving some 300 sorties a day, was Iraqi Scud missiles, 38 of which were fired against Israel, threatening to provoke the latter into retaliation which could have undermined the Arab contribution to the coalition. A combination of deployment of Patriot air defence missiles, air attack and operation of Special Forces neutralized the Scud missile threat after 81 had been fired, half of them against targets in Saudi Arabia. Only one caused serious damage and casualties. Before committing Schwarzkopf's land forces to an assault, which many thought could involve heavy casualties, there was a further spurt of diplomatic activity after Iraq had announced, on 15 February, that it would 'deal with Security Council Resolution 660 [the original one] with the aim of reaching an honourable and acceptable political solution, including withdrawal'. But the conditions attached were unacceptable and made it obvious that it was an attempt to play for time, divide the coalition and defer, if not prevent, the land offensive. Tariq Aziz visited Moscow and Teheran to no avail, and on 22 February the coalition governments set out conditions which Iraq must meet before noon (New York time) 23 February, in default of which the land offensive would be launched. On that day Iraq set fire to the 600 oil wells of Kuwait and rejected the ultimatum. In the early hours of 24 February Schwarzkopf launched his attack.

His general plan was to pretend that his main thrust would be near the coast. There the US Marines had two divisions, sandwiched between forces of all the Arab contributors, amounting to the equivalent of some seven divisions. The Marines also posed an amphibious threat with two brigades afloat. The main thrust was in fact to be made 200 miles inland, round the western edge of the Iraqi defences, by the 7th US Corps of one infantry and three armoured divisions, one of them the British, and a 'cavalry' or light armoured division.

This corps was to turn the flank of the Iraqi defences and head towards Basra to engage the Republican Guard, an élite force of armoured and mechanized divisions. Wider on the flank, the 18th US Corps of one infantry and two airborne divisions, one of them carried entirely in helicopters, and the French *division léger* were to seal off the left flank by occupying a series of positions up to the west bank of the Euphrates, aiming towards Nasiriyah. When the decision had been made to increase the British contribution from 7th Armoured Brigade to the whole of 1st Armoured Division, General de la Billière had asked General Schwarzkopf to employ the division with 7th US Corps in the main thrust instead of just providing tank support to the US Marines. This would exploit their training and equipment and would ensure that the British, the largest European contribution, would play a significant part in the main thrust. It would also make tactical cooperation easier, as the US Army divisions in 7th Corps followed NATO procedures, while the Marines had peculiar ones of their own. Once Schwarzkopf was satisfied that the British would be able to ensure the full logistic support of their forces from the base area round Dhahran and Al Jubayl – 350 miles to the start line and operations up to 200 miles beyond it – he readily agreed, although it meant that he had to switch a US Army tank formation from 7th Corps to support the Marines.

The attack was launched in the early hours (4 am local time) of Sunday 24 February by the Marines in the coastal sector and the 18th US Corps 250 miles inland. Both were initially so successful that Schwarzkopf decided to bring forward the attack by the 7th Corps, originally planned to start at 3 am on the following day, and launch it at midday. This meant carrying out an attack involving clearing gaps in minefields in the desert, where there is no cover to conceal what one is doing, in broad daylight, an operation that nobody in their senses would have undertaken in the desert in the Second World War. But the signs that Iraqi resistance was feeble, and the availability of overpowering fire support from aircraft and artillery, justified Schwarzkopf's bold decision. Unbelievably, the 1st US Infantry Division (The Big Red Hand) took only one hour and twenty minutes to break through the Iraqi defences and clear 16 lanes for the advance of the armoured divisions. The task of the 1st (British) Armoured Division was to protect the eastern flank of the corps advance by swinging right to attack the Iraqi reserves immediately behind their forward defences, which they did during the night of 25/26 February. Enemy resistance was weak and continued to be so, leading elements of the division reaching the Kuwait–Basra road half an hour before the ceasefire came into effect at 8 am (local time) on 28 February. In the land campaign of 100 hours, the division advanced 180 miles, destroying almost three Iraqi armoured divisions and capturing over 7,000 prisoners, including several senior commanders, at a cost to itself of 19 men killed, nine of them when two US Air Force aircraft fired on a British armoured personnel carrier. In all the operations since the air offensive began, the RAF lost six aircraft, all GR1 strike Tornados, but most of their crews survived, only five being killed, a remarkably low casualty rate for 4,000 combat sorties in which 100 JP233 airfield attack weapons, 6,000 bombs and 7,000 rockets were delivered. These losses, however, led to criticism of the RAF's addiction to very low level attack on airfields, using the JP233, particularly when it became known that the Tornados were changing their tactics to attack from a higher level, guided with laser-marking by a squadron of Buccaneer aircraft, flown out in January and February. It was later announced that only one of the Tornados lost was on a low-level JP233 mission.

The decision to call a halt on 28 February, when Schwarzkopf's forces were close to Basra and had reached the Euphrates near Nasiriyah, was controversial then and has become more so since, Saddam Hussein and his cronies having remained in power contrary to expectations that overwhelming defeat would lead to his overthrow. But none of the coalition partners wished to step into the politico-military morass which an attempt to occupy Iraq and support an alternative regime would undoubtedly have involved. World opinion was also withdrawing its support as the coalition forces appeared to be inflicting heavy casualties on Iraqi forces which were only intent on escape. Some air force pilots appear to have shared that view. The decision to call a halt was a rare example of voluntarily ceasing hostilities at the right moment. The British government was certainly no keener than the American to take a step into that bog, although it was instrumental in forcing the latter to join the UK and France in responding to the popular demand for intervention in Kurdistan to relieve the plight of the Kurds, fleeing from Iraqi forces but denied entry into Turkey. The Gulf War gave a considerable fillip to the self-confidence and morale of all three services at a time when their future seemed uncertain. The strong popular support which had been shown to them and their activities had been reassuring, and many hoped that it would temper the severity of the reductions which had been forecast just before Iraq invaded Kuwait.

11

OPTIONS FOR CHANGE: 1991 AND BEYOND

THE MINISTRY OF Defence took its time over announcing definite decisions about the future of the armed forces. Before the services themselves could work out all the implications of the reductions forecast in July 1990, action on which had been frozen while the Gulf war lasted, the future of NATO and of European defence organization had to be agreed. Although members of the Alliance had been involved in the war, NATO itself had not, apart from the despatch of German air force units to strengthen the air defence of Turkey. The Secretary-General, the German Manfred Wörner, and the American SACEUR, General Galvin, had continued active consideration of a NATO which no longer faced a clear military threat from the east and had to take into account, not only a unified Germany, but also the intention of all its members to reduce their defence expenditure and the forces it supported. A significant reduction in US forces stationed in Europe was seen as inevitable. The way forward for definite moves towards a new structure was opened by the signature of the Conventional Forces in Europe Treaty on 18 November 1990, agreeing to equal limits on major items of equipment between Western and Eastern Europe and the maximum individual holding of any individual state. These were respectively 20,000 and 13,300 for tanks, 20,000 and 13,700 for artillery pieces, 30,000 and 20,000 for armoured combat vehicles other than tanks, 6,800 and 5,150 for combat aircraft and 2,000 and 1,500 for attack helicopters. In practice the maximum holding for any individual state would only apply to the Soviet Union: no other nation was likely to come anywhere near it. Britain's declared totals were 1,198 tanks, 636 artillery pieces, 3,193 armoured combat vehicles, 842 combat aircraft and 368 attack helicopters, all likely soon to be reduced under 'Options for Change'. At the NATO summit meeting in July 1990, it had been agreed that, once the Treaty was signed, negotiations would be initiated to reduce short-range nuclear forces on both sides, including a mutual withdrawal of all nuclear artillery shells.

In discussions over the future military structure for NATO, a divergence soon appeared between those who wanted above all to ensure the retention of US forces, and a strong American influence in NATO as a guarantee of this, and those who looked for a move towards a more European organization. In general, the Americans themselves, the British, the Dutch and the Portuguese all kept to the former line, while the Germans, Italians, Belgians, Spanish and, above all, the French pressed for the latter. The Secretary-General of the European Commission, Jacques Delors, added a descant to the chorus with the argument that, if the European Economic Community was to advance towards greater political and economic union, as it was trying to do, it must have a defence and security aspect. The compromise reached by the time that the 1991 Defence White Paper (Cmnd 1559) was published just before Parliament broke up for its summer recess at the end of July, was to keep all the existing NATO commands in being, but to reorganize the forces, particularly in the Central Region, into 'reaction', 'main defence' and 'augmentation' forces. Reaction forces would be available at relatively short notice to provide an early military response to an emerging crisis; main defence forces would consist primarily of those of the countries themselves, which could rely more than they had done in the past on mobilization of reserves; and augmentation forces would be ones primarily dependent on mobilization of reserves, including those stationed elsewhere, for example in the USA. The reaction forces are to be formed into an Allied Command Europe Rapid Reaction Corps, which is to be commanded by a British officer with a multinational staff. The corps will have four divisions, two of them British and two multinational. The British will be the 1st Armoured Division of three strong armoured brigades, stationed in Germany, and the 3rd Division, stationed in the United Kingdom, of two mechanized brigades, an airborne brigade and, if required also, the Royal Marine Commando Brigade. Of the two multi-national airmobile divisions, one will be formed from the Central Region with a brigade each from Britain, Germany, the Netherlands and Belgium, and one from the Southern Region, the composition of which had not then been decided.

France, continuing to exclude herself from any NATO military structure, pressed for a separate European Reaction Force, to which she would contribute and which would not form part of NATO's military structure and command system. A compromise was reached under the umbrella of the Western European Union, which began to enjoy a revival. As has already been mentioned, France had for some years been favouring the strengthening of the WEU as an alternative to Eurogroup within NATO, in which she refused to participate; and, when the future of NATO began to be discussed, both the American and the British governments showed little enthusiasm for this, regarding it as liable to weaken American influence and support. But, as the Americans began to emphasize the need for Western Europe to make a greater proportionate contribution (not a new theme); as they considered more carefully the problems arising out of the unification of Germany, and saw with dismay the disappointing reaction of most of NATO's European members to contributions to the Gulf war, they began to accept that some strengthening of European cohesion within NATO was desirable. The British government's attitude also changed under the threat of defence becoming a responsibility of the European Community and falling into the hands of the Commission. Emphasis on the WEU could avert that danger, which would add greatly to the already sharp division within the Conservative Party over attitudes to Europe with a general election looming. Whitehall suddenly switched to near-enthusiasm for WEU and inserted a full page about it into the 1991 White Paper, from which the following are extracts:

> To thrive, NATO needs a strong European pillar. In building this we see a central role for the WEU . . . The WEU can serve as a bridge between the transatlantic security and defence structure of NATO and the developing common political and security policies of the Twelve . . . but would be subordinate to neither. In this way the Twelve could develop common foreign and security policies, but defence would be left to the WEU . . . To ensure that the WEU has practical substance . . . we have elaborated ideas for the development of a European Reaction Force.

The paper then explained that the force would be 'autonomous from NATO', possibly for use outside the NATO area, and would be 'drawn from forces allocated to the Alliance, along with national forces of countries not part of the integrated structure', opening the door to French participation, because 'neither we nor any other country could contemplate or would wish to retain separate forces for NATO and the WEU'. The paper went on to condemn 'totally distinct Western European defence entities, involving the eventual absorption of the WEU by the Twelve' as 'disruptive of NATO' and 'inviting confusion and a less reliable defence than we have enjoyed over the last 40 years'.

Agreement within NATO on Britain's contribution to the Rapid Reaction Corps signified a considerable achievement for the Ministry of Defence, freeing British forces on the continent from commitment to forward defence plans integrated with the Germans, and at the same time providing a clear training purpose for the army, although it would accentuate the problem of changing roles, equipment and organization, if the army was to stick to its preferred habit of keeping units together, but not tying them to permanent stations or roles. Much credit for this achievement was due to General Sir Richard Vincent, who, as Vice-Chief of the Defence Staff, carried on most of the discussion within NATO. Soon after the end of the Gulf war, he succeeded Marshal of the Royal Air Force Sir David Craig as Chief of the Defence Staff, the first holder of that post to do so without having previously been Chief of Staff of his own service.

Before announcing its firm plans for the future, the government was subjected to a concerted attack from retired senior army officers and Conservative Members of Parliament and Peers, and pressurized by honorary colonels and regimental old comrades, when the full impact of the reductions in the infantry and the cavalry dawned on them. Among the former, it came chiefly from those parts of the infantry which had successfully resisted transformation into large regiments in the reductions of the 1960s, complicated by the national factor of Scottish, Welsh and Irish affiliations. In their case, and in that of the cavalry, it was the linking of the so-called 'regimental system' to regiments consisting of only one unit which meant that any reduction involved either disbandment or amalgamation, in some cases following previous amalgamations. The usual demands were heard that the tail should be docked rather than the teeth, in spite of the experience of the Gulf War in which almost the whole of the army's tail had had to be used to support only a small proportion of its teeth. In the event, with only a few minor concessions, the government stuck to its guns, maintaining the reductions in forces announced in July 1990, reducing the manpower targets further: for the navy by 5,000 to 55,000 and for the army by 4,000 to 116,000, both including men and women under training. The army's actual trained adult UK manpower in 1991 was 135,500, of whom 6,300 were women, and is to be reduced by 1997 to 104,000. The strength of the army in Germany will be reduced from 55,000 to 23,000. This will involve the disbandment of six regiments of the Royal Artillery, leaving 16, the equivalent of four regiments of the Royal Engineers, leaving ten, amalgamations in the Royal Armoured Corps reducing its regiments from 19 to 12, of which one will be the training regiment and one the Mounted Regiment of the Household Cavalry, so that there will be only ten combat units, eight cavalry and two Royal Tank Regiment. Two of these will be armoured reconnaissance regiments, the rest all eventually equipped with the Challenger tank, Vickers having been given an order for 150 of the new Challenger II. Amalgamations in the infantry will reduce its strength from 55 battalions to 36, including bringing the number of Gurkha battalions down from five to two by the time that the Hong Kong commitment comes to an end in 1997. All the large infantry regiments, except for the Parachute Regiment, which will keep three battalions, two in the parachute role, will be reduced to two battalions. The Army Air Corps is to retain six regiments, losing the equivalent of another by the time that the Hong Kong commitment finishes. There is to be a major reorganization of the army's 'tail'. A new 'Adjutant-General's Corps' is to be formed, incorporating the Royal Army Pay Corps, the Women's Royal Army Corps, the Royal Military Police, the Military Provost Staff Corps (the army's prison service), the Royal Army Educational Corps and the Army Legal Corps. It will also include all clerks, both on the staff and in units, and will 'support' the Royal Army Chaplains Department. In future, women are to join the Corps 'appropriate to their specialization and serve alongside their male colleagues', as many women officers already do, instead of remaining cap-badged to the WRAC. The logistic services are to be reorganized into only two corps. One, for equipment support, will be based on the Royal Mechanical and Electrical Engineers, which will assume from the Royal Army Ordnance Corps responsibility for provision and distribution of all stores, including spares, concerned with equipment. The other, for 'service support', will absorb the remaining responsibilities of the RAOC, as well as those of the Royal Corps of Transport, the Army Catering Corps, the postal and courier functions of the Royal Engineers and, possibly, some supply functions of the Royal Army Medical Corps. This reorganization is almost a reversion to the pre-Second World War pattern before the REME was hived off from the RAOC and when the Royal Army Service Corps was responsible for almost all other supply and transport services.

Because the army's traditional organization means that every change is a traumatic experience, its problems attracted more attention than those of the Royal Navy and the Royal Air Force. The reductions announced in the 1991 Defence White Paper confirmed, with few exceptions, those proposed in King's announcement the previous year. The navy's ability to reduce its manpower by a further 5,000 had been, it was rumoured, the price it had to pay for assurance that its two ageing assault ships would be replaced and that an aviation support ship would be ordered to carry the helicopters to land the Royal Marine Commandos. There was to be no monkeying about with the programme to produce four of the *Vanguard* class Trident missile submarines to ensure that one could always be on patrol and the force would be 'assigned to NATO while remaining under the control of the British Government'. The third boat, HMS *Vigilant*, had been ordered and a tender for the fourth would soon be issued. The RAF would continue to provide a 'sub-strategic' nuclear force in support of NATO with four Tornado strike squadrons in Germany and four in the United Kingdom, a reduction of three instead of five, as the July 1990 announcement had forecast. Their free-fall nuclear weapon would be replaced by the end of the century by a Tactical Air-to-Surface Missile (TASM), developed with either the USA or France, delivering a British warhead. Naval helicopters and Sea Harriers would 'remain capable of carrying British nuclear weapons' and RAF Nimrod Maritime Patrol aircraft of delivering US nuclear depth-charges. The number of the army's missiles (Lance) and artillery with US warheads was 'likely to reduce as NATO's strategy evolves'. That evolution accelerated when, in September 1991, President Bush announced that all US battlefield nuclear weapons, delivered by artillery and short-range missiles, would be abolished.

The White Paper confirmed that the navy would continue to have three 'aircraft-carriers', as they could now be called, of which two would be manned at any one time, operating Sea Harriers and Sea King helicopters, which would be replaced by the EH101, prototypes of which were already flying. The last of the *Trafalgar* class nuclear-powered submarines would be accepted later in the year, and the successor to the *Swiftsure* class about the end of the century would be a development of the *Trafalgar* and not an entirely new design as the navy had hoped. As the destroyer/frigate force reduced from 46 to about 40, Type 23s would replace the older types and a new type of anti-aircraft destroyer would replace the Type 42s 'around the end of the century', its missile system to be developed in cooperation with France, Italy and Spain. Once again the future of HMS *Endurance*, the Antarctic ice-patrol ship, became a bone of contention between the Ministry of Defence and the Foreign Office, as it had before the Falklands war. The ship itself was badly in need of an expensive refit or preferably replacement. Pressure to keep *Endurance* or a successor came from both the scientific community and those who feared that failure to keep the White Ensign flying in the Antarctic summer months could encourage Argentina and others to stake their claims there, and was led, as always, by Lord Shackleton. It resulted in the chartering of the Norwegian *Polar Circle* and a government commitment to maintain it or a successor in the same role.

New equipment for the RAF centred round air defence of the United Kingdom. In the near future the Tornado F3, backed by seven Airborne Early Warning Boeing E–3Ds and supplemented somewhat unrealistically by 50 Hawk trainers in daylight only, would provide this, the Phantoms being phased out. The old Bloodhound surface-to-air missiles already had been. The European Fighter Aircraft was seen as 'having an increasing part to play' in this task in the future, while 'industry was being invited to make proposals for a replacement system to Bloodhound to be introduced into service in the mid-1990s'.

No estimate was given as to what peace dividend would eventually emerge when all these reductions had taken effect over a five-year period. The estimated out-turn for the defence budget for 1990/91 was £22,285m, an increase of £1,062m over planned provision, largely accounted for by the Gulf War, which in total was estimated to have involved additional expenditure of £2,500m, some of which would fall in 1991/92, for which a cash provision of £24,027m was to be made, reducing slightly to £23,350m and £23,390m in the two subsequent years. The White Paper expressed the hope that the bulk of the additional Gulf War costs would be covered by cash contributions pledged by other governments, of which £581m had been received in the financial year 1990/91, including £275m from Germany and £110m from Kuwait. £1,510m was expected in 1991/ 92, including £158m to add to the £25m already received from Japan, another £550m from Kuwait, £580m from Saudi Arabia and £190m from the United Arab Emirates, who had already contributed £85m. The other contributors were South Korea £16m, Belgium and Hong Kong £15m each, Denmark £8m and Luxembourg £1m. The peace dividend would be slow in coming, but the government stated that its aim was 'to secure savings made by the Options for Change proposals, and to reduce the share of GDP taken by defence in the coming years'. In 1990 it stood at 4 per cent, with France at 3.6 and Germany at 2.9, although it was below both as a total expressed in US dollars, and below France and above Germany on a per capita basis.

Critics of the government, who thought that the reductions went too far, maintained that events since the Options for Change study had been embarked upon showed that too optimistic a view had been taken about the reduction of threats and commitments. The Soviet Union, they argued, had made little progress towards internal freedom politically or economically, and its armed forces were still powerful, churning out new equipment. They could reverse the process of relaxation in East–West relations and resurrect a serious threat to Western Europe. Soviet forces were still in East Germany. Nor were conditions in Central and Eastern Europe reassuring. Recent events in Yugoslavia had shown that ancient animosities and rivalries could only too easily erupt once the lid of Pandora's Box, held down by the Iron Curtain, had been lifted. Further afield the Gulf War had demonstrated the need to be prepared to field forces in other parts of the world and that it was not only lightly equipped or peacekeeping ones that were needed. At home, we were no nearer peace in Northern Ireland, where an army garrison of ten battalions looked like being tied up indefinitely, while the commitment to retain garrisons in the Falklands and Belize remained. They complained that the changes had not resulted from a careful strategic review to reassess potential threats, but were based on a Treasury demand for reduction to a specific sum or percentage of GDP.

The government's answer was that, in spite of the fact that:

The process of political and economic reform in the Soviet Union and in Eastern Europe remains fraught with uncertainty; long-term stability is but a distant aspiration [and that] beyond Europe, the Gulf conflict has reminded us of the speed and unpredictability with which threats to international security can arise . . . the historic nature of the changes that have occurred is not in doubt . . . More than a million fewer troops will be ranged against NATO in Europe by the mid-1990s. The artificial division of our continent, most obvious in the Berlin Wall, has been removed and increasingly we can regard the former communist states as peaceful neighbours and partners.

Nevertheless a warning was sounded that 'we need as well to note the fragility of the new Europe, and the lack of stability outside it'.

During the short-lived and abortive coup in the Soviet Union in August 1991, the hopes of these objectors were raised. With cries of

171

'I told you so!', they called for a halt to the government's plans; but Major and King stood firm and were justified by the outcome which undermined the argument of the old and bold that NATO could again be faced by its classic threat as a result of a reactionary coup in the Soviet Union, backed by the military. This line was taken by both Mrs Thatcher and the House of Commons Defence Committee, chaired by a retired army lieutenant-colonel.

The normal source of criticism, the Labour Party in opposition, was muted. It had been struggling to cast off its old image – anti-nuclear, cutting down defence, anti-American and anti-European – and to be seen by the middle-class voters of the centre as a respectable alternative to the Conservatives. It somehow had to balance favouring a peace dividend, which could be used to boost the National Health Service, social welfare, education and better national infrastructure and public services, popular with its left wing and indeed most of its supporters, against the concern of the considerable number of trade unionists whose jobs were threatened by reductions in orders for defence equipment and supplies. Their ranks were joined by aged ex-servicemen and local interests, particularly in Scotland, Wales and the North of England, who objected to the amalgamation or disbandment of their familiar service associations. The threatened closure of the Rosyth naval base was successfully prevented, largely by well-organized trade union pressure exploiting the precarious Conservative political position in Scotland with an election in the offing. There was a resurgence of this criticism when the 1991 Defence White Paper was debated in both Houses of Parliament in October, preceded by a campaign in the media.

Almost all the critics of a reduction of the forces to a total of some 146,000 harped on the theme that no strategic review had been carried out to determine what forces were needed, and that insufficient provision had been made to meet the unexpected. They chose to ignore the difficulty of defining the threat. Since 1945 the Soviet threat, poised in the centre of Europe and supplemented by the world's largest submarine fleet, had been the principal justification for the organization and equipment of all three services and had provided a sense of purpose for which they trained. In previous times, when a continental commitment had been reduced, usually soon after the end of a war, the forces had been able to return to their traditional task of policing the Empire and its trade routes. That option is no longer open, with the exception of Hong Kong, which ends in 1997, Gibraltar, where the army garrison has already been taken over by the locally raised Gibraltar Regiment, the Falklands and Belize. The last has been independent for some time and the task of deterring Guatemala from invading it should surely be handed over to some peacekeeping arrangement, backed by countries of the American continent. The desirability of keeping a Gurkha battalion in Brunei, when the Sultan has adequate forces of his own, is also questionable, even though he pays for it. The commitment in Northern Ireland is unlikely to be significantly reduced, but a garrison of ten battalions should not be regarded as sacrosanct when the primary responsibility for maintaining law and order has for many years been in the hands of the Royal Ulster Constabulary, backed by the Ulster Defence Regiment.

Provision for the unexpected cannot easily be quantified. The Falklands and Gulf wars can be used by both sides in the argument: those who say that we must be prepared to do the same again, and those who maintain that what was done makes a repetition very unlikely. With the exception of the Falklands, any overseas expedition would almost certainly only be undertaken as part of a coalition, probably led by the USA. One cannot even imagine the United Kingdom fighting Guatemala over Belize without American intervention of some kind. The decision for the British government as to what contribution to make will always be based on a judgement of the political dividend to be gained, balanced against the economic or other cost, such as the likely bill of casualties. That judgement proved correct in the Gulf war, but, if its course had been different and the war had lasted longer and involved serious casualties, the dividend could have been seen in a different light. The decisions to set strict limits on our contribution in Korea and not to participate directly in Vietnam were undoubtedly sound, whatever the reasons for them. In any case, our contribution to the NATO Rapid Reaction Corps, and the concept that the same forces could act as a European Reaction Force outside NATO, are designed to cater for the unexpected.

The basic issue is the problem of what is needed to preserve the security of Europe. That cannot now be quantified in the manner of the annual 'strategic balance', listing the total of the nuclear and conventional forces on each side of the Iron Curtain. In reality that was never the main determinant of the size and shape of NATO's forces and of Britain's contribution to them. It was always a compromise between the vain hope of providing a balance of conventional forces, an estimate of the deterrent credibility of the NATO nuclear arsenal, and domestic political considerations affecting national defence expenditure and length of conscript service (or capability of voluntary recruiting) of members of the Alliance, as previous chapters have shown.

In considering Europe's security needs for the future, the attention of all governments of the Alliance, certainly of Britain, appears to be dominated by the short term, the next five years or so. Remarkably little attention seems to be being paid, at least publicly, to the longer-term need, on the assumption that events in Europe will proceed in the direction in which everybody, on whichever side of the Iron Curtain they have been, hopes that they will: a stable Europe, not divided by fundamental differences in ideology. After a spate of ideas involving the Conference for Security and Cooperation in Europe (CSCE), attention has been limited to how to preserve NATO and to consideration of what the organization should be for its European members. The wider, larger needs of Europe as a whole have hardly been addressed. As long as Soviet forces remain in Germany and until we can see more clearly how matters will develop within the Soviet Union, it is obviously prudent to preserve the structure of NATO in the military field and to rely on the European Community as the principal political institution, but we should regard that only as an interim solution. We should look forward to and prepare the ground for a scenario in which European matters, including security or defence – it is misleading to regard the two as different – are not dominated by a dialogue between the USA and the Soviet Union. That is already beginning to happen. If, and it is admittedly a big if, events move in the desired direction, it will not be necessary, appropriate or desirable that a European Security Organization should be dominated by the Americans, as NATO has been and still is, and it will be important that France, as well as Britain, should be a full participant. The future should not therefore lie in a development of NATO to give it a more political function nor in extending its organization to cover nations of Central and Eastern Europe; it should be changed into what it was originally envisaged as by the US government when the North Atlantic Treaty was signed in 1949 before the establishment of the military organization: that is a treaty arrangement for the support by the USA and Canada of a Western European integrated defence effort, except that in future that should not be limited to the present European members of the Alliance. A European Security Organization will have to provide reassurance against four potential threats: first, that posed to its neighbours, and perhaps to other countries, by the sheer size and military resources of the Soviet Union or, if it breaks up, the larger republics of Russia, Byelorussia and the Ukraine; second, a

174

resurgence of ambitions in a united Germany that all German-speaking peoples should be included in that nation; third, quarrels arising out of ancient animosities and rivalries; and, finally, threats to Europe's interests from beyond its borders. The way forward towards such an organization should be signed in stages, and the move from one stage to another should not be made unless it appears that political developments make such a move both desirable and possible.

The first stage should be to transform the current force contributions to NATO of European members into ones with a greater degree of European integration. The formation of the Rapid Reaction Corps is a step in that direction. It must be assumed for the present that the French will exclude themselves as long as the NATO command organization is as dominated by the USA as it is. They made this clear in the run up to, and at, the European Community summit meeting at Maastricht in December, as they had at the NATO summit meeting in Rome the previous month. But in this stage it is likely that there will be a significant reduction in US forces stationed in Europe and there is no reason why the relationship between US forces and integrated European forces should not be the same as it is within NATO between US forces and the national forces of European members. During this stage the WEU should assume the role which the Eurogroup and the Independent Programme Group now play within NATO, and should plan to develop itself into a European Defence Community, parallel to, but not necessarily with the same membership as, the Economic Community. Like the EEC, it would be subject to the authority of the European Council and Parliament. One of its main concerns should be arms procurement. The Defence Community should come into force in the second stage, if events in the Soviet Union and Eastern Europe make it appropriate and the USA can be brought to accept that it would provide an acceptable pattern for their future involvement in the security of Europe through the North Atlantic Treaty.

If those conditions are fulfilled, the second stage, which should certainly not be entered upon until all Soviet forces have been withdrawn into the Soviet Union, should see the abolition of the NATO commands of SACEUR, CINCNORTH and CINCSOUTH with their headquarters respectively at Mons, Oslo and Naples. CINCENT's command, based at Brunssum in the 'Dutch appendix', should be transformed into a European operational and training command, covering the area from the Alps to the Baltic, including France and Denmark but excluding Norway, and it should incorpor-

175

ate both CINCCHAN and CINCUKAIR. US forces in Europe would be associated with this command, but not be subordinate to it. Allied forces of other nations outside this area would remain under national command with direct links to CINCENT under the general authority of the NATO Military Committee, the chairman of which might always be the C-in-C of all US forces in Europe, as SACEUR now is. The Military Committee would be responsible for coordinating the plans of national commands and CINCENT, and the chairman would have a staff for this purpose. The C-in-C of the US Atlantic Fleet, who now has a NATO hat as SACLANT, would be one of these national commands.

The final stage would greatly depend on political developments, particularly on what sort of association other countries of Europe had by then established with the EEC. There would seem to be three possible options for the future of NATO at this stage. It could be associated with other countries of Europe, directly or indirectly, through their national commands; it could be associated with groups similar to CINCENT, formed in the rest of Europe; or it could be associated in either of those ways under the umbrella of the CSCE. An association of this nature should not involve a guarantee to do anything more than consult as to what military action was appropriate in the event of an associate being threatened. The whole question of the relationship of the Soviet Union to such an organization would be fraught with difficulty and would inevitably affect the relationship which the organization had with the USA. Political developments at this stage would determine whether the organization's forces remained ones designed to fight a sophisticated conventional war or were transformed into something more like a peacekeeping force, or a mixture of both.

Not the least of the difficulties would be the question of nuclear weapons. A perpetuation of the US–Soviet dialogue on this issue is more likely to prove satisfactory than involving all other European countries in the discussion. It is the two ex-superpowers which have the vast majority of weapons. Apart from Britain and France, none of the European countries have them, and the last thing one wants is to encourage them to think that they need them. The responsibility for bringing about an orderly reduction of the vast stock of nuclear weapons should be left to the USA to arrange with the Soviet Union and its republics, Britain and France becoming involved when reductions have reached a stage which makes their nuclear weapons relevant to the issue. But as long as the Soviet Union and its republics have nuclear weapons at all, so long will it be essential to preserve the North Atlantic Alliance, which binds the USA to support European defence. That will not necessarily mean that US forces, nuclear or conventional, have to be physically based in Europe.

One of the greatest problems involved in the general plan which has been outlined above would be to persuade the American Congress and people to remain committed to European defence, if they do not dominate it. That is clearly one of the principal reasons why the British government clings to the concept of NATO in much its present form. But it is doubtful if Congress will allow future US administrations to remain committed on anything like the scale which the present administration envisages. The best policy will be to show that Europe can and will assume a much greater responsibility for its own security, and that essential American support, particularly nuclear support, can be provided at much less cost in terms of manpower, finance and risk to themselves.

If the future arrangements for the security of Europe, on which the security of Britain will depend, were to develop in this direction, the changes that will be required in British defence policy and armed forces will be far more radical and involve a much deeper departure from tradition than anything envisaged under 'Options for Change'. The armed forces, particularly the army, would do well to prepare themselves for adaptation to such a possibility. In their devotion to past traditions, they have seldom been prepared to do so willingly except under the pressure of war.

Britain's defence policy since 1945 has fundamentally been based on that pursued throughout the Second World War by Winston Churchill: to persuade the USA to help to protect British interests both in Europe and elsewhere in the world, because she was not able to do so by herself and no longer had the resources of her Empire on which to draw, not that the latter had in reality been of great benefit. The military commitments which the Empire, and later the Commonwealth, entailed had for a long time outweighed the benefits to be gained from the military resources which they contributed. The days are long past since the British Commonwealth could be regarded as a pillar of support for the interests of the United Kingdom. The size and shape of our conventional forces has been determined by a judgement of what was needed to persuade the Americans that we were doing enough ourselves, and setting a good enough example to other European members of NATO to deserve their support, and to a certain extent that, in comparison with other members, especially Germany, we carried sufficient weight in the

Alliance. Our own nuclear weapons were introduced to persuade ourselves that, in the last resort, we did not need American help.

There is little sign at present of any basic change in that policy of dependence on the USA towards one in which Britain regards Western Europe as the principal pillar of support of her interests, rather than America, but political and economic influences are moving in that direction. They should determine defence policy, which should not be driven in the wrong direction by clinging to outmoded military concepts – 'Keeping a hold of nurse for fear of finding something worse'. Those who oppose a move in that direction cite the poor performance of the European members of NATO over military contributions to the Gulf war and the reliability of the USA as an example. But that argument can be turned on its head: that there was a sad lack both of the concept that Western Europe should deal with the USA as a community and not independently on a national basis, and of any institution through which such dealings in defence matters should take place. As Lord Carrington, with all his experience as a former Secretary of State both for Defence and for Foreign and Commonwealth Affairs, and as Secretary-General of NATO, said in the House of Lords on 6 September 1990:

> For those of us who believe, as I do, that, if the Community is to have any influence in world affairs and that after 1992 there must inevitably be a closer political element to match the economic integration, there are urgent lessons to be learnt from the past month.
>
> In the future, the Community must concern itself with its own security and . . . there are, it seems to me, ways in which that could be done in association with an evolution of NATO in a rather different form from what it is now.*

One must hope that Britain will take the lead in moving its defence policy and that of the North Atlantic Alliance in that direction.

Looking back over the near half-century that has passed since the end of the Second World War, what verdict should one pass on the degree to which British governments have succeeded in achieving the right balance in order to remain on the tightrope of defence policy? It is not an easy question to answer. Treasury mandarins

---

*House of Lords *Hansard*, Vol. 521, No. 130, Col. 1827.

and many economists would say that we fell off it during – or even in the years before – the Second World War and never managed to get back onto it; that the advice they gave Neville Chamberlain in 1938 – that our economy could not support the rearmament programme then proposed – was proved correct, and that the level of defence expenditure maintained since then, particularly overseas expenditure, and the demands defence made generally on the nation's resources, have prevented successive governments from curing the underlying malaise of the economy; that they have prevented, or at least discouraged, British industry and commerce from escaping from their outdated patterns and methods of trade and from adjusting themselves to new methods and markets, as nations which had not emerged victorious – Germany, Japan, Italy and also France – had been forced and able to do.

Foreign and Commonwealth mandarins and defence chiefs would take a different view. They would stress the real danger of the communist threat in the 1950s, both from the armed forces of the Soviet Union, occupying the eastern half of Europe, and from its support of international communism in Europe and all over the world, exacerbated by the victory of Mao Tse-tung in China. The only hope of continuing this lay in the support of the USA, and at the time no nation other than Britain was in a position to act as its partner in this mission. Even if the French had been willing, they were too entangled in their own colonial problems in Indo-China and Africa to do so. There were large areas of the Commonwealth in which we could not expect help from the anti-colonial Americans in maintaining the imperial or ex-imperial burden. Even if the government of the time wished former parts of the empire to become independent, as India and Pakistan had done, too precipitate an advance in that direction ran the risk of their falling into communist hands. The Middle East was a special case. We had important interests there in oil and transit facilities by sea and air. If we moved out, either the Soviet Union or the Americans would move in. The former would have been a disaster. To the politicians, mandarins and defence chiefs of the time, the latter appeared to be greatly to our disadvantage. However, in the light of recent events, to have handed over all the problems of the Middle East to the USA, as we had landed them with those of Greece and Turkey and, to a high degree, of Palestine in 1948, can now be regarded as possibly a profitable policy, in spite of the loss it might have entailed of foreign currency earnings from oil.

Our influence on the USA in persuading them to support policies which furthered our interests and security depended on showing ourselves both staunch European partners in NATO and firm opponents of communism throughout the world. This could not be done on the cheap. The Foreign Office often thought that the defence chiefs over-insured in their plans, while the latter maintained that they were stretched to the limit to meet the commitments which the Foreign, Commonwealth Relations and Colonial Offices imposed on them. Nevertheless the defence chiefs were seldom in favour of a radical reduction in those commitments.

In comparison with France, and with the American commitment in Korea and Vietnam, Britain's tightrope walking in between these two opposing views can be judged to have been adroit and economical. In terms of lives lost, the withdrawal from empire was not expensive, and it did not involve the political turmoil which France suffered as a result of her attempts to stay in Indo-China and Algeria, or which afflicted the US during their intervention in Vietnam. But there is little doubt that the emphasis laid by governments of both political persuasions on the importance of maintaining Britain's status as a world power led, and continues to lead, to the preservation of certain aspects of the defence establishment which were, and are, not justified by more strictly military requirements, or even by the need to pursue political and economic policies in the best interests of the nation. Often the opposite was true. Withdrawal from the Indian sub-continent in 1947 should have led to a major reappraisal of defence policy outside Europe, but that did not take place or was fudged. The Chiefs of Staff's Global Strategy Paper of 1952 (still not released in the Public Record Office), with its emphasis on reliance on nuclear weapons, deceived some influential people into thinking that this would make resources available, without too great a strain on the economy, to support the worldwide defence role. The Suez affair of 1956 was the moment of truth, as Harold Macmillan recognized. But his Conservative colleagues appear to have scotched an objective consideration of the Future Policy Study by officials, which he commissioned in 1958 (also not released in the Public Record Office). That study addressed the basic underlying issues, one of which was the need to recognize that the Commonwealth was no longer of any great importance to the United Kingdom in political, economic or military terms: indeed, was more of a liability than an asset. Its sole remaining significance was cultural and sentimental. The other important point it made was that we should think more in terms of securing our interests 'by combining with friends and allies' than by action on our own, for which we had not the resources.

This was a clear pointer to joining the European Economic Community.

Sandys and his immediate successors, although realizing that radical changes were needed, made the error of thinking that changes in the defence apparatus would adjust the balance without the need for a radical shift in political and commercial attitudes to Britain's world-wide presence. Not even Healey accepted that, until it was forced on him by the financial crisis of 1967. Thereafter the problem of balance was less one of commitments against resources than as between different forms of expensive equipment, especially ships versus aircraft, and between them and the manpower requirements of the army and all that was needed to keep it in Germany.

The prime example of the emphasis on status as a world power has been Britain's nuclear weapon programme. It had never been needed as an addition to the US nuclear arsenal on strictly military grounds, and has not, as was hoped, helped to influence the nuclear weapon policy of the USA. To a certain degree it has been a millstone round the neck of those responsible for planning the defence equipment programme, particularly at times when new systems had to be introduced. The irony is that it cannot be said to have enhanced Britain's power in any field, political, economic or military. We have not been able to do anything with it that we could not have done without it.

The radically different situation in international relations which has developed in recent years gives Britain the best chance it has had for years – perhaps for centuries – to adjust itself to the realities and opportunities which the twenty-first century will soon bring, and to exploit them. But we will only be able to do so if we cast off the shackles of the past, which bind us to a vision of Britain as a world power, which was almost always an illusion, created, first, by ousting the French from India and North America in the eighteenth century, and then by a temporary advantage in industrialization in the nineteenth. The armed forces tend to cling to sentiment about the past, partly because they are, fortunately, generally precluded from practising their craft to a full extent in the present. They face the problem of the manager of a football team, trying to maintain them in good training and spirits to play their rivals at any time, but forbidden to practise with a real ball against a real opponent. He would have to fall back on memories of past victories. Even the youngest service, the Royal Air Force, is prone to that. It is to the future, not to the past, that sailors, soldiers and airmen, and those who are responsible for them, should look. Trying to keep their

181

balance on the tightrope between many conflicting interests and pressures, their only hope is to look ahead. If they look back, they will fall off.

INDEX